QUINCEAÑERA STYLE

# QUINCEAÑERA STYLE

*Social Belonging and Latinx Consumer Identities*

RACHEL VALENTINA GONZÁLEZ

UNIVERSITY OF TEXAS PRESS ᐊᐅ *Austin*

Requests for permission to reproduce material from this work should be sent to:
    Permissions
    University of Texas Press
    P.O. Box 7819
    Austin, TX 78713–7819
    utpress.utexas.edu/rp-form

♾ The paper used in this book meets the minimum requirements of ANSI/NISO
Z39.48–1992 (R1997) (Permanence of Paper).

LIBRARY OF CONGRESS CATALOGING-IN-PUBLICATION DATA

Names: González, Rachel Valentina, author.
Title: Quinceañera style : social belonging and Latinx consumer identities / Rachel
Valentina González.
Description: First edition. | Austin : University of Texas Press, 2019. | Includes
bibliographical references and index.
Identifiers: LCCN 2019008100
    ISBN 978-1-4773-1968-0 (cloth : alk. paper)
    ISBN 978-1-4773-1969-7 (pbk. : alk. paper)
    ISBN 978-1-4773-1970-3 (library ebook)
    ISBN 978-1-4773-1971-0 (nonlibrary ebook)
Subjects: LCSH: Quinceañera (Social custom)—United States. | Hispanic
Americans—Social life and customs—21st century. | Hispanic Americans—Ethnic
identity. | Hispanic American consumers—United States.
Classification: LCC GT2490 .G66 2019 | DDC 394.2—dc23
LC record available at https://lccn.loc.gov/2019008100

doi:10.7560/319680

FOR TONY AND HIS INFINITE POTENTIAL

AND IN MEMORY OF MARIA GONZÁLEZ SANCHEZ, WHO LEFT HER
HOME IN BAJA CALIFORNIA AT AGE FOURTEEN TO START HER LIFE
IN THE UNITED STATES

CONTENTS

I never had a quinceañera of my own. But I distinctly remember that Emilia was late, very late. The invited guests and close family had all caravanned together from St. Elizabeth's Catholic Church in East Oakland to the lavish Cameron-Stanford house on the edge of Lake Merit. The historic Victorian house and grounds was a common site for the celebration of weddings and other large private gatherings. To everyone's surprise, Emilia's white limousine hadn't directly followed her family and friends to the reception site as anticipated.

It was 1990. I was eight years old and wearing my repurposed first-communion dress to serve as *damita*, little maid, in my godsister Emilia's quinceañera celebration. My role was to represent the childhood the quinceañera girl was leaving behind. Emilia was actually turning sixteen, and the celebration was a cultural compromise, as most quinceañeras are. This one blended her own desire for a sweet-sixteen celebration legible to her non-Latinx peers and her mother's wish to reinforce her Puerto Rican heritage. Emilia herself was Puerto Rican Jewish and South Asian, her mother Puerto Rican Jewish and a transplanted New Yorker. The quinceañera celebration was a cultural practice that the two could share, even if Emilia's mother had not celebrated her own. The event was a symbol of intersecting subjectivities made manifest in material goods—dress, limousine, historic venue, and food.

Emilia's mother paced along the edge of the veranda area filled with folding chairs and tables that had been rented for the late-afternoon event serving a predominantly Latinx audience of family and friends from other parts of the city, parts of the city with less architectural beauty and historical significance. The interior of the house remained off limits to our party except for the bathroom and kitchen area, as it was only the veranda and patio that were formally rented for our use. Even standing in the grass, watching my godsister's mother smoke frantically by a back gate and looking down the main street for the limousine to enter her line of sight, I felt exposed. I was unsettled because I was accustomed to my invisibility. The wide-set, wrought-iron fencing made the entire event and everyone celebrating visible. When I was a child, it wholly escaped me that for once we were on the inside of the fence, not peering in at elite experiences that were just out of reach. On weekends my family would drive into the Oakland hills to admire the mansions that overlooked the bay from our repurposed commercial minivan. My grandmother would call it "Shangri-la."

Emilia finally arrived, nonchalantly, with a small group of friends. She had the limo driver first take her home to change out of her full-length, peach-hued gown with thick off-the-shoulder straps, a dress she decided she no longer wanted to wear, and then to her next and primary stop, a nail salon where she had her acrylic nails fixed because one had cracked early in the day. What stood out to me that day was not the mass or even the composition of the crowd. It was the way Emilia celebrated and at the same time still resisted the strictures of the day, ultimately questioning the very point of the celebration that supposedly dictates the social and cultural norms of Latinas expected to behave as good girls. Emilia's resistance to her dress, to obedience, to selflessness denaturalized the dangerous social fantasy of the happily self-effacing Latina woman. Her defiant teenage performance also reinforces how genuine initiation rites like the quinceañera that serve as a bridge onto the long road to adulthood are characterized by their fundamental banality—boredom, expense, infighting, and an amazing amount of tedious labor (Grimes 27). Emilia was a typical narcissistic sixteen-year-old USAmerican teenager.[1] This is the true sign of successful initiation into the US mainstream, the privilege of being rendered unremarkable.

Seeing Emilia's criticism through action requires that observers question the practice of quinceañeras among US Latinas beyond the tradition's capacity to serve as a symbol of ideal feminine social performance and religious conservatism. Instead, we need to imagine it as a product of consumption that defies totalizing logics of the primacy of ethnic categorization within contemporary Latinx-identifying populations. Or, to pose this assertion as a question, What kind of social citizens are Latinas *allowed* to be?

ACKNOWLEDGMENTS

In truth, this book would have remained an idea in my head if not for the generosity of all the individuals whose experiences are shared in these pages. My special thanks go out to Jazmin Alcazar, Christina Garza, and Doña Lupe, who were the first family to share their quinceañera story with me, in the summer of 2009. To my collaborators, friends, and each of the quinceañera girls and their mamás who intimated their dreams to me, I thank you.

This book has had many iterations, but none of them would have been possible without the generous institutional support of the Department of Mexican American and Latina/o Studies and the College of Liberal Arts at the University of Texas, as well as the Woodrow Wilson Foundation's Early Career Fellowship. To my colleagues who read early drafts, Regina Marchi, Nicole Guidotti-Hernández, Juan Colomina Almiñana, Laura Gutiérrez, Mary Beltran, Kerry Webb, Dustin Tahamahkera, and Julie Minich, I appreciate your sharing your time, energy, and ideas with me. I thank my mentor and friend Domino Renee Perez, who generously read every word of this before anyone else. This book is a direct reflection of her commitment to thoughtful collaboration and compassionate scholarly practice.

This book would never have been finished had I not had the daily support of Doug and Tony Martin. I thank my parents, Jesús G. González and Jane López, and my extended family for motivating me to keep working even when it meant we wouldn't be together. I am especially indebted to my tía and madrina Thelma Lawler, who always said I could do it, even when I didn't think I could. I am forever grateful.

QUINCEAÑERA STYLE

## COMING OUT LATINX

Quinceañeras are the manifestations of possibility. The term "quinceañera" refers to both the fifteen-year-old Latinx birthday celebrant and her celebration, a rhetorical shorthand that collapses a young woman's personal identity with an elaborately styled and deeply rooted initiation ritual meant to spur social transitions into cultural womanhood. Bilingual Latinxs, those with life experiences that are divided among the linguistic resources of Spanish, Spanglish, and English, squabble over the correct use of the Spanish-language term, with purists defending the tradition on grammatical grounds as belonging to Latin America. However, the doubling of meaning and social use of the term as celebrant and event illustrates the tradition's roots in a USAmerican milieu and its outgrowth as a hybrid form. To encompass this hybridity in text I employ the term "Latinx" precisely because it is open to possibilities of inclusion that mirror how I am thinking about quinceañera practices in the book. As Richard T. Rodriguez warns in his article "X Marks the Spot," I am not succumbing to the "easy embrace" or an eliding of the "spliced genealogical roots" from which the terms "Latina/o" and "Latin@" arose (202, 205). Rather, in working with gay Latino, gay Mexicano, unidentifying, queer, and transgender Mexicana collaborators, I found that the use of the "x" marks a pivot point toward decentralizing heteronormativity in conversations about the quinceañera tradition. I use "Latina" when I specifically refer to groups of young women and terms of address that my collaborators offered me. I am an American folklorist and Latina/o/x studies scholar, and my academic lens emerges from US Latinx communities that are predominantly English-speaking; therefore the "x" over the Spanish neutral "e" is also part of this story of Americanity. The use of the "x" holds space for defiance and reminds the reader to critically consider how audiences interpret public markers of race, class, and gender subject formation.

~

The anonymous quinceañera girl was caught on camera at her local mall in the summer of 2011, photographed like a rare creature in the wild. Her image circulated through Facebook and Twitter and appeared on the site guanabee.com of a Hispanic media agency owned by Gawker Media. The "chuntara quinceañera," as she is named in online comments, stands sucking down her Slurpee with her bright-pink and black hair that clashes with her metallic purple ball gown, milling around a shoe store as her *chambelanes*, her male escorts, dressed in bright-pink, fitted, bedazzled Western shirts and colorful *botas* shop for trendy sneakers. "Chuntara" and "chuntaro" are terms for Latinx individuals who display a socially determined low-class aesthetic, identified with a lack of sophistication or mainstream style. This public encounter with a self-righteous cell phone camera likely documents an encounter embodying the tedious hours between morning mass and evening reception. As an archetype of aloof nonchalance, she is the antithesis of the glossy and airbrushed commercially instituted images of ideal coming-of-age style that encourage young women to obsessively attend to each of the tiniest details of their day in order to make their quinceañera dreams come true. Dream fulfillment is a public process of self-actualization and is completed through likes, shares, and representations of material success. This young woman, hunched in an unflattering photo position, in danger of staining her gown, and clearly not the center of this portion of her day, rather simply being herself, flouts commercial and social expectations that would monetize her body as a collective cultural symbol but discount her individual aspirations.

I see the quinceañera wherever I go: seated in front of my laptop, scrolling on my phone, in the car, updating my inbox, at the mall and the library, the grocery store, the bank, on campus, and in my home. I hear it on the radio and see it on television. I have a consciousness of all things related to the practice, and this is reality not simply because I have lived and breathed it for the past eleven years. Photos and videos, books and magazines, YouTube videos and Instagram posts, Facebook and Twitter feeds, the hum of Latinx cultural life in material and immaterial US cultural imaginary is real. The quinceañera practice is but one material manifestation of this imaginary, one that integrates cultural communities around the common acceptance of commodity fetishism. Regarding consumption as a social phenomenon, in the case of cultural practice in use in material, digital, and psychic spheres, the commodity is the self. In the above example, our chuntara quinceañera works as the material manifestation of a street-style phonetics because it "symbolically challenges the capitalist logic" of the United States that implies that a culturally neutral and racially unmarked identity holds "immense Western value" and therefore is the surest route to mainstream cultural acceptance and social success (Hinojosa and Casillas). Our mediagenic chuntara illustrates how theatricality is a social resource both in and outside of the quinceañera ritual.

What we must understand about quinceañera practice, though, is that it sits in the interstitial space between US Latinx peoples and wider US culture, a space separated by the border of the young, feminine, brown body. As such, young women leverage their bodies in the service of belonging to neither community fully, instead finding themselves in a space of constant vacillation, transition, and transformation. Their transitional roles are mediated by affective economic relations in which memory and shared nostalgia are imbricated with the coordinated material practices of ritual to conjure dreams of material wealth and social success.

In the United States, where American folklore studies situates most of its intellectual labor, being receptive to the work of folklore involves understanding how the work of folklore in marginal communities functions to assert the right to exist and be seen in American society. Communities use folklore as a catalyst for social presencing and asserting their right to social survival into an undetermined future. For Latinx communities, an investment in sustaining cultural practices becomes a mode of both documenting the self in present space and time by restaging the past and contributing to the potentiality of Latinx futurity. In this way, the staging of quinceañera events by US Latinxs is interpretable as one of many contemporary "strategies of selfhood" (Bhabha 1). In *The Location of Culture*, Homi K. Bhabha interprets such strategies as inhabiting interstitial spaces, and recognizing their existence and value is a theoretical project that requires retreating from the narrowness of "originary and initial subjectivities" to contemporary processes that emerge in the recognition of existing at the uneven, jagged seams of cultural difference. In such an undefined groove, Bhabha asserts the need for "new signs of identity, and innovative sites of collaboration, and contestation" (1–2). Using a lens of Latinx folkloristics, I interpret cultural practice and performance in the United States as located in the interstitial space between creation and reception, where practices become locations for the negotiation of transitional intersubjectivities of race, ethnicity, class, gender, sexuality, region, and citizenship.

Observing quinceañera consumer practice allows us to see how a new generation of Latinx youth is curating its own everyday cultural logics. Doing so in the face of symbolic annihilation is both difficult and powerful. Living an accented life, verbally or visually, choosing to see one's demonstrable Latinx cultural heritage as a social asset is a daily challenge to centuries of western cultural hegemony. The quinceañera as a representation of inter-American Latinx identity carries with it a visual accent. This accent is a strategic ideological code switch from institutional English to informal Spanglish channeled through material arts and embodied performance. Therefore, coming out Latinx is to do more than assert cultural pride or ethnoracial family values through tradition, but to self-consciously occupy a social stage as a cultural other and expressly demand to be recognized as a social, economic, and political force.

Quinceañera events materialize one way young Latina consumers are manifesting their social values and ideologies on the borders of their bodies as spaces for the curation of visual self-portraits that in essence sell themselves to social networks in person and in mediated digital networks. A sense of the self as commodity or a process of self-objectification is also a process of self-awareness and evaluation. This creates a self-reflective ideology in which young women see themselves as social animals surviving in a world of visual currencies that stand in for an understanding of the neoliberal economy of objects and western cultural values. What is often forgotten is that Latinx youth are very much part of western culture and at the same time, western cultural hegemony. What these youth of color also understand is how their racialized identities affect their place in that western hegemonic system. They do not live in ignorance of its bias, of its colonial history, of its violence. As I put forward in this book, they have learned how to push back on a system that rejects their humanity while appropriating their cultural capital. This process gentrifies cultural expression, calling for cultural austerity or a flattening of cultural identifiers on the part of people of color and fostering palatability through invisibility.

## METHODS: CRITICAL LATINX FOLKLORISTICS

This book is not intended to give voice to anyone. Instead, I am using it to hold space for folks who strategize daily about how to make space for themselves in a neoliberal US society that "invisibilizes" their experiences until they are deemed legible and therefore profitable (Gottschild 2). My prerogative as an author and collaborator is to translate community experiences onto the page. This role as culture broker, particularly fomented in research conducted in highly visible minority communities, is easily co-opted for personal profit—academic job stability, economic gain, personal fame and acclaim, or even simply a smug sense of benevolence, to name a few potential perks of academic authorship. Despite the experiential gap between community creativity and academic discourse, I endeavor to keep the priorities of collaborators rather than academic audiences in mind. I am an ethnographer and a storyteller. I weave firsthand experiences into textual narratives, only to realize that the words on the page are no comparison for the complexity of the textures of fabrics, the sounds of family voices, and the consuming chaos of public encounters. What I am able to bring to these community experiences is a brand of strategic legibility—to recontextualize community narratives in places where they are yet allowed to exist.

My goal in investigating contemporary quinceañera practices interconnected across the United States is to reconcile the hypervisible imagining of Latinx culture that foregrounds poverty, undereducation, unstable migratory status, and patterns of mass incarceration with the lived experiences that emerge as self-documentary practices of community solidarity, upward social mobility, cultural adaptation, and flexible citizenship. The experiences shared through this work are many, and each of them serves to strip away the mystery and aura of ritual, shifting the view of the quinceañera from esoteric "ethnic" rite to secular social performances that together exemplify and amplify a contemporary stateless inter-American identity of the consumer citizen. Individually each event is a vivid exemplar of creative ingenuity and genuine care; together they weave a more enduring collective narrative than has yet been revealed by scholarship that has focused on institutions such as a the Catholic Church or on singular examples of personal aesthetics and family experiences. Engaging with the quinceañera as a series of interconnected fragments that are simultaneously partial and complete stories, depending on observational positionality, grounded in commercial flows of goods, bodies in and of space, ideologies, and digital ephemera serve as mutually informing intertexts and as "the unauthored codes of culture" that "form the threads through which we weave new patterns" (Grimes 27). With a conceptualization of a national Latinx collective identity, the informed meanings also take on emergent meanings as groups renarrate the coming-of-age ritual as an extension of aspirational middle-class American identity. To make sense of the narratives, which take on visual and aural forms, we must agree on the premise that Latinx folklore, the everyday creativity of US Latinx–identifying communities, must be academically approached through three key concepts explored throughout this book in a theoretical framework of critical Latinx folkloristics, which brings together an approach to form that is intersectional, interdisciplinary, and translocal.

Critical Latinx folkloristics methods are not in themselves new to American folkloristics. The specific methods have never been framed as a collective body of interpretive practices; instead they have been filtered through professionals and writers who derive their analyses and community practice from a blend of theoretical sources often external to folklore studies. Among their interdisciplinary sources are literature, cultural studies, anthropology, critical ethnic studies, women and gender studies, media studies, queer theory, and feminist geography, employed to respond to Latinx community practices faithfully and holistically. Critical Latinx folkloristics is an approach to research collaboration with Latinx communities that attempts to systematize the exploration of such communities by any folklorist, not limited by race or ethnic affiliation, to help ground fieldwork and analysis in ethnic methods to account for the realities of being an American Latinx person.

I am an anthropological folklorist and Latinx cultural studies scholar in that my research focuses on the everyday artistry and practice of Latinx-descent communities in the United States whose culturally invested art production encompasses social strategies whereby creativity is a cultural resource and a method of resisting oppressive systems of power, be they structural or personal. Folkloric cultural productions that intentionally and tacitly function as readable social texts become semicontained, self-representative, autobiographical accountings of Latinx lives. Inspired by Marivel T. Danielson's *Homecoming Queers: Desire and Difference in Chicana Latina Cultural Production*, I assert that in order to prioritize community perspectives of enactments of Latinx folklore and especially Latina spectacle, we must account for such creations' explicit orientation in wider, racialized "public perceptions of excess" such as the appearance of quinceañeras in public space (Danielson 2). This manner of personal autotopographic social positioning serves as a way of creating a sense of "home" through flexible modes of "creative expression and critical consciousness" that requires invested scholars to attend to notions of shared alterity, cultural specificity, and a subversive aesthetics (4).

In the following chapters I examine the quinceañera as a cultural practice from a variety of interconnected vantage points by drawing on a mixed-methods approach. Unlike studies that have focused on personal life experiences or ethnographic observations outside the United States, my work engages directly with ethnographic interviews, media analysis, and field observations conducted among quinceañeras and industry professionals over a seven-year period in California, Nebraska, Iowa, Missouri, Illinois, Texas, and Mexico City. I draw on fieldwork I conducted at twenty-four commercial expositions wholly dedicated to quinceañera products and the voices of ten interlocutors whose work has intersected with quinceañera consumer culture materially and digitally. My goal is to mobilize a dynamic notion of practice rather than static interpretations of folklore-as-object to examine common culture-in-use as it informs larger popular understandings of race and class divisions within US Latinx populations. As I have previously asserted, a merger of Latinx folkloristics and cultural studies methodologies that foreground notions of practice "offer a framework through which we can discuss how individualized cultural performances are rendered part of a collective process of resistance through attention to public creative acts that create communities of practice in the process" (González-Martin 59). In the case of quinceañeras in Latinx communities, such a process involves examining the representations of quinceañera practices rather than ritual structures, emphasizing the way materiality is used to index aspirational social mobility.

Ethnography of the ephemeral also draws on the work of scholars focusing on the cultural productions in placeless locations such as online sites and communities. Quinceañeras find common ground through the use of online retailers and blogs that encourage girls to share their wishes and experiences as well as social networking sites that offer girls a chance to display their lives and experiences in real time; thus, examining the life and practice of twenty-first-century quinceañera celebrations involves conceptualizing the events as placeless and ephemeral. Placelessness means that this ethnographic work is one not of people and places but rather of practice. As such, the practice is always moving, and its meaning is not primarily defined by geographic location. Quinceañeras do not belong to any one area over another. Their practice is a product of inter-American circuits of knowledge. While the tradition is taken up in nuanced forms across the United States, thinking of it as being of one particular area is erroneous because of the movement of Latinxs across the United States at different social and historical moments in history. Therefore, we need to consider the quinceañera, as I have come to understand it, to be a reflection of place and of people's flexible connections to space over time while simultaneously analyzing the tradition as one that can exist outside a realm of geographic formality.

In *Quinceañera Style* I examine how twenty-first-century Latinx communities negotiate social belonging through consumer intervention in ritual coming-of-age spectacles known as quinceañeras. Spectacle here is based on a definition of performative speech acts. In *Queen for a Day: Transformistas, Beauty Queens, and the Performance of Femininity in Venezuela*, the anthropologist Marcia Ochoa interpolates the relation between performative speech and the concept of spectacle as she investigates feminine spectacle as social strategy among transgender beauty pageant contestants. She asserts, following Judith Butler, that the link between performed speech and spectacle is identifiable by the presence of three factors: theatrical production or staging, presentation to an audience, and interpretability, "subject to the conditions and possibilities of reception" (Ochoa 209). These three key elements are found within quinceañeras as elaborately planned and staged fifteenth-birthday celebrations that expand beyond neighborhood and close-knit families into manifesting material and digital publics. These events, more than being religious rituals or commercial products, are spectacles of Latinidad that amplify the presence of Latinx communities in everyday life across the United States and shift the acceptability of ethnoracial visibility for future generations.

### AUSTIN, TEXAS

A line had formed on the walkway, just beyond the grassy area surrounding the Tejano monument. I sat on a bench to watch the teenagers in tuxedos and evening gowns sweat and fidget as they waited for their turn to pose with history. They had to rotate between waiting for tourists who wanted to see the statue and read the plaque and other quinceañera courts and the photographers waiting to find unique angles that best suited their clients. That particular day the capitol grounds were bustling with quinceañera traffic, tourists with large cameras who emerged from a group tour bus, and a poorly attended pro-life rally that was occupying the south-facing steps and using a bull horn to decry a woman's right to choose. It was an intense and complicated spectacle of diverse femininities on display. Passengers from the large tour bus were photographing the protest and then turned their lenses toward the Tejano monument to take photos of the quinceañera girls as they crowded under the fleeting shade of a large tree. The concentrated spectacle of racialized femininity in that moment represented a notable emblem of Americanity.

### SAN FRANCISCO, CALIFORNIA

I saw her running across the street with her court. You couldn't miss her, stopping traffic around the square in her bright-pink dress with layers of tulle and crinoline that made it appear hard for her to maneuver in busy city streets around the civic center. It was a Saturday afternoon, and we were just exiting San Francisco City Hall, where my brother and his bride had just gotten married. Tina, their event photographer and a native San Franciscan, said she photographed quinceañeras there all the time. Just like brides and grooms, quinceañera celebrants choose the site for its beautiful marble architecture, sweeping staircase, and giant dome, which is a full forty-two feet taller than the dome at the nation's capitol.

### DES MOINES, IOWA

I had seen one of Oscar's promotional photos circulating on Facebook through the *Quinceañeras Magazine* Iowa page.[1] I was accustomed to seeing the photographic tableau of the church steps adorned by the court of honor and the close family or maybe just the quince girl and her parents. But this photo was interesting, different. Rather than a traditional portrait used to adorn invitations or to decorate the reception hall, this image was not a typical portrait-studio image, with the quince girl centrally located and looking directly into the camera lens. This image, photographed by Oscar Ramos, depicted a quince girl in a voluminous seafoam green dress holding onto a bundle of balloons and jumping off of steps of the state capitol building in Des Moines, Iowa. The image was being used to advertise Oscar Ramos Photography, in particular to showcase innovative photo shoots. With innovation as the goal, this photographic ethos of unanticipated backdrops was a pattern I had been seeing evolve since my fieldwork began. I noticed how significant preserving quinceañera images was to families and how circulating those same images was a powerful draw for new clients who saw a version of their dream represented by other girls. In many ways the visual cultural economy of social media helped bolster these photographic innovations, as girls could witness quinceañeras from across the hemispheric Americas from their bedrooms with the touch of a button and a swipe of the screen.

MEXICO CITY, MEXICO

Lía and I had just walked through the Zona Rosa toward the financial district. She shared how the area was still tense for the city's trans community and was primarily populated by moneyed, white, gay men. We stood on the east side of the busy roundabout on Paseo de la Reforma facing El Ángel (Monumento a la Independencia). Inaugurated in 1910 to celebrate the centennial of Mexico's War for Independence, in recent years the spot has become a popular place to meet for large protests. The city's Pride parade began there, and it is the site for public celebration of national soccer victories. Yet, more importantly to me, it is a spot where brides and quinceañeras come to take commemorative portraits. It was raining that day, and there were very few tourists or locals ascending the steps to pose. One must take a shot from across the street to capture the entire 118-foot Corinthian-style column and 22-foot-tall bronze statue of Nike, the Greek goddess of victory. The memories made in this historic location manifest in photographic portraiture that places young women into public space and then brings the aura of public recognition into private homes.

*Quinceañera Style* is a story of representation and materiality, not ritual. Representations index cultural practice in revision and integrate different ideological and material elements of wider social, political, and cultural environments into intimate personal narratives of social belonging. An accumulation of such performances in everyday life has the capacity to affect social environments by changing the dynamics of socioracial reception. The accumulation of representations of quinceañera practices in a US social imaginary rejects cultural austerity that would ask people who live in marginal states of difference to smooth their edges for the convenience of mainstream audiences. Rather, the representations form a demand to be consumed, and to be consumed on one's own terms, and the knowledge that Latina youth in particular have the power of being both producers and consumers when it comes to quinceañera folklore practice. As such, through their mobilization of choice in an ideological architecture framed by neoliberal possibilities, quinceañera girls are re-creating their performance environments into places where their life experiences have value. Spectacle is an interpretive tool that allows others to see how social actors fashion their own social niches through artistic intensification. Making a spectacle of oneself becomes a social strategy to control gaze.

The use of spectacle as a unifying framework first allows quinceañeras to be acknowledged as part of a cultural performance repertoire and at the same time plays with the politics of drawing in others' interrogative gaze.[2] The notion of making a spectacle of oneself is inflected with criticism and induces shame and even a sense of danger for one who is subject to racist or classist social judgments. Quinceañera events draw in gaze, and individual girls base the success of their celebrations on attentive local and mediated viewership alongside circulation of their images. Willful Latina spectacle is an acknowledgment of the power of being seen, instrumentalizes the reception of the brown feminized body to generate intimate relations between social actors, and rejects erasure on the basis of presumed social illegitimacy. The Latina spectacle is an embodied *testimonio*. It is a strategy that uses the external fetishization of the Latina body as a site of guerrilla social warfare to disrupt presumptions of normativity about the singular body and collectivized subjectivity.[3] Such a social assertion rendered through flesh is dangerous, as it reveals the ambivalences and indeterminacies cemented in canonical cultural identities and at the same time contests neoliberal social logics of hyperindividualism. It is collective and personal, intimate and public, joyous and interrogative. In this way, the collectivized subjectivity of the Latina spectacle transfigures neoliberal logics of individual social success.

Guy Debord argues, "*Spectacle* is not a collection of images, but a social relation among people, mediated by images" (36). Society is made manifest in the spectacle, and the spectacle has discernable impact on the everyday lives of the oppressed who find pieces of themselves at the edges of the spectacle. Ochoa critiques Debord's conceptualization of the spectacle as an overreaching monolith (Ochoa 204). My goal is to mobilize Ochoa's concept of spectacular femininities to highlight the ways that Latinas employ spectacle through quinceañera performance. While Ochoa's work is located in Venezuela and her argument foregrounds transgender beauty queens, her assertion of feminine spectacle as commodity articulates a bridge between discursive formation and bodily realities of race, class, and gender in the hemispheric Americas; such a connection allows us to examine shared symbolic resources and technologies of feminine and hyperfeminized bodies in public space. The forms of US Latina spectacle are the everyday artistic practices that centralize cultural production where individual bodies are key locations of cultural negotiation and possibility. These mobile canvases manifest visual narratives that are at the same observational moment complete and interrupted, recognized and cryptic, and legible and confounding. The spectacle is desire made material and an amplification of personal autonomy. And feminine desire counters self-abnegating cultural scripts by creating a space for generational resistance, with elders who support the scaffold of spectacle and youth who are exposed to new cultural scripts through it.

This work traces the life of the quinceañera as a circulating social text between ethnic, territorial, and gendered boundaries in the contemporary United States. At the same time, from the vantage point of professionals, the quinceañera becomes a representation of the monetizing of Latinx culture in contemporary America. Constituting new social meanings, these diverse regional ethnographic encounters among quinceañera industry professionals, performance artists, and individual quinceañeras reveal the ways the tradition has been reimagined, with economic integration into modern circumstances designed for consumption. This additional lens of consumer practice, the commoditization of ritual objects turned material adornments, is directly connected to the identification of Latinx Americans as a national consumer demographic with increased impact on the wider US economy.

In her foundational ethnographic monograph on racialized mass media and cultural institutions, *Latinos Inc.: The Marketing and Making of a People*, Arlene Dávila examines the "production of commercial and mass-mediated culture" directly linked to Latinx populations in the United States and reflects on how inclusion in consumer marketplaces is part of a discourse that links consumption and targeted advertising to nationalism and citizenship. Dávila looks toward mass media collectively as a structure that grants and negates belonging at a national level through the mediation of representation (11–12). Her argument, that as ethnographers and cultural critics we cannot examine marketing to Latinxs without foregrounding their "peripheral status in US society," especially influences my desire to examine quinceañera cultural productions as a form of marketing and cultural production that has implicitly responded to racialized inequity in marketing representations. As such, these productions are creating new generations of cultural entrepreneurs who enact a social critique of Latinidad in public life while also blurring the lines between hemispheric nationalisms and presumptions of juridical citizenship. Moreover, the quinceañera itself becomes a place of informal community marketing, promoting not only the value of objects in use but also community practice as engines of social and personal possibility.

An expression of a developing Latinx middle-class style, the quinceañera celebration therefore becomes a coordinated performance of class signification. Integrating regionally varied ethnographic fieldwork, observational case studies offer an unprecedented perspective on the coming-of-age process as a product of multiple, interdependent cultural economies that defy regional geography as they spill into digitally mediated consumer spaces. Moreover, a focus on these economic relations draws attention to a stable Latinx middle class and forces the reevaluation of the social mobility of a group that has been largely defined by stereotypes of poverty, undereducation, and social dysfunction.

My work cultivates the contemporary field of critical Latinx folkloristics by specifically drawing on the intellectual histories of folklore and anthropology as extensions of colonialist premises. My goal in each of the chapters that follow is to forge a new intellectual frame rather than simply draw on existing frames of even Latinx anthropology in order to focus attention to community agency and authorship. With my emphasis in folklore studies, I am able to assess communities of practice. Rather than taking on a lens of voyeuristic ethnographic gaze of a people in a place, I examine *practice* as a primary informant in my methodology. Geographic provenance, a stalwart determinant of the power of ethnographic fieldwork in anthropology, is less significant in my work. At the same time, even digital ethnography, especially that which draws on digitally mediated experiences, often fails to account for race and class as part of spatial identities. Mobilizing a critical folkloristic frame allows me to draw on agency in practice while also assessing the politics of space and place without limiting the texts under investigation by assumptions of race or ethnic difference.

On a wider level, these narratives of social mobility offer insight into larger theoretical conversations about social citizenship in the twenty-first-century United States. My research intervenes in the rather limited scope of previous scholarship by centralizing cultural economics or socioeconomic integration in a conversation of culturally informed social practice. In this way, the case studies expand beyond traditional narratives that oversimplify feminine signification at the heart of this increasingly public cultural performance. Instead, the diversity of quinceañera practice illustrates the way that Latinx cultural practices might actually be fundamentally American and economically driven behaviors. The stylistic diversity exhibited in quinceañera offers a new framework from which to understand social belonging in multicultural and multiracial consumer networks in a neoliberal United States, where an accumulation of goods has historically signaled the potentiality of realizing the American Dream.

## AN AMERICAN QUINCEAÑERA

Quinceañera celebrations are practiced among Latinx and Latin American communities throughout the hemispheric Americas. The ritual event's historic branding as a family-based, religious celebration has relegated the complexities and transfigurations of the event to relative obscurity. This obscurity has allowed the ritual practice's identity to languish in an antifeminist social imaginary, one interpreted to be more harmful than helpful to Latina youth. As much as we can identify the divide between feminism and Latina feminisms, and with few Latinx voices contributing to this narrative as a national spectacle reflective of a shift in Latinx social practice, we need to rethink the way in which Latinx social actors are transfiguring the event to suit their personal, social, and political needs in the present day. My first task is then to rhetorically parse out the varying elements of the celebration to better understand the materials being used to rebrand and repurpose Latina spectacle.

The average quinceañera celebration is divided between secular elements and sacred elements, with secular aspects gaining greater traction across diasporic Latinx communities in the United States. Its practical patterns are manifest in the United States but ideologically rooted in practices across the material and digital hemispheric Americas. In Cuba and the Cuban diaspora, large-scale parties are often supplanted by extravagant professional photo shoots that practically offset the costs of a full party and capitalize on the creation of memories through photography (Pertierra). After travel to Cuba was reinstated under the presidency of Barack Obama, there has been an influx of wealthy Cuban exiles who return to the island just to celebrate their daughters' quinceañeras.[4] Such heritage trips offer a boon to local economies, even if the events have little precedent on the island since the revolutionary period began. In the United States, the event is broadly divided into two phases: a religious blessing and a reception celebration. This pattern of practice is commonly recognized as typical and traditional. It is not uncommon to hear of Mexican American families with transnational ties celebrating in Mexico, where, as in Cuba, costs are lower and more family members may attend.

In the consumer-driven twenty-first-century Americas the more popular reception phase of the event has subsumed the religious markers of the quinceañera. That change has troubled leaders in the Catholic Church who, despite the event's informal affiliation with the Catholic faith, feel it necessary to exert creative controls over the dress and presentation of the celebrants within church walls; some have gone so far as denying young Latinas the right to celebrate if they choose not to attend mandated preparatory seminars and adhere to formal rules of dress and propriety coded in the modesty of dress design. Such strictures appear to mobilize similar logics of school dress codes, particularly those finding currency in contemporary news stories of public schools denying young women the right to choose their styles of clothing, as those choices that reveal skin may elicit sexual desire. The tension between church and consumer culture is less about morality and more about control, in particular over the creation and demonstration of desire. When quinceañeras were products of private family planning, it was the church that guided and validated the tradition but did not have to acknowledge it as an official sacrament. As the practice of quinceañeras is lauded and supported outside the church, parishes are being rendered marginal as incidental influences on the larger celebrations. They are losing control of the event that is seen as not only a singular coming-of-age moment but also a chance to share the Catholic faith with larger audiences.

As the numbers of Hispanic Catholics in the United States are shrinking (Dias), in 2008 the church took an official stand in claiming the blessing of the quinceañera as a documented custom of Hispanic Catholics in the United States. Within my fieldwork in California, I found that the religious ritual, although adhered to, was less a worry or focus for families than the development and staging of the later reception. In fact, because of the commercial focus and the increased influence of burgeoning professional quinceañera planners, staging the reception and its internal customs—micro rituals such as changing from flats to heels and dancing the group waltz—has become a more pronounced element of the celebration. At the same time, as families are becoming more aware of the celebration as events that reflect the prowess and values of their families, they are spending a great deal of time reflecting on events and how those events are part of a larger shared system of community involvement in which one event comes to index another, creating intimacy or distance between participants. This is in part a by-product of the strong drive toward creating a uniquely personal event. In sum, the quinceañera tradition has shifted in the twenty-first century from private households to public display through consumer and media intervention; the events are styled by individuals but serve to narrate wider community experiences of social transition, and their efficacy now resides in their capacity to engage communities on a secular level.

In the chapters that follow, I draw on observational experiences from two additional phases of cultural production that offer different insights into the event's social efficacy. The initial phase is one of shopping and buying, which I term "the consumer rite." The preamble of the event has a complex correlation to social meanings, especially as shopping and buying happen in brick-and-mortar US and Mexican businesses or as domestic and international purchases over the internet. In a final review stage, young women and other participants come to evaluate the material and digital memories of the event, whether days or decades later. Rather than examining the event as bounded by a singular day and time, I illustrate the layers of social politics involved, as the quinceañera becomes a metonym for larger shifts in Latinx life in the United States.

## PREVIOUS SCHOLARSHIP ON QUINCEAÑERAS

Since the turn of the twenty-first century, quinceañera industries have grown alongside the visibility of quinceañera culture in the US mainstream. Despite the event's popularity and presence amid regional and national marketing campaigns drawing in Latinx consumers to buy Dr. Pepper and watch Monday Night Raw wrestling, and in popular young adult fiction, coupled with the primacy of Latinx positions in recent national political debates, the quinceañera ritual has remained conspicuously absent in studies of US Latinx folklore. Before the edited collection of articles was published by *Quinceañeras* in 2010, only one other was published, in 2000. There have been quinceañera planning guides mostly for younger girls (Hoyt-Goldsmith; King; Salcedo), articles on the topic from within Mexican and Mexican American communities (Cantú "Chicana," "La Quinceañera"; Dávalos, "Making Gender"; Horowitz; Napolitano; Potowski and Gorman), resources of multicultural psychology and social work (Romo and Mireles-Rios), and a memoir broadly exploring US quinceañera culture (Alvarez). Yet very little critical attention has been paid by Latinx folklorists to the intricacies of the phenomenon, especially to the material elements that have come to set the event apart from other coming-of-age celebrations practiced within the United States.

Although Eva Castellanoz was made a National Heritage Fellow for her work as a quinceañera corona maker and spiritual leader in her Latinx community in Nissa, Oregon, in 1987, folklorists in the United States have written few works dedicated to the documentation of the quinceañera celebrations among broader Latinx enclaves. Scholars who have investigated the tradition in the United States have approached the topic in two ways—as a marker of gendered Latinx identity among migrant communities with clear links to family and cultural histories (Cantú, "La Quinceañera"; Davalos, "Making Gender"; Horowitz) or as a practice that highlights the continuing prominence of Hispanic Catholics within the church (Deiter; Erevia). These studies position the event in a generic form, as though each event were a carbon copy of another, revisiting and recapitulating the same message each time. I expressly draw from the strongest pieces of research on US quinceañeras by Chicana feminist scholars Karen Mary Davalos and Norma E. Cantú, who have observed the tradition as performances of femininity and ethnicity but within a framework of cultural preservation. Dávalos's work, completed in the 1990s, approaches the quinceañera celebration as an unexpected source of cultural knowledge, one way of asserting how Mexican Americans in Chicago continued to express their cultural identities in socially meaningful ways. Her use of quinceañeras was incidental, as she found herself attending events over the course of her fieldwork but was not invested in documenting the celebration. Rather, her focus was on the retention of a range of cultural traditions, language skills, and ideologies that were part of a Mexican immigrant sensibility, of which the quinceañera became a useful example.

Cantú has documented Chicana quinceañeras in South Texas ("La Quinceañera"), focusing on a feminist framework that prioritizes acknowledging and documenting Chicana traditions while at the same time looking deeply at the intersection of origins and expressive elements that reify the complexity of lives lived along the US-Mexico border. Cantú identifies the potency of the religious ritual and shows how familial beliefs are routed through this female coming-of-age rite by emphasizing structures of spirituality. Her work stands out as one of only a few focused, critical ethnographic attempts to document the celebration as a living cultural tradition in the United States; she demonstrates that the quinceañera is more than the sum of its parts, as something much larger and deeper, and has the capacity to speak for a larger community of Tejanas. Cantú's work speaks to how quinceañera traditions materialize local community histories, and she sets the groundwork for practical ethnographic documentation of quinceañera celebrations among US Latinas, particularly through the study of material culture. I have chosen to expand her assessments by indexing the array of material choices mobilized to customize events, while I also investigate how consumer competition offers young women a broader swath of aesthetic choices for self-adornment that reveal changes in social and cultural expectations of Latinas.

The novelist Julia Alvarez takes up such a critique of materiality in her memoir, *Once upon a Quinceañera: Coming of Age in the U.S.A.*, the first text to foreground the presence of commercial intervention in US quinceañera celebrations. She documents a year of personal observations of different elements of quinceañera planning across the country. She observes the realities of twenty-first-century quinceañera practice, in particular noting how sites of cultural knowledge transmission relocate from kitchen tables to commercial spaces in such venues as quinceañera expositions. These expositions of cultural and consumer products serve as primary informants in my fieldwork.

The multiple spaces that quinceañeras occupy require rethinking ethnographic investigation from the perspective of participant observation, oral history collection, and ethnography of the ephemeral. While traditional ethnographic inquiry focuses on the importance of a durable field site, ethnography of the ephemeral develops out of a desire and need to observe socially significant sites of temporary or limited duration (Dávila, *Latinos Inc.*; Paulsen). This form of ethnography becomes particularly important as my work with quinceañeras developed into an investigation of personal performance situated within public spheres of consumer sales promotion such as consumer expositions. These events are particularly important as they exist as cultural and consumer resources for Latinas who are the first in their families to plan quinceañera events. In addition, these events take place where Latinx identities become reified in public space, open and visible to a larger, diverse populace, and draw attention to the often ubiquitous yet overlooked Latinx presence in an area. Ephemeral spaces are often divided by their connection to larger society; either they are viewed as reinforcing "existing social norms, such as weddings," or they are seen to introduce new elements into a culture "in the case of trade shows" (Paulsen 510). Quinceañera expos actually serve both these claims, being invested in promoting a traditional practice while introducing material innovations into its performance practices whose trickle-down fashion changes almost daily. While these events are short-lived, lasting for a mere five hours on a Sunday afternoon, they are spaces of intense social and cultural expression on the part of organizers, vendors, and consumers alike.

Quinceañera expos are unique cultural and consumer zones that function as material inspiration for shopping and buying quinceañera accessories as much as ways to spend time with one's family on a Sunday afternoon. I follow the quinceañera tradition from girl to girl, house to house, but also into the public commercial spaces of quinceañera expositions as well as the more remote and literally placeless space of digital media, where quinceañera culture thrives at the creative fingertips of young consumers, marketing agencies, creative directors, and professional event planners. Expos are spaces where these influencers converge.

The expo environment, whether devoted to brides or quinceañeras, is a complex, multipurpose commercial and social environment. These group-specific venues provide not only space for businesses to feature products but also a place in which consumers are courted while they see active demonstrations of their potential purchases in one cohesive, meticulously organized, glamorized space. Quinceañera expos offer a space in which to see the convergence of cultural and consumer environments. While difficult to track, the expos seem to have cropped up in Latinx areas across the United States such as California, Texas, and Florida since the "quinceañera boom" of the mid-2000s, as Pamela Colloff dubs the phenomenon in her 2009 *Texas Monthly* discussion of extravagant quinceañera traditions in the Rio Grande Valley (143). While some observers like Colloff emphasize the financial burden encouraged by over-the-top industries, the expos represent part of the previously opaque backstage planning process, a venue that contributes to the shared vision of a ritual coming-of-age tradition. Expos also provide a social platform from which to sell consumer goods by implicitly marketing dreams of consumerism and embedded within them, dreams of social and personal acceptance and success in US society. This topic becomes particularly relevant as a new generation of undocumented yet acculturated Latinx youth are clamoring for a space in mainstream cultural settings. Vendors' desire to sell products merges with the specialized expectations of consumers to transform this basic commercial space into a multitiered performance space. Central to that space is the use of language; expos become spaces of translation in visual and aural registers.

As a folklorist I have followed diverse iterations of the quinceañera practice, placing the most effort on observing consumer-focused trade shows hosted by *Quinceañeras Magazine*, a regional, Latina, teen magazine that circulates in Latinx enclaves across metropolitan areas such as Los Angeles County; the San Francisco Bay Area; Chicago; Washington, DC; New York City; and San Antonio. The editorials and articles in English and Spanish offer seasonal advice to young Latinas in the process of planning their coming-of-age celebrations. In 2015 the magazine celebrated its tenth anniversary with the inauguration of its Quinceañera Foundation, which holds an annual beauty pageant where regional contestants compete for the title of National Miss Cover Girl and a college scholarship. The print magazine is designed to help young women and their families plan their quinceañera events and features full-page, bilingual advertisements encouraging and promoting the acquisition of large sums of money through home refinancing. Booths are set up by banks offering credit cards with low introductory interest rates to help offset the initial costs of coming-of-age events. These new financial offerings imply that families will sacrifice quite a bit to host ideal events for their daughters regardless of cost. The investments are also part of a cultural understanding of spending in which the emotional commitment to one's family and community represents a form of necessary collectivism that reaffirms social relationships (Falicov 314). With the expansion of consumer industries, the material reality of quinceañera party planning has shifted in focus from internal familial exchange to a system of atomized private borrowing. The change in economic strategies repositions Latinx consumers as active and central participants in the US debt economy on a characteristic path toward leveraging the American Dream.

One of the primary strengths of the expo environment is that it is engineered to fill the service gaps that have been left open by internet-based quinceañera resources and local dress shops. Latina culture is being constructed and Latino consumers manipulated. The journalist Maria Hinojosa expresses similar suspicion as she and a young producer on her *Latino USA* podcast team visit one of the largest expos on the East Coast in the September 16, 2016, episode "You Are Cordially Invited to Hailey's Quinceañera" (Cereijido). While only devoting a few pages of her lengthy memoir to these emergent consumer venues, Alvarez delivers an extremely personal narrative confronting cultural change and intergenerational tension; her responses to commercial developments around the celebration are familiar and generationally specific. Alvarez reveals her dismay in personal, textual outbursts such as "Crazy, crazy, crazy, I think the world's gone crazy" (61). She finds herself personally disoriented by chile con carne fountains and photo-booth demos, by the cacophony of competing sounds advertising DJ services and plasma screens, in essence by the growing marketplace that is buying and selling culture and that excludes *abuelitas*, grandmothers or elders whom she interprets as being demoted from vital cultural gatekeepers to party guests. In celebrations of previous generations, those of the 1970s and 1980s, informal networks of family and friends grounded the celebrations in communally gifted labor or services, but that group practice has been exchanged for an engagement with the debt economy that prioritizes personal control rather than communal compromise. The new process of depersonalization and commodification marks a shift from informal to formal economies of procurement and practice. Although Alvarez never claims to analyze the celebration, as a madrina of Latinx bildungsroman in the United States she draws together personal stories that document a snapshot of cultural change that signals a shift in the way American Latinxs are intellectualizing culture practice through rather than despite trends in the US consumer system. The consumerist quinceañera cannot be confined to geographically confined consumer practice.

In the United States and Mexico, patterns of practice unify traditions despite geographic divides. In *The Beauty Trade: Youth, Gender, and Fashion Globalization*, Angela McCracken offers an international perspective on quinceañera practice that specifically explicates the relations between global commerce and beauty products among quinceañera industries located in Guadalajara, Mexico. McCracken, a feminist political economist, investigates quinceañeras from the perspectives of international studies and global political economy. She uses the quinceañera as a lens through which to examine how global consumer beauty culture plays a foundational role in guiding beauty practice in middle- and upper-class Mexican quinceañera traditions in Guadalajara. My intervention in cultural conversations concerning the representative materiality of the quinceañera draws on key themes posed by Alvarez, but like McCracken, I analyze quinceañeras as part of larger, macro contexts of cultural and consumer trade not limited by geographic borderlands or ethnically specific discourse. I assert that the quinceañera represents an intersection in private and public space, complicated by means of twenty-first-century technological and social shifts. A focus on the transition of the ritual among a new generation of Latinxs becomes particularly relevant as one better understands how the celebration has been narrated in history.

The majority of quinceañera-inclusive scholarship published in the 1980s and 1990s consists of "feminist fueled studies of beauty that sought to understand how it served as a tool of oppression, made powerfully dominant through patriarchal and capitalist circuits of meaning" (Estill 174). My work instead focuses on quinceañeras as representations of Latinx lives from a secular, consumer perspective that embraces "neoliberal contexts of possibility" (Grewal 1). Rather than thinking about what dominant social forces are being thrust on feminine social actors, I consider what the same actors are doing with the social resources they have. While Dávalos focuses on Mexican American communities, I explicitly draw on Latinx cultural experiences that are rooted in home communities as a unified national marketing demographic that cannot be ignored as twenty-first-century cultural and social communities find themselves implicitly linked by trends in media, popular culture, and national consumer marketing.

Forms of success, when made public, become defiantly visible as the materialization of violated expectations where problematic hypervisibility is repackaged as a form of oppositional aesthetics that I term "quinceañera style." This aesthetic cannot be limited to ethnoracial categories but emerges from a process of community intellectualizing that asserts personal agency and influences community narratives of citizenship and nationalism, gender and sexuality, and activism in multiple sites populated by Latinx communities. This state of *amasamiento* (kneading) is a concept mobilized by the Chicana feminist theorist Sonia Saldívar-Hull to elucidate the gendered, raced, and classed intellectual labor invested in practices of social change in Latinx community spaces. She cites the work of Gloria Anzaldúa, who, finding herself at the margins of so-called traditional Chicano culture, defines her cultural identity as defying the comfort of precedent:

> I am cultured because I am participating in the creation of yet another culture, a new story to explain the world and our participation in it, a new value system with images and symbols that connect us to each other and the planet. *Soy un amasamiento.* (Anzaldúa 103)

Amasamiento is an admixture of the familiar and the unknown, what is seen and what is felt, of working to blend elements together to synthesize something new. One might imagine hands kneading *masa* (dough) or as I do, hands working to glue or stitch beads and lace onto quinceañera dress bodices. What is most powerful is not simply the act of creating but also the intellectual process that precedes it and the emotional dissonance communities must master as they live between the traditional and the dynamic, as communities steeped in histories of oppression have a different relation to instabilities than dominant ones. Anzaldúa notes that the product of such kneading "has not only produced a creature of darkness and a creature of light, but also a creature that *questions the definitions* of light and dark and gives them new meaning" (Anzaldúa 81; emphasis added). I assert that this practice of adaptive kneading can be likened to Dávila's conception of culture work or the instrumentalization of culture in the service of neoliberal agendas (*Culture Works* 1). However, I understand this kneading as the insight and value added from perspectives of communities that understand how to navigate neoliberal economic agendas in the twenty-first century as actors and agents rather than subjects. Amasamiento is a vulnerable state of constant emergence in which familiar meanings are being redefined—where the legible is made illegible so that everyone might see what is possible. This is the work of quinceañeras as representations of a new generation of Latinx youth in which precarity and risk are transfigured into a recalibrated socioracial imaginary where their lives have value.

In drawing on archives of folkloric knowledge of distinct communities of practice, amasamiento becomes a lens through which Latinx cultural practices serve as a platform for ensuring cultural relevance. Latinx communities must work outside the expectations of dominant social narratives to place themselves in mainstream western space. These practices become part of a sociocultural documentation process of which form, context, and content become metadiscursive representations of community—regardless of the accepted function of the practice. My goal is therefore to make visible the creative processes by which quinceañeras move beyond characterizations dominated by heteropatriarchal and conservative religiosity to imagine them as secular strategies of selfhood, that is, processes of self-determination that push back against the problematic hypervisibility that haunts US Latinx communities daily—in particular the specter of illegality. In the case of American quinceañera practice, such strategies of folkloric amasamiento recast shallowly interpreted moments of indifferent, even misguided pageantry into forms of multidimensional artifice, defiant visibility, and embodied commemoration.

## CLASS PERFORMATIVITY

The efficacy of quinceañera events transcends their immediate representational contexts by becoming, in addition to internalized qualities of honor versus shame, opportunities for personal branding among local and deterritorialized peer networks and performances of class aspirational "success theater." Success theater is a framework adapted from the rhetoric of internet startup companies that estimate high market value despite their lack of tangible products. The term has since been adapted to describe ways the increasingly mediated engagement of twenty-first-century communities leads to the curation of online lives that rarely match lived reality. Whether such narratives of self can be verified by outsider interpretations is uncertain; as a shared form they illustrate how social mobility begins with sublimated personal narratives before they can become reality. This becomes particularly true for youth communities still living as dependent minors who build narratives of self out of rhetorics of possibility over experiential reality.

"I spend, therefore I am." This, a crass rephrasing of Descartes's famous pronouncement "Cogito ergo sum" (I think, therefore I am), is a jaded sentiment that in many ways gets at part of the subsumed motivations and intellectual labor guiding quinceañera industries and consumer practices in the service of traditional practice. But rather than saddling quinceañera practice as the vacuously interpreted cultural practice being stifled or defamed under the pressures of consumer capitalism, it can be approached as one of many intersecting strands of self-documentary practices utilized by a new generation of young adults of color eager to insert their social narratives into a wider US society. Such visual interjection is a reckoning with social invisibility and the injustices that stem from seeing diversity as a mongrelizing of "American" (read: white) culture. At the same time, such practices manifest a desire to visibilize and make legible their shared subject position on their own terms, impacting the possible images of an American public.

In this book I examine class as social experience that is not completely tied to bank accounts, homeownership, or even education level. I understand class as bell hooks describes it:

> Class is much more than Marx's definition of relationship to means of production. Class involves your behavior, your basic assumptions, how you are taught to behave, what you expect from yourself and from others, your concepts of a future, how you understand problems and solve them, how you think, feel, act. (*Feminism Is for Everybody* 39)

Quinceañera markets are saturated not only with the sale of material goods but also with tutorial-style reading materials and classes in which girls and teens can learn the soft skills necessary for seamless social mobility. Walking in heels, public speaking, skin care, healthy eating, and makeup tutorials are topics covered in *Quinceañeras Magazine* and themes that extend into planning services and online vlogging spaces. These skills index how to be one's best self by being fully engaged in the geotemporal present, that is, by being ideologically located in the present as a constant confrontation with subjugations of the past and hope for the future. Cultural practices help channel those seemingly paradoxical polarities. Quinceañera practice offers an accessible mode of class performativity in which class-as-achievement is a matter of instrumentalizing tradition to court audience reception and acceptance into social memory. Such a strategy purposely entangles the cultural logics of Latinx experiences and USAmerican priorities as social performance of an ephemeral logic, that of the inter-American.

## LATINX CULTURAL ENTREPRENEURSHIP

Latinx cultural entrepreneurship is the ideology and practice that allows individuals within cultural communities to draw on ideologies of neoliberal capitalism while also promoting community solidarity. The Latinx entrepreneurs examined here are a mixture of business owners, performance artists, activists, and aspiring cultural influencers whose labor orbits around the practice of quinceañera celebrations in the United States. The notion of cultural entrepreneurship embedded within these pages is a nod to individual research practice and collaborative theorizing where cultural practices meet popular culture. In our introduction to the anthology we edited, *Race and Cultural Practice in Popular Culture*, Domino R. Perez and I theorize the capacity of popular representations as consumer productions that function precisely because minority communities in the United States are gaining traction as profitable market demographics. This is especially true among contemporary Latinx communities whose newly recognized diversity of middle-class, upscale, and working-class spenders remarks on a variety of other intersectional experiences in wider society and at the same time offers a more nuanced reading of social inequities and aspirations that cannot simply be attributed to presumptions of ethnoracial solidarity. We distill the idea of cultural entrepreneurship:

> Individuals who provide products, services, or specialized knowledge about enacting ritual practices or trade in the signifiers of race or ethnicity are cultural entrepreneurs. These professionals, operating in both formal and informal economies, provide material goods, services, or knowledge to signify or enact the traditions and practices of a cultural community. These culture brokers determine, produce, and reproduce culture primarily through material goods used in ceremonies, performances, or other cultural practices. (Perez and González 23)

Following Thomas Aageson, I understand cultural entrepreneurs to function as "cultural change agents" who, using often unrecognized and undocumented skill sets, "organize cultural, financial, social, and human capital" with the end result being economic survival and even the capacity to live well (96). Cultural entrepreneurship is only a partial response to social inequity, and for many scholars and readers it may appear antithetical the values of social revolution, yet it makes no claim to do social justice work. What it does is offer social success to entrepreneurs and recognition of social presence to the consumers who partake of it in their service. It has the capacity to embolden communities while at the same time acknowledging that success—economic and social—does not completely elude US Latinx communities, nor are entrepreneurs wholly invested in radical movements of social justice. While that may not be my personal politics, this book is only partially about my authorship, as diverse audiences may variably read it between the lines. Instead, the stories I share here are meant to challenge the social expectations of audiences and the stakes under which people find themselves alternately living and surviving. Such stories include narratives of resistance and profit, side by side and fully entangled in one another not as creative indulgences but as necessary intersections of genuine lived experience. Rather than offering certainty, I distill multiple interpretations of shared potential crafted within communities that furnish a reimagination of individual futures by renarrating a collective past. The experiences created from US quinceañera culture and practice textualized here reorient the event from a ritual that locates an individual in a singular, linearly experienced past to a visualization of a web of collective futures.

## CONSUMER CITIZENSHIP

In *Transnational America: Feminisms, Diasporas, Neoliberalism*, Inderpal Grewal asserts that "American" is a descriptive framework that functions as a discourse of neoliberalism, making possible struggles for rights through consumerist practices and imaginaries that came to be used in and outside the territorial boundaries of the United States (2). The term "American" represents western power, privilege, and cultural imperialism through the spread of neoliberal capitalism around the globe. Embracing a consumer identity in these neoliberal conditions of possibility indexes belonging within national borders but also within gentrified narratives of western hegemony on the global stage. The ideas of America and being a diasporic transnational citizen are mediated through a capacity to place oneself into the social mainstream through integrated processes of consumption, implicating consumer goods and services as unconventional sources of cultural knowledge. The quinceañera practice and its deterritorialized representations become part of the inter-American chain of knowledge, while they also produce transnational connectivity through consumption of art, culture, and goods across borders.

Approaching quinceañera celebrations from a perspective of representation and material practice implicitly entails the intertextual examination of multiple related quinceañera texts. This disrupts discourses rooted in a connection to an authentic past and instead examines patterns of practice in the present that are centralized in discourses of contemporary intersections of class and gender formations. The value of this approach hinges not on singular stories but on an accumulation of visual texts that speak to the prevalence and power of the social phenomenon of continued quinceañera practice as an adaptive sociocultural technology of selfhood; in its current state, quinceañera practice is as much a product of US consumer culture as it is a complex of diasporic cultural imaginaries. I draw inspiration from the conceptualization of Afro-futurism, in particular from Juliet Hooker's 2016 book, *Theorizing Race in the Americas: Douglass, Sarimento, Du Bois, and Vasconcelos.* Hooker draws on myriad sources to distill Afro-futurism as "an aesthetic and literary movement that aims to counter the overwhelming absence of people of color and concomitant assumptions of racelessness in dominant conceptions of futurity" (119). Contemporary quinceañera practice is a reinterpretation of the past and Latinx communities' social and economic futures. As a folkloric tradition, the display of such prescience reveals itself as the productions of memories of and in the service of the future. Memories are mediated not only by oral narratives of experiences being recounted from one generation to another but also through the creation of a tangible and digital legacy of visual documentation that becomes a product of coming of age.

Considering a theoretical lens of intertextuality requires the examination of the power of accumulation not unlike the artistic method of bricolage. The accumulation of art objects, in this case quinceañera images, emphasizes a framework of intensified meanings that are contextualized on the canvas of social media, where they then become the products of social networks that circulate images based on an esoteric logic of shared value. These internal systems of value intersect in media spaces where social actors author visual narratives of themselves, turning personal pages into digital artistic installations representing their very best selves. The body is where culture and materialism meet, and this best self is self-consciously realized through the consumption of goods and experiences as a Latinx consumer citizen "whose individual freedoms are guaranteed not by the state or other institution but by the freedom of the market and of trade" (Banet-Weiser 44).

## ORGANIZATION OF THE BOOK

As I draw together these case studies of quinceañera practice in the twenty-first century, I consider them not as rituals but as representations. While a ritual perspective would examine the internal intricacies and psychosocial interpretations of the meaning of certain actions in situ, a representational analysis is centrally concerned with the circulation of ritual practice, its textured public presentation, and its reception from one audience to the next. This focus on representation of cultural practice allows one to consider how folklore is part of community methods in social change that, as Audre Lorde asserts, dismantle the master's house but do so with the tools of the oppressed. While this process of dismantling occurs in simple ways, its larger goal is to denaturalize images of Latinas in the United States from micro-local to macro-national perspectives.

In the first chapter, "Quinceañera Style and Class Performativity," I examine style from a material and ideological perspective. I examine how materiality is used as a tool for expressing aspirational class mobility. I discuss how style is a mediator between quinceañera practice and the monetizing of Latinx culture in the US marketplace as performance of middle-class identification. In the second chapter, "Identity off the Rack: Selling Quinceañera Dresses and Manufacturing Identities in the Experience Economy," I examine the consumer turn in quinceañera practice that has led to increased accessibility of the ritual through the availability of inexpensive, imported dresses that become repackaged as luxury goods as they are sold to those planning their events in the United States. The dress functions as a boundary object moving through space and accumulates relative social value as it is modified across branding strategies. Through manufacturing adaptive interpretations of an authentic quinceañera dress, personal investments in goods become acts of nationalistic class performances.

In chapter 3, "Coming of Age in the Digital Barrio: Quinceañera as a Product in Cultural Economies Online," I discuss how quinceañera practice changes among new generations of "digital natives," those exhibiting a facility with digital technology and a dependence on social media outlets. While many consider the church and the ballroom the key sites for interpreting quinceañera celebrations, more than ever Latina youth are using physical celebrations as part of a personal branding process that takes place online. Beyond personal presentation, these spaces quickly turn from self-portraiture to fertile platforms for cultural niche marketing. In digital consumer space, online cultural influencers digitally circulate the newest themed products and critique ongoing practice, creating a sense of consumer desire and risk while intensifying the need for professional intervention to plan and fund the fantasy of coming of age.

Chapter 4, "Made in Mexico, USA: Beauty Professionals and the Manufacturing of Quinceañera Beauty Culture," draws on ethnographic fieldwork with professional makeup artists and hair stylists who spend much of their professional lives styling quinceañeras for public presentations; field research conducted in the Midwest reveals where personal transformations meet globalized beauty economies. I document the work of two queer men, from Kansas City, Missouri, and San Antonio, Texas, who style young women on the verge of social debuts. Using their philosophies of makeup and the currency of beauty in the US visual economy, I discuss the ways Latina physical transformation and the creation of dramatic material narratives communicate young women's own personal values and styles in these visually complex coming-of-age ceremonies. Both migrant, queer professionals rebrand the quinceañera "looks" as self-representations that are products of a complex web of cultural mediation made possible by queer Mexican men, family desires, and media technologies.

In chapter 5, "Ambivalent Embodiment: Reconstituting Quinceañera Performance Space," I discuss the role of queer aesthetics and subject positions within quinceañeras' practice that are continuously framed by Latinx social critics as oppressively heteronormative. I analyze the work of a Mexican performance artist who uses the quinceañera as part of her own queer identity-building project. The dominant case study shares the story of Lía la Novia Sirena. As a self-identified trans woman, Lía dedicates her time to artistic social interventions in which she stages quinceañera performances around her home in Mexico City, including at quinceañera consumer expositions. Through quinceañera performance, Lía has changed the affective topography of public space, and queerness becomes part of a cultural marketing schema in which Latinx heterosexuality is being repackaged and sold back to conservative, straight communities. This reality reorients the process of quinceañera performance as moments to "disrupt hetero-normativity" in public space (Puar), and in the process it questions the ways gender and sexual identities are constructed within conservative Latinx households.

In the conclusion, "Rights/Rites and Representation: Reading Latinx Social Performance," I examine how my approach in this book is actually part of a larger vision of foregrounding cultural practice as self-documentation in a world built upon representational authority, that is, links to gender, class, and citizenship status as part of a neoliberal economy of stateless personhood. Agentive, self-conscious documentary practices are economic investments in social representation in a world that foregrounds seeing and being seen as ways to assert belonging that is seemingly outside of strictures of rigid governmentality and fragmentation. Implicitly responding to alienating narratives of history, emergent quinceañera culture functions as an extension of politicized remembering.

## CHAPTER I

# QUINCEAÑERA STYLE AND CLASS PERFORMATIVITY

Quinceañera style recontextualizes the viewing and reception of Latina bodies in public spaces, as young women render themselves publicly visible, and the shaping of imagined communities in public space by instrumentalizing a Latina spectacle that is rooted in the notion of discernable style. Style—sartorial, affective, or environmental—works as a vehicle for public spectacle that is designed by participants and enacted in a racialized state. To recognize quinceañera style is to acknowledge the celebrant's right to objectify and choice to appropriate oneself as a valuable commodity. Choice "emerges in relation to how identities themselves are produced through a nexus of nation, state, gender, race class, and a number of other factors, then ethnic identities produced through consumption cannot be seen as being chosen or willed" (Grewal 119). The process of commodification relies heavily on stylistic choices that make young Latinas adornments of the state. The same process also privileges young consumer preferences, integrating style of adornment on their own terms. Under the rubric of tradition, assertive styling practices flout expectations of unassertiveness and self-denial as expected coping strategies for Latina youth raised in strict households. Quinceañeras use personal style within tradition to change their environments rather than change themselves. As a psychological coping strategy, modifying one's social environments has been characterized as "American," when Latinas, Mexican-origin women in particular, are interpreted to cope with controlling home lives through self-modification, as illustrated by a mother's self-sacrifice for her family (Solís-Cámara et al. 355).[1] Patterns of physical adornments reflect an admixture of ritual significance, costuming, and everyday dress but also come to index the reimagination of social relations of power through a rejection of self-denial.

Style is classed. Quinceañera style comes with an aura of upscale Latinidad. *La Opinión*, a Spanish-language news source on US Latinx issues in and around the Los Angeles metro area, ran an article in 2014 with the headline "Upscale Latinos Drive the U.S. Market." The author, Danielle Restuccia, reports on research released from the Association of Hispanic American Advertisers that newly recognized Latinx consumers,[2] "upscale" Latinos, "represent one of the most important consumer demographics" in the United States, worth $500 billion, making them valuable to companies interested in an "economic edge." Upscale consumers at the time were those whose "household income is between 50k–100k." Upscale Latinxs in the same income bracket displayed other characteristics that reflect ethnic and racial factors: "They are often bi-cultural, young, dual income earners and may have large families" (Restuccia). The "bi-cultural" identity implies an ethnic nationalist identity that is not wholly subsumed in a USAmerican culture, but the implication is that these consumers live on a line dividing clear distinctions between ethnic Latinx and national US identity. The report also presumes that such individuals live in this sociocultural space but also that there is a market being built along an upwardly mobile trend. The trends implicate families, not just individuals, and the youth identification implies a younger generation, possibly the same that is targeted by other media outlets such as MTV[3] or the wider "millennial" market, an identification that transcends ethnic nationalist distinctions. They are an attractive economic niche that is defined by spending power, not by liquid wealth or property assets. In the twenty-first century, style becomes a way to make visible the spending power of Latinx consumers, in particular the role played by Latina youth. Expos provide spaces where market trends meet personal experiences.

With a theme of "Eco-Chic," a fashion show in Commerce, California, was not the main event. Girls surrounded the stage, smartphones in hand, waiting to document taffeta and tulle and instead getting repurposed garbage. Admirably, the inventions were creative and interesting, a real shift from typical quinceañera offerings. On this Sunday afternoon, the expo was featuring a different, haute couture–style fashion exposition featuring products of local retailers as well as professional designers. What proceeded was a show of a small collection of dresses designed by young women reflecting aspects of their lives that were important to them. Ramona was passionate about environmental sustainability and elected to make a one-off quinceañera art dress completely of recycled materials. The dress represented quinceañera style as flexible and personally customizable rather than limited by a set of cultural rules that simply recapitulated the dictates of feminine expressive culture. It opened a space for the expansion of quinceañera dress designs but also deregulated the performative space to allow the garish, the gaudy, the revealing, and ultimately the oppositional. These oppositional choices usher in a performance aesthetic that flouts the racialized signifiers that link assumptions of stereotypes of racial identity markers to perceptions of class.

The dress was impressive and environmentally aware but unlikely to make it to the reception. As the emcee described the dress, she explained how selecting a dress is about reflecting personal style and making it known publicly. For Ramona, her passion for environmental sustainability could be part of her quinceañera design, specifically through fashion choices that had the capacity to materialize consciousness, and share them with audiences. In public recirculation, quinceañera style becomes the vehicle for informing the social reception of the tradition and the community of practice.

Quinceañera practice is ephemeral, and what remains when practice is over is representation through isolated material elements that when brought together envision a new reality that audiences can view as a shared style. I use the term "style," in particular "quinceañera style," to address the accumulation of a performative aura that the spectacle of Latinx femininity infuses into everyday life. Such a theatrical infusion is made possible not only through the direct presentations of young women in public spaces in self-representative practices but also through television, internet, and cinematic venues that circulate representations across the globe. In an inter-American representational circuit where social geographies and political regimes control linked yet decidedly different public spheres, style is not about standards of beauty or of ugliness. Instead, style is about efficacy—What draws in gaze best, and how does a social actor benefit from drawing in such gaze? In this way, style is about the spectacle of the everyday. The concept of spectacle as a social technology links the work of the Latin American anthropologist Marcia Ochoa and the French Marxist theorist Guy Debord. Quinceañera style facilitates a social space for the staging of a Latina feminine spectacle that instrumentalizes a Latinx interpretation of "beauty and glamour" as a self-conscious performance of femininity (Ochoa 231).

Debord's 1967 work *Society of the Spectacle* addresses the reality of living in an image-saturated, consumer culture. He interprets an all-encompassing, spectacle-driven social environment as a tool to distract and pacify the masses. In the United States a half century later, such a relation is manifest in the masses walking in silence even among friends, heads buried in portable digital media that separate individuals from fully experiencing their environments. This critical assessment only holds if individuals relate to their public environments the same way as generations past did. The boom in accessibility of different forms of digital media has fundamentally changed how individuals expect to interact with the world outside their homes, as smartphones have become naturalized extensions of their lived experiences. While some who have theorized public life before the era of digital media saturation see the retreat into technology as a distancing from "reality," for younger generations reality is digital living. Technologically mediated social and consumer lives are how people see their world and are taught to be seen in the world. In his third thesis on the spectacle Debord asserts that "the spectacle reduces reality into an endless supply of commodifiable fragments" and through this process "encourages us to focus on appearances" (7). But what if we can recontextualize the spectacle into the twenty-first-century United States among populations of color and consider that perhaps new generations, raised in environments saturated in cultural consumerism, are reclaiming the spectacle, shifting their role from passive audiences to agentive artists?

In choosing to be publicly Latina in a social milieu that rejects Latinx cultural difference and profits from neoliberal economic strategies that embrace the disposability of migrant Latinx labor, the choice to make oneself a racialized subject of public consumption is defiant and dangerous. In "Fashion Crimes," Chon Noriega asserts that display and fantasy are integral to public life. While he specifically speaks to the sartorial excess exhibited in 1940s-era pachuco zoot suit culture, the notion is that style, particularly modes of personal display, serves communities who find themselves marginalized in contemporary society. Such embodied curations have the capacity to speak back to demoralizing social conditions through a process of self-objectification—a demand to be seen, consumed, in essence repurposing the damaging power of racialized and sexualized hypervisibility. Quinceañera style can be qualified as consumer-driven, aggressively visible, predominantly secular, unapologetically femme, situationally narcissistic, and conceptually fluid.

At the 2010 expo in San Jose, California, I saw a host of innovative dress designs that included a silver and purple zebra-print bodice on a black and white dress, a bright-red dress with a leopard-print corset accented by black piping, and a white ball gown layered with rainbow tulle ruffles cascading down a removable full-length skirt that easily converted into a minidress. The expo space helps foster a sense of style that primarily appeals to Latinx consumers and does not need to satisfy the expectations of wider publics. Thinking back to our chuntara strolling the mall in her quinceañera gown, these models and the girls who idolize them clearly know the attention their dresses and escorts would garner; they understand the state of spectacle that they occupy.

Quinceañera style, as an aesthetic of inter-American transnationality, engages Latinas in a process of self-othering, in essence controlling visuality by instantiating an oppositional aesthetic in white middle-class America. The young woman in the Galleria photo, who may or may not appreciate the moniker "chuntara," was exerting a manner of working-class taste resembling what Tomás Ybarra-Frausto terms "rasquachismo":

> In the realm of taste, to be *rasquache* is to be unfettered and unrestrained, to favor the elaborate over the simple, the flamboyant over the severe. Bright colors (*chillantes*) are preferred to somber, high intensity to low, the shimmering and sparkling over the muted and subdued. (133–134)

This description perfectly encapsulates the quinceañera aesthetic being promoted in the twenty-first century, and yet it is one that still garners criticism from audiences confounded by their own inability to reconcile style and form. Quinceañera style is a confrontation with stereotypes of race and class.

Cultural entrepreneurs working in the US quinceañera industry lean into an understanding of captivating visibility as a mark of social power—as manipulators of gaze and therefore finding power in the spectacle through control over their own self-representations. In his first thesis on the spectacle, Debord distances his ideology from that of Marx, who claims that where capitalist modes of production prevail, social success is represented as the accumulation of commodities. Debord claims that under "modern conditions of production," life becomes an "accumulation of spectacles" (166). He explains these spectacles as new realities devoted to representational living. In this interpretation cultural texts reflect both an aesthetic sensibility and a cultural condition in a society where the effects of power are apparent though their structural organization is obscured. This representational living is akin to Baudrillard's notion of the "hyperreal." Any spectator patrolling social media on a daily, hourly, or momentary scale has likely come to unflinchingly accept the constant stream of images and commentary as real rather than a filtered interaction with individually and institutionally contrived representations of self. But nuance in the communities one watches and follows, such as among youth, women and girls, people of color, the historically disenfranchised, reveals patterns of articulation that are purposefully and thoughtfully working within the system to engineer personal visibility and social success in a world that has come to respect representational practice as a component of competitive modern living. Quinceañera style is an extension of will that emphasizes young Latinas as active culture producers. This is not to say that such attempts at representation are always successful in the way artist-authors would ideally desire, and yet these producers are in control and seeing a way to affect a process that offers communities a sense of home and agency in a world saturated by representations of themselves by others.

## STYLE IN THE FACE OF CULTURAL AUSTERITY

Cultural austerity is a social milieu that encourages socialization through common culture that implicitly calls for the scouring of ethnoracial difference from the public sphere for the sake of national unification. In a society that values civility over equity, race and class differences are to be feared, and the physical and structural violence that ensues is interpreted as justified. From the perspective of cultural practice, folkloric forms are rendered legible through a process of cultural and geographic gentrification. In my current home of Austin, Texas, murals are literally being whitewashed out of existence. The vernacular art forms that tell stories of generations of black and brown communities living on now coveted East Austin properties are simply disappearing overnight. This racescaping is being done by new property owners with little social or cultural investment in the history of this area of the city and who are buying foreclosed or vacant businesses of owners unable to retain their properties as their taxes skyrocketed. An organic locavore coffee shop only needs a trace of diversity to thrive as they serve a newly arriving clientele equally unaware of the ethnoracial history of these places. Such patterns appear all over Austin. Local cafes often serve "hibiscus tea," which is a common *agua fresca* drink in local Mexican American communities known by its Spanish name, *agua de jamaica*. Cultural distance is maintained as the use of Spanish signifiers is a presumed detriment. This steeped, iced beverage is verbally deracialized as a mode of linguistic style and made appealing to anyone who doesn't want to feel self-conscious saying "Haah-mY-Kah" out loud.

Quinceañera style, on the other hand, exhibits cultural difference and definition as a point of pride, racializing spaces and offering a critical interpretation of performative class formation. As quinceañera style utilizes signifiers of neoliberal social values such as conspicuous consumption, it does so by shifting a focus toward Latinx audiences while also maintaining a legible ethnoracial profile. Quinceañera style has basic characteristics that makes it efficacious not simply as a way of exhibiting bodywork but also by creating ambivalences in meaning that support neoliberal consumption while also questioning its implicit invocation of white supremacy. First, it contains self-expression in a legible cultural practice, the coming-of-age ritual. Second, an emphasis on style foregrounds consumption and self-branding through innovative fashion. Third, it illustrates the wealth capacity of Latinx markets as willing economic actors. Finally, it vividly and unapologetically materializes aspirational class mobility. Latinx families learn early that to thrive, children must to learn how to utilize their material environments efficiently and creatively. Style functions as social technology to modify and control social perceptions and becomes the vehicle through which girls are creating a social environment in which their experiences have value, one that is neither wholly ethnoracial nor fully USAmericanized.

Quinceañera style as a material and ideological reality is facilitated by a drive toward consumer integration as a form of recognized cultural citizenship that allows self-identifying Latinx communities across the United States to document their own versions of an ideal self. The idealized self-images draw on the legibility of deeply embedded cultural traditions and mobilize a kind of social futurity in visual narratives of innovative personal style and social potential where families believe that the production of happy memories of one's youth will socialize a child into a healthy and confident (socially successful) adult. Style of vestments and mannerisms are rooted in two psychosocial faculties: memory and desire. Affecting desire in Latinx quinceañera practice is conceptualized in Danielson's *Homecoming Queers*, where the author posits how desires and erotics of creativity mobilize conceptualizations of home. At the same time desire involves connection with the past, personally and historically narrated to inform the present and envision the future. It in turn informs the inevitable construction of Latina subjectivities from vestiges of colonialism. These tenets illustrate what Latina women know about who they are and who they want to be. With this framework in place, style comes to modulate much more than clothing choices and physical adornment; it negotiates social status through aspirational longing and the staging of potential through material arts. Memory and historicity play a role in how the quinceañera celebration has been and can be received in US Latinx communities.

## HISTORICITY AND THE QUINCEAÑERA AS HISTORICAL FACT

To understand the work of quinceañera style in the 2000s–2010s, one first needs to take a closer look at how quinceañera traditions are rooted in community histories. Discussing tradition is in many ways the deconstruction of unremarkable histories, those left out of the official logs of documented history and relegated to the category of memory or nostalgia, often via raced and classed interpretations of value. In *The Decolonial Imaginary*, Emma Pérez reinterprets the narratives of the past through a Mexican diasporic third-space feminist lens, theorizing from a Chicana perspective to address the interstitial gaps of previous narratives presumed to be facts but that actually blur the lines of real and imagined (xv). The origin stories of the quinceañera event as a practice of and in diaspora, Pérez asserts, must be considered on both sides of the border as a product of national political discourses and practices in which women becomes central social actors. At the same time, the reader must accept that the "historian's subjectivity imagines and produces historiography, even when it is revisionist" (Pérez 32). The historical narratives around quinceañeras are divided between academic theorizations rarely accessible to community members and the folklorized discourses shared among communities and entrepreneurs in the promotion of the event. I assert that the popular narratives are just as important as or more important than those of scholars, as they are the fuel that motivates the continued practice of this coming-of-age spectacle.

In popular discourse the origin of the quinceañera tradition is discussed as part of ancient indigenous rituals of social transition. More recent assertions claim that the quinceañera lay dormant until the 1960s, as "Latin populations" were supposedly eager to "assimilate quietly into suburban America" (Marling 3). In contemporary form, the quinceañera is anything but "quiet," where such an auditory reference leads to an assumption of subdued invisibility.

Historically, quinceañera celebrations have been defined as a cultural product of the syncretism between religious and social rituals of Spanish and indigenous communities of Latin America, primarily rooted in the history of the conquest of Mexico (Cantú, "Chicana," "La Quinceañera"; Dávalos; A. McCracken). Quinceañera rituals are narrated as a version of pre-Columbian rites of passage. In "Quinceañera: The Mexican American Initiation Ritual of Young Women," Bert Watters claims that "the quinceañera originated in the everyday life of the Aztecs in ancient Mexico" (151). In Chicana feminist discourse, the foregrounding of "indigenous" (Aztec) origins remakes the signification of the quinceañera into a narrative of race in which participating American Mexican communities are characterized as reclaiming a tie to an indigenous Mexico while at the same time taking on the material aesthetics of European colonizers. The mobilization of this indigenous motif despite a lack of direct historical evidence speaks to the celebration as a sensitive receptacle for the social and cultural values of different intracultural social movements. In part, this connection relies on an ideological cornerstone of the Chicano movement of the mid-twentieth century, the desire to be seen as descendants of an indigenous past. Fetishization of Mexican Indianism enacts an implicit form of symbolic violence against living, breathing indigenous Mexican populations who do not include the quinceañera as part of a repertoire of indigenous cultural performance but rather as an adaptation to western influences on youth culture integrating narratives that reflect idealized Mexican nationalism. On the quinceañera Ronald Grimes notes, "There is no compelling evidence that this coming out celebration is a synthesis of these [Aztec and Spanish] traditions, since most accounts of the quinceañera date from the 1920s to the present" (128).

The journalist Chris Kudialis reports on the thriving quinceañera industry in Las Vegas of dress shops like Casa de Calderon that price dresses from "$900 to $3,000 depending on size, colors and carefully stitched jewels" and Enrique Montes's Dream 15 Boutique, which sells custom gowns for "$600 to $4,000" to a client base who will pay "whatever it takes" to make a quinceañera memorable. This consumer traditioning in which retail practice influences the character of performance is not a product of the ancient Aztecs or religious syncretism between Spanish Catholicism and Maya spiritualities (Dávalos 16). The connection between indigenous Mexican roots and contemporary practice can be viewed as the product of a social and cultural moment in which communities were desirous of creating a cultural bond between Mexican Americans and Mexican history—and the authentic quinceañera lives in an ancient past (Dávalos; Marling). Such discourse is part of a popular imaginary that continues to this day to frame the tradition of quinceañera as "centuries old."

While there is little documented reference to quinceañera practice in the United States and accounts rely on oral histories of experience, at times a blend of auto-ethnographic retellings such as Norma Cantú's *Canícula: Snapshots of Girlhood en la Frontera*, these narratives cannot speak to the wider practice of traditions across space and temporality beyond the immediate performative moment. It is clear that contested origins complicate the interpretation of the practice in the present, as changes to elements of practice such as religious aspects are interpreted as a violation of some authentic original. The sociologist Valentina Napolitano, who has studied the ritual in the Lomas de Polanco area of southern Guadalajara, notes a much later, mid-twentieth-century inception of the quinceañera tradition that calls into question assertions of the event's deep historical presence:

> The origins of the feast are unknown to people in Lomas de Polanco. Old women do not recollect it in their accounts of the past. Middle-aged women remember that rich families in their villages of origin did celebrate the feast, but it was a custom of the "gente de dinero" (rich people). . . . The first reports of the feast started to appear in the *Sociales* (social events) section of Guadalajara newspapers during the early 1940s. There are no church records, since the ritual is not a sacrament. . . . Nowadays, press reports still present an "ideal" model of the celebration of the fifteenth birth-

day, a standard unattainable by the population of Lomas de Polanco but still deferred to by *quinceañeras* (girls fifteen years old) and
their families. (66)

Her reports from Guadalajara mirror other documented social histories from South Texas (Cantú) and Cuba (Mitchell and Reid-Walsh) that
function to evoke racialized difference and elite class mobility, respectively.
The continued ruminations around the connection of the quinceañera to
an "Aztec initiation rite taken over by the Catholic Church in the sixteenth
century . . . [or] a ceremony begun in the nineteenth century by Carlota,
the Austrian Empress of Mexico and the Duchess of Alba" (Marling 3), add
a legendary quality to the celebration that speaks more to the values of contemporary communities than to the provenance of traits of practice. Such
a process blurs the lines between legend and history when a desire to believe romantic origin stories and their acceptance as truth is more revealing
of Latinx cultural logics than realizing that official records care little for the
social culture of women. Similarly, families continue to circulate anecdotes
of the Aztec origins of quinceañera rites, as families eager to mobilize the
tradition as a heritage practice include elements of Aztec dress and dance
that cannot be classified as anything but sincere and examples of a process
of customization of the ritual. Adaptation of the tradition, in the case of the
indigenizing of origin narratives, becomes fundamentally necessary to the
continuation of the tradition into future generations, especially as height-
ened value is associated with traditions that have deep historical precedents.

In *The Writing of History*, Michel de Certeau writes, "In the case of historiography, fiction can be found at the end of the process, in the product of
the manipulation and the analysis. Its story is given as a staging of the past"
(9). Quinceañeras as tangible cultural practices stage a revised historical narrative. Assumed historicity or the perception of historical authenticity of the
practice plays a role in how the quinceañera event has been socially valued in
Latinx communities and how such experiences are narrated as history. This
desire to foster a historical link between pre-Columbian Central America and
the US Latinx diaspora speaks to the social and emotional needs of communities that through generations of at times violent and desperate migration
lack a clear connection to their imagined homeland. Quinceañera style as
practices and narratives manifest such a bridge. The aforementioned indigenous link serves to validate the existence of the event as a deeply rooted ancient tradition. Much like the narrative of indigeneity, heteronormative aesthetics have also been part of building an idealized ethnic-national imaginary.
Quinceañeras, more than the individual events, represent patterns of prac-

tice that enforce gender and social roles of both women and men, although women are staged for the purposes of nation building. Such strategic uses of feminine beauty and the female body as tools for social advancement resonate with gendered tensions seen during early twentieth-century migrations of Spanish-speaking migrants to the United States.

In her desire to reconstruct adolescent aspirations and experiences of Mexican American women from 1910 to 1930, the historian Vicki Ruiz has found that as Mexican American women became educated, employed, and media savvy, they became agents of Americanization in their households through a rhetoric of personal aspiration ("Star Struck" 120). Although Ruiz notes that the histories of women at the time were minimal, in her search through archival field notes and oral historical research she has found no reason to mention the quinceañera celebration within the period when Spanish-speaking immigrants were flocking to the United States fleeing political and social turmoil in Mexico. What she does note is the way Mexican American adolescents of the time actively engaged in the cultural economy of American life as consumers on a variety of levels. "Teenagers chatted about [American] fads, fashions, and celebrities," she finds, and they had access to "movie and romance magazines . . . [that] enabled adolescents to experience vicariously the middle-class and affluent life-styles heralded in these publications and thus could nurture a desire for consumer goods" ("Star Struck" 112). While those interests might seem a far cry from quinceañera celebrations in the twenty-first century, what this historical narrative allows is rethinking the origin stories of quinceañera practice and recontextualizing its value away from racial and religious roots and toward a discourse of economic cultural relations. Rather than framing the quinceañera as part of a social economy as new, its twenty-first-century manifestations may be seen as a continuation of a shared process of customized social integration through a culturally inflected engagement with consumer products.

If the quinceañera can be placed within a process of cultural engineering based on an imagined romantic Mexican past, then the practice in the United States was not started as a tradition of courtship but as a social drama designed to satisfy the desire of Americanized youth to be acknowledged as adults. The celebration, though criticized as a sublimated wedding designed to draw in the male gaze, may actually be the product of a compromise between youth and parents to acknowledge adulthood while keeping daughters in their natal homes for a few more years.

What Ruiz also offers through her examination of adolescent consumer engagements of the early twentieth century is that at this social historical moment, young women of fifteen and sixteen years of age sought out early marriage as a way to escape socially controlling families whose hypervigilance put a damper on their desires to be "American" women:

> A more subtle form of rebellion was early marriage. By marrying at fifteen or sixteen, these women sought to escape parental supervision; yet . . . many of these child brides exchanged one form of supervision for another. (*From out of the Shadows* 118)

Ruiz's acknowledgement of marriage as a form of rebellion offers a new lens through which to interpret contemporary quinceañeras. Alongside narratives of the oppressive heteropatriarchy promoted by the event, a key criticism of the quinceañera is that it promotes early marriage, sometimes as a product of teen pregnancy. The origins of the practice can be reframed not as an indigenous ritual inspired by the spiritual colonization of the New World but as a creative project of postrevolutionary nation building in Mexico designed to bolster state identity and promote a cohesive social imaginary as communities bartered culture practice across the US-Mexico border (Cantú, "La Quinceañera" 84). Such negotiating loses its relational capacity as transnational cultural relations, filtered through new media, splinter US and Mexican axes into the wider hemisphere, characterized by cultural bartering and transculturation that in the United States is broadly considered "Latino." Quinceañera style was born in the postrevolutionary era when extravagant cultural production, in this case a coming-of-age ritual, served as "a manic release from the tension of war" and began to "gain needed recognition in a world without stability" (Russell 450). While Douglas Russell is referencing a brief period of male sartorial excess during the French Revolution, the evaluation holds as social and political chaos led displaced Mexican immigrants northward seeking order in their lives by ordering the bodies and lives of their daughters. The quinceañera ritual was fashioned for male heads of household to furnish a material embodiment of a romantic nationalist state, a memory through which young women hold borders on their bodies while also being adornments of the state.

At its inception, the quinceañera served as a rhetoric of cultural identity linking gender, class, and race. I would like to think about the quinceañera as read through style, as a rhetoric of social potential and personal aspiration. In his discussion of style and social mobility, Stuart Ewen connects style with magic, and such a merger may be used to frame how quinceañera style can serve as a vehicle for social potential: "Part of the promise of style is to lift us out of the dreariness of necessity" ("Marketing Dreams" 31). The true functionality of style is to allow a break from needing to attend to the functional in everyday life. Although seemingly individualistic, such an aspirational narrative, made manifest through material forms—first through ritual objects of adornment and then through the circulation of composite images of success, dream fulfillment, and personal achievement—must be examined through a narrative of accumulation linked to the patterns of practice that engineer a living social profile of a particular segment of American Latina youth. Such patterns of accumulations layered on the body serve as the materialization of style and represent artfulness as social survival when one makes oneself a product of consumption.

## STYLE AS STRATEGIC VISUALITY

Quinceañera celebrations as public representations of US Latinx subjectivities reject unfavorable presumptions of the hypervisible Latinx experience. The temporary performative spectacles engineered as marking teenage coming of age in the United States disrupt public and private spaces alike, creating a new, third space from which to view Latinx bodies as products of self-oriented practice, group representation, and a unique brand of consumer citizenship mobilized by hemispheric Latinx communities.

Critical visuality applied to twenty-first-century cultural practices interrogates social hierarchies relative to larger schema of social and culturally mixed visual culture. In the field of visual culture and the study of folklore, particularly Latinx folklore, I examine the dialectic between the loaded designations of "vision" and "visuality" as explicated in Hal Foster's volume *Vision and Visuality*. I draw on Foster's application of the terms as differentiated by limits of context, social, political, and historical in nature, that implicate "how we see, how we are able, allowed, or made to see, and how we see this seeing or the unseen therein" (ix). Rather than discuss visuality as an ability to see and be seen that is simply a product of biological capacities, I view it as a set of ideological categories through which visual stimuli are interpreted and alternately categorized as cultural or consumer, authentic or false, real or imagined. In the case of quinceañera practice, a secular (re)visioning process has modified the public narrative around the coming-of-age celebration, minimizing the religious ritual and emphasizing consumer practices. Such practices manifest in consumer goods as dresses, limousines, elaborately styled hair and makeup, curated portraiture, and custom invitations, staged and popularized through commercial expositions. Each of these elements contributes to an ethos of an aggressive visuality—a demand to be seen on one's own terms, and a refusal to be ignored—now potentially filtered through a quinceañera celebration.

As curated images of quinceañera girls circulate through mailed invitations, posted digital photography, framed portraiture, magazine covers, news coverage, and billboard advertisements, the quinceañera celebration becomes more than a representation of biological transition or social maturity; it expands to a larger discourse marking the unapologetic presence of US Latinxs in American society and in particular the national consumer marketplace. Quinceañera celebrations embody the values of the Chicana feminist movement, of self-determination, social success (via education), and unapologetic racialized social visibility, now manifest in young Latinas donning sparkly bustiers, sequins, and stilettos who serve as unanticipated ambassadors of an ethos of feminist independence in the twenty-first century.

The functionality of gaze has been part of the rhetoric of construction and deconstruction of Latina subjectivities in the United States since Spanish-speaking women have been unfairly judged as generalizable and reprehensible social subjects with respect to Anglo-dominant American identity politics. Quinceañeras and their characteristic ritual dress code are one node in a larger conversation about the place of Latina women in American public space. Quinceañera girls reflect twenty-first-century patterns of a Latina youth citizenship—social presencing through extravagance—asserted in visual public space and referencing specific identities of practice. While this discussion is rooted in practices that employ the narratives of millennial youth culture in the United States—Latinx millennials being legal citizens but not cultural Americans (Flores-Gonzalez)—such contingent discourses have continuously been among narratives of self-determination of Latina women living in the United States since before political nationhood was solidified.

In her work *The Woman in the Zoot Suit: Gender, Nationalism, and the Cultural Politics of Memory*, Catherine Ramírez discusses the place of 1940s pachucas in light of a long history of gender policing of women of Mexican descent in the United States that is rooted in issues of normative, heterosocial views of femininity and critiques of deviant performances of social class. Ramírez notes that while pachuca culture and performance represent salient examples of the way American women have been rebuked for visually resisting social norms of class and gender politics, they are by far not the first women to use everyday performativity to disrupt oppressive symbolic categories. The *pelona*, a Mexican American flapper with a characteristic short, bobbed hairstyle, is one of the earliest performances that serves as a "spectacular affront to her immigrant parents' standards of feminine beauty and comportment in the 1920s" (Ramírez 19). The images that serve as public disruptions of ideal citizenship through defying ideal feminine practice give way to other publicly performed Latina subjectivities in the latter part of the twentieth century, including the *feminista* of the civil rights movement and the *chola* of the 1980s. The public image of the chola as highly eroticized and public subject finds representation on the hoods of lowriders, in tattoo designs, and on T-shirts. Cholas are subjects of consumption. They and their pachuca predecessors are relegated to the margins of discourse. "Fashioned as a deviant in studies of adolescent girl gangs, her story remains unauthorized and untold" (Fregoso 73). Rather than isolating images of Mexican American femininity, interpretations would benefit from integrating regional public performances of various Latina femininities that converge around the notion of empowered deviance.

In a 2009 article, Jillian Hernandez asserts that *chongas*, working-class urban Cubanas in South Florida, represent a "hypersexual, hyperethnic, underclass inscription" that even among Latinx youth communities is described as "antithetical to the efforts made by second and third generation Latinx youth to assimilate into American culture" (74). Chonga visuality represents a public identity couched in sartorial displays that are noted to misuse or misinterpret valued commodity items, swapping high-end designer clothes and jewelry for inexpensive imitations. This is quite similar to the way quinceañera style, although costly, is racialized to index a performance but not the reality of social mobility. Here value and worth are synonymous, making high prices equivalent to high social capital. Chongas are predominantly but not exclusively Cuban American, often further criticized as "recent immigrants" whose primary social sin is a failure to acculturate fully to American life (Hernandez 75). Oppositional gaze expands interpretations of quinceañera celebrations beyond celebratory, once-in-a-lifetime moments to artistic processes of young women collaboratively curating temporary, public self-portraiture that serves to elevate a co-ethnic community profile.

The art historian Stacy E. Schultz asserts, "The female body and traditional and religious expectations of demure and self-sacrificing femininity collide in contemporary performance practices" of Latinas (13). Schultz references the work of professionally trained Latina performance artists, acknowledging the agency of young Latinas poised between family expectations and diverse sociocultural environments. My claim is that quinceañera celebrations, more than being personal narratives of social and biological transformation, become artistic performances in which material prosperity meets ethnic-cultural capital.

Quinceañeras are often demographically associated with Mexican-descent communities, although as cultural objects in the United States they have become decidedly pan-ethnically Latinx, and young women collaboratively curate material space to construct a common Latinx cultural space in the twenty-first century. In this sense of generational parallels, chonga girls and quince girls have much in common as they work in a medium of dress coding that flouts the rules of racialized capitalism and intellectualizes extravagance and excess. Gaudy dresses and loud fashion that are unmistakably part of the ritual fifteenth-birthday celebration are often characterized as embarrassing to US Latinas eager to assert intellectual and political awareness over bodily and sexual development. In the contemporary United States, judgments of what is considered "gaudy" rather than "elaborate" are class- and race-based assessments. Ewen notes that in feudal Europe the advent of production in particular allowed for mobile forms of wealth such as certain clothing styles to be made available to those who became entrepreneurs rather than those with generational wealth. Mimicking the elaborate attire of the wealthy allowed a merchant class to ingratiate itself beyond the social margins. "Elaborate clothing, a commonly understood mark of power was now available to the successful merchant" (Ewen, *All Consuming Images* 26). Likewise, chongas and quince girls mobilize commodity goods to express their relations to class performance in the United States, and both groups falter, mobilizing "the 'right' commodities (jewelry, trendy clothes) in the wrong way" (J. Hernandez 75).

Unlike chonga girls, whose style is viewed through a lens of foreignness, the spectacle events of the quinceañera celebration often draw criticism as being pathologically American. Part of the pathology is the obsession with drawing in rather than mitigating critical gaze. There is much distinction between the two performances, but both communities of young women are demanding a place in the public sphere—a space of discourse relations as visible social actors who are "not going to be shamed into invisibility" (Fraser 75). Chonga style is an enduring subculture that is cultivated over the long term, while quinceañeras are single-serving styles that accumulate over generations as their continued performances bolster a wider, subsumed process of mobilizing middle-class style aesthetics. Quinceañera style has a pan-Latinx following and a compressed temporal window.

The generation and circulation of quinceañera-themed portraiture in popular media—television, film, advertising, and social media—offer public venues for what bell hooks terms "oppositional gaze," which she defines as "the ability to manipulate one's gaze in the face of structures of domination," which in turn "opens up the possibility of agency" ("The Oppositional Gaze" 121). In this sense, quinceañera style, a product of bodily aesthetic and folklore practice, speaks to one way young Latinas coming of age in the hemispheric Americas inhabit space visually and their bodies are recognized and mobilized as tools of self-expression nested within larger cultural, social, and political tensions.

The stylistic tropes employed in quinceañeras in twenty-first-century US mainstream culture represent a culturally and temporally defined collective sense of gendered performativity. Rather than meeting sociocultural expectations (variable by home, location, economics, race, and more), they transform bodies into sites of contingent resistance mobilized through oppositional aesthetic choices that challenge the limitations imposed upon Latinx identity formation as unquestionably raced and classed in the public sphere.

Controlling gaze and drawing in viewership are a hallmark of modern social media realms where worth is determined by likes and shares. With the development of social media outlets that place personal control over public narratives of self, digital natives and marketers who endeavor to earn their consumer loyalty collaboratively shift relations of representational power through a collectively visualized coming-of-age process in the twenty-first century. Before the advent of social media sites, quinceañera photography never left one's family living room. Claudia Alvarez, who came of age in San Jose, California, in 1997, said in our interview in Oakland in 2009 that she felt self-conscious about the staged photographs that continued to adorn her mother's living room two decades after her quinceañera. The photos of her two daughters' quinceañeras materialize the memories of the two monumental events in the life of their mother, Ana Maria Guzman, in a manner that becomes readable to anyone visiting her home. Families invest in formal portraits, but those images often remain private. The idea of privacy is not shared among contemporary, digitally integrated Latina youth communities.

In the digital and material public sphere, changes in quinceañera style are the by-products of movement and adaptation. The adaptive patterns I am concerned with here are the product of a secular revisioning process in which the key influences on the practice are not rooted in the dual legacies of hegemonic Spanish colonialism and Catholicism (Franco). The social immobility of women in Latin American society was mandated by the church and served to "ensure the purity of bloom that Spanish society had imposed after the war against the Moors" (Franco 507). In contrast, stylistic practices are drawn from the spaces previously deemed too dangerous for women, the public commercial sphere. Revision has wrought glossier presentation and performance of the celebration but also changed the system of social viewing through which the event is interpreted by new generations of audiences. The understanding of a quinceañera celebration as a social space in which to transform one's public image requires acknowledgment of how the traditionalized act of personal portraiture, in particular formal photography, has shifted from being exclusively shared in material forms to being widely shared in digital formats. That shift enables greater circulation of images of the successful dream event and digital personal branding rooted in a social trade of images of an ideal self.

The digital shift also allows a visual representation of personal transformation that is both ethnically inflected and cross-culturally intelligible. These visual narratives find their greatest salience on social media sites such as Facebook, Instagram, Pinterest, Snapchat, LinkedIn, Twitter, and WhatsApp, among others currently cultivating digital youth markets. Manny Ruiz, the chairman of Hispanicize, a leading social media resource for Hispanic marketers, explains, "Social media represents the most powerful medium Latinos have ever had to find their voice and harness their growing strength socially, economically and politically" (qtd. in Llopis). Alexandre Hohagen, the vice president of Facebook Latin America, asserts in 2013 that "23 million Hispanics are active on Facebook every month [giving] Facebook one of the largest audiences for Hispanic affinity in the United States" (qtd. in Llopis), and user numbers have continued to grow. In the United States, Facebook is most popular with Hispanic users, boasting 73 percent of adults polled who identified as "Hispanic" ("Social Media Fact Sheet").

Targeting those with "US Hispanic affinity," not limited to Latinx-identifying people, Facebook has identified this group as the most mobile and socially active group in the United States. The cluster is identified as "actual users who are interested in or will respond well to Hispanic content." There were 26.5 million monthly active users defined as part of this US-based affinity group for Hispanic content ("US Hispanic Affinity"). This perspective builds from a 2013 report from Facebook's internal data sources that claims in a thirty-day period active users in Hispanic affinity groups uploaded 338 million photos and 4 million videos, made 1.1 billion comments, clicked 5.83 billion likes, and checked in more than 7 million times.[3] Those numbers, the valuation of the Hispanic market at $1.7 trillion in purchasing power in 2018, and the demographic of more than half the US Hispanic population under twenty-nine years old speak to the long-term consumer impact potential through digital environments that privilege a currency of visual exchange (Morse). Images of quinceañera style in situ, as part of this informal economic sphere, serve as intertextual markers of Latinx cultural production and call attention to emergent community patterns of practice. Images of young women in elegant vestments leaning against trees and looking wistfully into the distance, posing by rugged wooden fence posts, or stopping traffic on a busy city street with a capitol building in the background become documentation in the experience economy. Such documentary practices supplant discourses of cultural wealth with images of potential albeit ambivalent signifiers of monetary prosperity.

The performance of visuality, of electing to be seen while also denying processes of social erasure, is not enacted without performative risk. The risk emanates from intercultural sources outside of Latinx-identifying communities and intracultural sources in critiques from Latinx-identifying individuals. Intercultural dialectics are often compounded by cultural translation, a lack of understanding that needs to be resolved from one interlocutor to the next and yet must include a desire to educate. In such cases, eroticizing frameworks are often utilized to explain away unintelligible cultural practices as simply vestiges of foreign histories. To outside audiences, the quinceañera resembles a debutante ball for women ages eighteen to twenty-one, often at the end of high school or before college graduation. And so the quinceañera celebration has been interpreted as working in the service of heteronormative courtship. This is a product of a perspective that conflates sensuality or an engagement with the senses that is intensified in a ritual setting—such as the aromas of characteristic foods and scent of a grandmother's perfume and the sounds of music, laughter, and high-heeled shoes on the dance floor as well as, most potently, the onomatopoeic swish, swish, swish of a ball gown rushing to the stage—to become narrowly construed as having explicit sexual value as they are seen as in the service of the audience rather than potent connections for the formation of memories for the celebrant. Such hypersexualizations normalize the peril of Latina teenage marriage and parenthood.

Intracultural tensions and critiques are specifically wrought from observers' inability to recognize the practice because of illegible cultural logics and lack of direct engagement with contemporary communities. The quinceañera in the twenty-first century, as a product of intersecting consumer industries, is unrecognizable for many older community members; it fails a test of authentic visuality and is criticized as having lost an intrinsic value because its presentation has changed. Such judgment about shifts in aesthetics results from value differences between generations that often are intensified by shifts in relation to American consumer culture and new media technologies that resignify the celebration as a social spectacle in which families become viewing audiences. Through the reception of local and remote audiences, style renders quinceañera performance a readable social text separate from the young woman's everyday life; celebrating manifests an image of potentiality. Aspirational social status is connected to the circulation and reception of images coding family life, and elevated status is read through curated consumer choices.

## MIDDLE-CLASS PERFORMATIVITY

Quinceañeras as ethnic-specific versions of success theater denote a symbolic practice contributing to the cultivation of an image of a discernable Latinx middle-class style. Class, as a racialized social resource, is thus a relational experience. Observing the ways Latina women are portrayed in marketing media, one can see them defined by their relation to white women rather than by their own standards of sexual and social propriety. Dávila's explication of Latinas in marketing is that they are reduced to stereotypical images (*Latinos, Inc.* 132). Those images are disjointed from mainstream interpretations of idealized femininity and thus obscure methods of visibly projecting legible social success to mainstream audiences in commercials or in everyday life. Middle-class construction as a mode of advanced cultural citizenship—one that shows rather than simply states inclusion—is fundamentally dependent upon representations as much as realities of individual lives. Middle-class style acknowledges class as a resource in the service of social maneuvering; class status is a transient state that an individual can access through the vehicle of cultural practice.

Jody Agius Vallejo, in *From Barrio to Burbs: The Making of the Mexican American Middle Class*, narrates class formation as racially dependent and notes that the pathways toward upward social mobility look different for Mexican Americans than for African Americans or Asian Americans. Her assertion is hardly surprising in view of how class status is bestowed and fueled by racialized capitalism. Gregory Rodriguez, in "The Emerging Latino Middle Class," finds that unlike the individualistic path of social mobility characterizing immigrants to the United States, the Latinx path to upward mobility is "marked less by rapid individual educational progress and more by nuclear or extended family members engaged in blue- to pink-collar labor pooling their money to improve the status of the whole family unit" (3). Rodriguez frames middle-class identity as one mediated by education and labor.

The anthropologist Sherry Ortner, who discusses middle-class identity broadly, asserts that those aspiring to a middle-class ideal are

> simply all those who have signed up for the American dream, who believe in a kind of decent life of work and family, in the worth of the "individual" and the importance of "freedom," and who strive for a moderate amount of material success. . . . It is everybody except the very rich and the very poor. (236)

Ortner uses fluid distinctions, framing middle-class identity as a state of mind as much as the capacity to live above the poverty line. The question that needs to be addressed is how middle-class identity fits into scholarly discourses about US Latinxs. Gregory Rodriguez boldly claims that a Latinx "path to upward mobility is often ignored or even derided by academics" (3). He contends that scholars choose to revel in narratives of cultural alienation and social inequity while ignoring communities that do not fit into a narrative of romantic poverty.

In "Transnational Triangulation: Mexico, the United States, and the Emergence of a Mexican-American Middle Class," José E. Limón discusses the rise in a specifically Mexican American middle class in Texas. Like Rodriguez before him, Limón identifies the absence of scholarship dedicated to this population as "middle class erasure" (239). The metaphor reflects the importance of the visual encounter with the modern quinceañera as a visual counternarrative that does not erase endemic poverty but attempts to add to a conversation of social mobility and consumer integration.

The subtext of Gregory Rodriguez's claims is that being upwardly mobile is only lauded when one moves from abject poverty to working-class status. Advancing past poverty implies that in the transition, culture and indeed authentic ethnoracial identity are being sacrificed. In reality, this is true. Communities change and adapt to new surroundings at the micro and macro levels of society. Limón notes that the perspective missing from discussions of middle-class growth among Mexican-descent communities in the United States is "anthropological assessment of the worldview and activities of such a class" (240). And with this mandate, I have endeavored to discuss quinceañera celebrations as part of the social and economic development of Latinx middle-class and aspiring middle-class communities, thinking about an image of quinceañera style that has the potential to mirror a broader Latinx middle-class style.

The notion of a middle-class style can be viewed through a lens of quinceañera performance as more than a coming-of-age drama—but also as a product of a developing sense of material prosperity. While Limón finds middle-class identity tainted by the "tragic flaw" of rampant consumerism, my work here foregrounds consumer practice and indeed romantic consumerism as the hallmark of Latinx middle-class identity but not in a pejorative way. Although consumerism is a highly complex process, variable acts of social consumption empower individuals to author discourses of self seemingly on their own terms. Examining the quinceañera from a perspective of consumer intervention allows for a different type of narrative about the tradition to emerge, one that does not rely on notions of pathological femininity or endemic patriarchy. Consumerism within the quinceañera celebration changes the cultural discourse of an individual's coming of age to a national US Latinx process. The emergent Latinx middle class is in continuing development, and scholars of Latinx studies and those working in Latinx communities can no longer pretend it does not exist. A Latinx middle class encompasses transitional communities that have been judged to have assimilated successfully, at least in partial ways, and are creating and re-creating cultural practices that make them fundamentally and unapologetically American. The process is mediated on one front through images of personal success that demonstrate Latinx consumer power. Quinceañeras therefore represent generative cultural spaces that speak to the experiences of a new generation of middle-class and aspiring Latinx populations around the country transforming cultural wealth into indicators of material prosperity.

Quinceañera style is complex. It encompasses more than present financial or social expenditures and material adornment; it also is a modeling of prosperity. At their most focused, entrepreneurs are selling quinceañera style in whatever material form they can because style functions as a vehicle for the reproduction of class and images of luxury. "If one was repeatedly made aware of *self as other*, of one's commodity status, style became a powerful medium of encounter" (Ewen, "Marketing Dreams" 46). Style facilitates an illusory transcendence of class, yet it also can be seen as a testing ground for a classed spectacle. What style truly does is allow "a symbolic ability to one's own name" (Ewen, "Marketing Dreams" 46).

I began my research on quinceañera cultural practices in the United States during the economic downturn of early 2009 that the National Bureau of Economic Research declared the Great Recession, the worst since the 1929 Depression. The effects of the Great Recession that I observed as I began my research in the San Francisco Bay Area included families losing their homes and being unable to make balloon payments on questionable bank loans that triggered the subprime mortgage crisis in an inflated housing market, but also quinceañera industries around the Bay Area flourishing and growing.

In 2010 Quinceañeras Magazine Inc. welcomed two new franchises in California alone, Monterey Bay on the central coast and Santa Rosa in the Napa Valley. The Santa Rosa expo served new Latinx micro markets that were expanding even during dire economic times on a national scale. Just as economic upturns and job prospects often differentially have affected Latinx populations, particularly working-class folks who may work and live by informal economies in addition to documented labor, the downturns also affected communities in ways that do not exactly mirror the average economic status. In reality, my work around quinceañera consumer industries should have fizzled, and instead of examining growth of the public presence of Latinx consumers, I could have documented small-scale, simpler celebrations that reflected the economic conditions that terrified stable middle-class Americans watching the evening news. That was not and is not the case. In truth, Latinx families, those who identify as migrants and legacy migrants, those who have lived at the end of political and social marginalization by way of language politics and racial inequity, are adept at surviving at the margins. The narrative of quinceañera expenditures does not take away from the grit and tenacity of working-class narratives and those of people living and continuing to thrive in poverty and social precarity. Quite the opposite— the continued and renewed investment in Latinx social practices like the quinceañera need to be read as intentional and thoughtful expenditures— investments in extravagance in times of austerity.

Such relations mirror the donning of a zoot suit by Mexican American men and women in the 1940s United States, where the austerity of clothing style reflected support of wartime rationing (Noriega 199). Noriega notes that resistance through dress serves as both display and fantasy that brings together integral elements of public life—being seen on one's own terms and embodying dissent. Much like that interpretation of pachuco style manifested through the donning of a zoot suit, quinceañera style mobilizes public "display and fantasy . . . over use and practicality" (Wollen 9). This interpretation complicates a dichotomy between an ethos of economic minimalism that is read as practical and an economic extravagance by brown consumers that is read not simply as frivolous but also as irresponsible. The style of spending examined through quinceañeras in a politicized climate of cultural austerity implicitly contrasts the socioeconomic precarity felt by those whose lives are newly touched by financial struggles. Extravagant spending on folkloric practices is a specific investment in the public visibility of ethnoracial cultural life. Rather than use the word "fantasy" as Peter Wollen does, to mean conspicuous Latinx social performance among USAmerican publics, quinceañera style in theatrical costuming for the ritual event gives substance to social potential. Its conceptualized potential becomes specifically dangerous and transgressive as fear of the "un-American" has flourished in Donald Trump's America.

## CHAPTER 2

## IDENTITY OFF THE RACK

Selling Quinceañera Dresses and Manufacturing Identities in the Experience Economy

*I feel as if I've wandered into the back room where the femaleness of the next generation of Latinas is being manufactured, displayed, and sold.*
                    JULIA ALVAREZ, *Once upon a Quinceañera*

The quinceañera dress represents the central icon in a larger, wider circle of critical analysis surrounding quinceañera practice in twenty-first-century Americas. This book began as an object study, my intention being to follow and narrate the life of a quinceañera dress. The dress moves through space and time, interweaving communities and ideologies that inform cultural production of Latinx quinceañera celebrations. My hope continues to be to complicate the discourse around both the Anglo Americana of USAmerican folklore studies while also illustrating the political importance of focusing on tangible material markers of cultural heritage that turn individual bodies into cultural spectacles. Here "culture" does not refer to either USAmerican or any singular ethnoracial category of Latin America, but some other interstitial subjectivity vacillating along a spectrum between those two—the inter-American. This in-between zone categorizes both psychic and material reality and affects the ways individuals acquire and are received by the world at large, moving in scale between depersonalized national discourses and invested personal publics.

The quince dress is a stateless garment reflecting flexible transnational affiliation and serves as a boundary object between Chinese manufacturing, Mexican and US marketing and consumer distribution, and ethnoracial Latinx personal publics creating a transgressive style. Stylistic innovations are then fomented by USAmerican social pressure toward cultural austerity. "Quinceañera gowns," those made, manufactured, and branded for that occasion, are a recent inter-American social phenomenon. Before there was a currency in recognizing multicultural traditions, these were simply formal gowns used to mark the special ritual occasion in religious and social contexts. They function more like ethnic costumes, intensifying specific traits in the wearer that are also linked to ethnoracial histories. For US Latinxs the quinceañera has always indexed migration and removal, and the manifestation of the tradition was linked to a retaining of natal traditions that unquestionably belonged to territories once part of Mexico and serving as a gateway to Latin America. The role of the dress has intensified since the early 2000s, when dresses began to take on bold colors and revealing silhouettes that racialized quinceañera style realized in USAmerican culture and customs. Here I examine the role of the quinceañera dress as a material representation of the individual wearer and the sociopolitical history of the event as well as a platform through which young women are allowed and expected to exert personal creativity. Rather than examine the quinceañera gown as a form of confinement and control of feminine Latina subjectivity, I explore its use as a platform for creative engagement; in this understanding, creativity is a strategic social action, and creativity in the face of oppression is revolutionary.

The history of this symbolic garment is obscure. I find that its mystery is both political and personal. The event itself has only been formally documented in US Latinx history since the early 1940s, and it has little social presence outside of family narratives. The obscurity is not surprising, as the event is a marker of women's symbolic social transformation that is interpreted as domestic and private. The invisibility of the tradition to larger audiences and public record also contributed to cultural conservatism rooted in a romantic narrative that the celebration finds its inspiration in pre-Columbian Mesoamerica. However, such a historical through-line, linking contemporary US Latinx practices to Latin American origins, has never been established. Rather, the legend of the quinceañera as the product of indigenous and Spanish syncretism in the "new" world serves as a historicizing discourse that links the tradition back to an idealized heritage community. The styling of quinceañera gowns, especially in the United States, has been a product of current US fashion and of a desire to make tangible a class-conscious narrative that would liken Mexican Americans and other Latinx-identifying communities to elite, prerevolutionary Mexico.

The earliest gowns worn for quinceañera-in-name events were being made and procured by Mexican Americans in South Texas and Cuban Americans in South Florida in the early 1940s and 1950s, a decade after the end of the Mexican Revolution and just before Fidel Castro took control over the island. In *Canícula*, Cantú writes of her girlhood on the *frontera* in Laredo, Texas, and of her own quinceañera celebration as a family- and community-driven affair. Dresses were made for quinceañeras whose priorities would be preparedness for adulthood in the church. Dresses were simple gowns, in white or light pastel colors, and were sacred objects infused with value and love through the labor of familiar, skilled hands. Through acquisition and use, the gowns became something new in Cuban communities and distinct from Mexican American traditions. In the twenty-first-century revisioning of the Latinx tradition of quinceañera, dresses embody narratives of migration but also Americanization; they are wielded as commodities in their own developing transnational marketplace that recognizes Latina consumers as a powerful economic force in the Americas.

## EL MERCADO DE LA LAGUNILLA, MEXICO CITY

"Llevatelos, si otros caen" (Take them, in case others fall off). Evelyn reached out a clenched fist toward me from behind a cash register concealed under an elevated dress display that made the most of the crowded vendor space on a corner of Pasillo 10. I struggled to grasp the offering, as I was holding a thick, gray, no-tear garbage bag full of quinceañera dress parts and two synthetic woven paper crinolines made from industrial interfacing fabric that promised to create the characteristic volume expected under the ball gown worn for a quinceañera celebration. Unlike traditional hoop skirts made with metal wire, this newer version is completely collapsible and would be transportable in my packed suitcase. Offering a freed hand, Evelyn dropped a handful of sparkling, plastic crystals matching those that adorned the neon-coral corset I had just purchased. I stuffed them into an internal pocket of my purse, eager to not drop them all over the uneven concrete floor of the busy public marketplace, exposing my outsider status.

Evelyn was not selling me the idealized quinceañera experience. She was selling me working-class practicality. If the hot-glue workmanship of the adorned bodice failed, I would have crystals to replace any that had been dislodged in transit from Mexico City on my trip back to Austin. Such a transnational shopping pilgrimage is not an uncommon practice of Mexican and Mexican American families living in the United States who maintain strong familial and economic ties to Mexico. I wondered in that moment if Evelyn hands out loose crystals to everyone or just me, the self-identified folklorist looking to buy a dress to display, rather than a bright-eyed young woman with her family, eager to use sartorial magic to transform herself into a princess for a day.[1]

The Mercado de la Lagunilla in Mexico City, in the barrio of La Lagunilla, adjacent to barrio Tepito, and ten blocks north of the Zócalo, offers inexpensive goods to area residents and on Sundays spills into the street in the form of a *tianguis*, an open-air market. As my companion Lía and I made our way through the labyrinth that is the internal marketplace on an average Wednesday afternoon, I was in awe of the volume of quinceañera dresses on display and the tightly packed vendor stations that fostered a sense of both communalism and competition. La Lagunilla vendors sell quinceañera dresses cheap, thousands of pesos cheaper than in the individual dress shops that line Avenida de la República de Chile, also called "la calle de las novias," a colloquialism that needs to be updated to "novias y quinceañeras," as the merchandise for brides and quince girls, though distinct, is for sale side-by-side in many shops. I bought the gown from Evelyn for 2,500 pesos, a steal at roughly US$130, reflecting an 18:1 peso-to-dollar ratio at the time of our transaction in the summer of 2016. Shopping anywhere in the United States, one would be hard pressed to find such an inexpensive handmade, new gown; even used brand-name dresses listed on online classified ad sites like Craigslist sell for many hundreds of dollars.

I got what I paid for, a beautiful dress fashioned together with simple hand and machine stitching along major seams and bodice ornamentation secured with hot glue. It is a practical homage to the single-use status of these gowns, made to be worn and discarded, with disposability a function of the dress as a representation of an exact, transitory moment in life and style. I purchased exactly what I expected, as the market is not only an economic space but also a generative creative space where quinceañera style is intellectualized and sold. Even before we happened upon Evelyn at Originales Mary, I watched dressmakers gluing lacy appliques, sequins, and crystals onto plain bodices, adding feminine touches and outrageous embellishments before my very eyes. Buying a quinceañera dress is more than the acquisition of a product or consumption of goods; it is an investment in experience that takes on a distinct character in the United States among Latinxs preparing to celebrate a quinceañera.

The example here clearly references Mexican workmanship in the production of quinceañera fashion; in the United States, product provenance gets complicated as dress production becomes an implied reference to class status and national loyalty. In a celebration that has been dominated by claims of its status as a marker of ethnic pride and social difference in the United States, advertisers and marketing arms of fashion suppliers use product provenance in their campaigns. Cantú writes of the celebration as it exists in South Texas: "The *quinceañera* allows Chicanas to perform their cultural identity outside the realm of US mainstream culture" ("Chicana" 16). Her observation may hold true along the southern border, where traditions of dress may still very well be located in handmade gifts. From the vantage point of the quinceañera as a consumer practice, the consumption of the tradition and the goods that make it manifest in the world is centered in neoliberal capitalist logics of a recognized US Latinx marketplace. In mass-produced commercial dress culture, the idea of performing identity outside of a supposed mainstream culture gets complicated, as the tradition has become increasingly commercialized by Latinx cultural entrepreneurs who are allying the process of planning the traditional event with other modes of American consumer capitalism. In following the quinceañera dress through a situated object history, I am examining the social phenomena that impact methods of acquisition and consumer choices that affect how the dress is framed from one quinceañera marketing season to the next.

Following the dress as a stylistic manifestation of Latinx American identity through consumer spaces facilitates a conversation at the intersection of traditional art and consumer agency. Latinx consumer landscapes made manifest through the labor of cultural entrepreneurs capitalize on the rhetoric of collective ownership of traditional knowledge and monetize cultural knowledge through individual business ventures that create a quinceañera consumer culture alongside the ritual. The quinceañera ritual is not under discussion here, but instead, I focus on the less-known planning phase, when the roles of ethnic culture actor and consumer actor merge. Consumer spaces become more than areas for negotiating purchases; they are also for negotiating values and virtues that are in flux from one generation to the next. It is within these consumer spaces that the ritual event of the quinceañera becomes a comingled construction, mutually manifested by an American capitalist system and a generation of adolescent Latinas who embrace their status as hybrid, postnational citizens of a fluid multicultural imaginary.

## INSCRIBING VALUE INTO A CONSUMER PROCESS

We sat at the kitchen table and chatted. Jazmin's grandmother Lupe was cutting a bright-orange cantaloupe into large, even pieces that she would later blend with ice into characteristic *agua de melón*. We sipped our melon drinks and discussed the idea of value, and Jazmin in her shy way reminded me how these large celebrations were often less about the will of the daughter and more about the vision of families. In her case, her mother, Christina, wanted more than anything for her daughter to have good memories of her youth. Jazmin was not eager to claim that she would celebrate the event again should she have her own daughter. She was more interested in remaining the same than in shifting to a new life stage. She was happy in sneakers and jeans and not eager to assimilate the trappings of idealized womanhood into her personal performance repertoire. Her lack of interest in a complex performance of ideal femininity was not a failure of the event but reinforced her mother's specific goals for the event—to showcase the beauty of youth and the joys in simply being young and unfettered by grownup responsibilities. Christina more than gifting her daughter womanhood was giving her a moment to revel in simply being young. That youthful moment is marked by the ability to access a quinceañera celebration and the possession of social and economic currency to make such an event possible.

As I was preparing to leave Sanger and make the three-hour return trip to the Bay Area, Christina came up to me with a rumpled Macy's dress bag. She offered me Jazmin's dress. Not just the dress, but her floral bouquet, her tiara, and her headpiece. I was flabbergasted. I confirmed that she was sure that Jazmin didn't want to keep these mementos for herself, and she replied in a very matter-of-fact tone that the objects were simply taking up space in Jazmin's closet. I assured her I would take good care of them, and it took the entire car ride home for me to realize that the aura of these objects—their material and ideological value—was confined to the moment of performance. They were now decommissioned, out of service, and beyond their initial usefulness to Jazmin and her mother. After the months of searching and the battle that ensued when mother and daughter clashed over accent colors and price tag, the balled-up dress, replete with dinner stains, was now simply a fluffy ball of wrinkled polyester. As someone who watched the celebration grow and develop and never had a quinceañera of my own, I saw this object as a treasure, as the material manifestation of everything that the event stood for in this one family, but in reality, that was the academic interpretation. The practical interpretation lay in valuing what was next, not what was in the past. The documentation was in the formal photos, the carefully crafted memory objects that revealed the dress in use. Beyond these two-dimensional representations, the gown's ideological value was siphoned away into other efforts. As I absconded with my treasure like a raccoon who found a tasty bit of trash, I found myself thinking deeply about the life of the dress and how its display and use within a quinceañera celebration is but one leg of its journey through different social and economic realms of value.

## QUINCE DRESS CULTURE AND THE RISE OF EXPERIENCE ECONOMICS

Since the early 2000s, quinceañera consumer industries have shifted in character from goods providers to experience stagers. It would be erroneous to claim that quinceañeras have only recently engaged with consumer industries. Rather, the celebration's relation to consumer industries has changed, and the change has affected the use of material artifacts associated with the event, in particular the ubiquitous quinceañera dress.

### THE TÍA-SEAMSTRESS

Any Latina who came of age before the later 1990s can attest that the character of the quinceañera celebration has different qualities than those taking place after the turn of the millennium. Nostalgic and disgruntled quinceañeras would wax about overbearing female relatives who were responsible for engineering events with love and *fuerza*; the women would make food, help rent halls, and more importantly, make and gift a quinceañera dress to a young quince-to-be. The construction of the dress, handmade by any member of a young woman's family network of support, was a representation of group identity mixed in with requests made by the young woman. Regardless of the percent of contribution on either side, the dress was a collaborative adventure, a representation of family love and pride. At the same time, the dress was laden with expectation and anxiety. The dress became the quintessential referent of Latina womanhood for families practicing the tradition and as such, was the material site of ideological negotiations. How much skin can she show? What color represents a "good señorita"? What did her sister wear? These and a thousand other intimate questions plagued the production of the ritual garment, meant to help the transitional process by staging the young, still developing body as a woman—as the desired result of idealized femininity and womanhood. This theme would haunt many young women who by donning the dress made with the hopes and dreams of female relatives, mothers, grandmothers, tías, and cousins, would betray their own sense of gender and sexuality. Such young women would be forced by traditional expectations into a "cynical" presentation of the self (Goffman 18).

In these compulsory heterosexual social niches, identities of proto and assuredly queer women of color would be erased from their familial history through the contortions of fashion and respectability politics. While many things were exchanged between families and good friends in the informal dress economy, money often was not. Dresses were produced as part of a communal construction of the birthday event, fabric and time were a gift and for some, as offerings of intergenerational connections of shared womanhood. Labor was a sign of love and affection, even if the regulation of that labor was out of the control of the quinceañera girl or her family. At that point the dress was part of the event but not the center of the event. It was one location in the celebration, the most intimate location through which the ritual exerted itself onto a Latina, revealing and concealing, contorting and accentuating, molding womanhood onto young brown bodies. For many young women whom I call "reluctant quinceañeras," those whose practice of the event came from the gentle cajoling or mandate of mothers and fathers, narratives of the dress linger as moments of self-realization and difference. Even for those whose quinceañeras did not leave a lasting fond memory on their psyches, dresses made by relatives and friends, even if they emphasized antiquated styles or values, maintained their value as representations of affection and the networks of support that would continue to surround the quince as her life progressed.

As the dynamics of family life changed, as women were increasingly entering the workforce by desire and need and becoming breadwinners, and as families were being transplanted through transnational migration, the patterns of quinceañera production also shifted. Quinceañera celebrations were becoming variable parts of diverse Latinx experiences across the United States. The journalist Michele Salcedo notes how Cuban quinceañeras in 1950s Miami would acquire gowns in wedding-dress boutiques as their only outlets for shopping for the gown. In her narration of the history of the tradition, Cantú notes that in the 1960s and 1970s the practice of quinceañera took a dip ("La Quinceañera" 17). Chicana Rita Torres from Oakland, California, shared with me that Chicanas like her who would have come of age in the late 1960s had no desire to don "poofy pink dresses" and chose to come of age in the streets demonstrating for civil rights and other political actions. In that moment, the quinceañera as a celebration was antithetical to her social circumstance and social values. In *The Overspent American*, Juliet Schor observes that the 1980s and 1990s brought on a spending culture in the US economy as "middle-class Americans were acquiring at a greater rate than any previous generation of the middle class" (2). Acquisition of goods, class-based spending, and a desire to return to traditional values spurred cultural forms, and it is around that time that the quinceañera celebration gained new traction among US Latinxs. Extrafamilial and extracommunal influences began to permeate the porous boundaries of the celebration, offering goods and services to families planning their quinceañera celebrations, but the most apparent of shifts came in the form of the lavish quinceañera gown. At this same moment, niche marketing that deemed the 1980s "the decade of the Hispanic" was making way for the "Latino boom" and the advent of a Latino national imaginary (Valdivia 5).

The gifted, handmade quinceañera dress is one experience of quinceañera practice in contrast to the development of the experience economy. Cultural entrepreneurs maneuver in the experience economy in which businesses sell more than goods and services; they profit from the staging of personalized experiences. As quinceañera style developed within US Latinx communities in the 1980s and 1990s in a socioeconomic context that established consumption as a national pastime, the labor of dress production became increasingly externalized from informal family networks. For some this distancing from a family labor force invokes a sense of loss of familial engagement, but for those who never had such engagements or who have gaps in their family trees due to circumstances of personal loss and systemic oppression, this loss is not felt. In fact, for those without a personal link to the tradition, the externalization of the tradition makes a consumer access point through which a Latinx family living far from relatives and who desire to do so can still plan and enact a quinceañera celebration. These quinceañeras are staged by swapping communal family labor for capital investment. Such families invest in the labor of local dress boutiques that function to Latinize public space across the country.

## THE CONSUMER TURN IN QUINCEAÑERA PRACTICE IN THE UNITED STATES

Since the late 1970s the "Hispanic" consumer sector has represented the next lucrative frontier in ethnic-specific niche marketing in the United States; by the early 1980s systematic studies of the community were in place to help determine the Hispanic consumer potential in key demographic areas like Los Angeles and New York (Halter). Such studies emphasize the buying power of a Latinx youth market that is now in the twenty-first century visible in the success of big business offshoots like MTV Tr3s, a network claiming to offer "superservice" to bicultural, multilingual, American-born, Latinx teen market. Such ethnic customization can be seen in English-language national advertising. In early 2016 the Coca-Cola Corporation released two ads that feature quinceañera themes as hooks to draw in Latinx consumers. The first depicts a girl dancing with her father around a small kitchen, learning her waltz steps, and laughing over Cokes (Maines). Diana Alejandra Perez from Houston, then seventeen years old, played the role of quinceañera and was accompanied on screen by her father, who was cast after the two were observed video chatting before the formal audition. Alejandra did not have a formal quinceañera but said due to the commercial she did have one, after their father-daughter waltz reached her family in Honduras as part of Coke advertising campaigns across Latin America.

Another commercial is a montage of flashing images of Latin American cityscapes and skylines. It contextualizes quinceañera practice in a few frames of a quinceañera girl swirling across a dance floor. These advertisements draw on the representation of quinceañera celebrations in the United States and Latin America as markers of the social success and upward mobility, real and aspirational, of diverse Latinx consumer audiences. In popular cultural venues, the quinceañera tradition is represented not by the depiction of church spaces or specific ritual gifts but by the characteristic gown. Patterns in acquiring this gown have developed hand-in-hand with the larger presence of Latinxs in nationally visible pop culture outlets. As social citizenship in the United States is entrenched in complex relations of shopping and buying, quinceañera practice becomes more than a question of family history and ethnic pride but a window into larger consumer politics in which heritage traditions are instrumentalized by buyers and sellers as markers of intimate connections to American consumer citizenship.

The origins of the quinceañera ritual are opaque and subject to multiple generations of social and cultural politics in their interpretation, but the onset of the intense commercial presence in quinceañera practice can be traced back to 1987, when the first telenovela marketed toward Latin American teens was made in Mexico and titled *Quinceañera*. It stars the singer, actor, and global entrepreneur Ariadna Thalía Sodi Miranda, known professionally as Thalía, in the first major role of her expansive telenovela career as Beatriz Villanueva Contreras, a fourteen-year-old from a wealthy family on the precipice of celebrating her quinceañera. The winding plot is plagued by romantic entanglements, social climbing, and the drama of teenage pregnancy. *Quinceañera* was produced by the Televisa network, "a leading media company in the Spanish-speaking world" ("Company Overview"); the program was distributed in the United States on the Univision Network and in 1988 won the Telenovela of the Year award by Premios TV y Novelas. It would go on in 2010, twenty-three years after its original air date, to make *People en Español*'s list of Twenty Best Telenovelas ("*Las 20 mejores*"). The show had such an impact that Televisa produced two remakes also targeting teen audiences, in 2000 renamed *Primer amor, a mil por hora* and in 2012 *Miss XV*. The popularity of the original not only inspired remakes but also affected a generation of Latinas who for the first time were seeing the tradition of the fiesta de quince años played out in a public, popular culture context.[2] Until this point the quinceañera was a decidedly family affair, and its social and cultural frame was viewed through the lens of private family networks.

The telenovela *Quinceañera* reflects the onset of a public narrative of quinceañera practice built around a consumer frame where the tradition is part of market appeal to target Latinx youth audiences. The show's young star and co-protagonist, Thalía, who received the Best New Actress award alongside the show's lead, was only a teenager herself when the show aired. Her quinceañera performance became one that girls idolized as they saw themselves being represented on screens across Hispanic America (*"Thalia recibe premio"*). Thalía and her co-star, Adela Noriega, also appeared on the special "Mis quince años" cover of Mexico's *Ultima Moda* magazine in 1988, anticipating a trend that would develop into the twenty-first century as a competitive quinceañera magazine industry whose sole product is quinceañera material culture. The archived image, without provenance, is posted to Los Angeles–based Quinceanera.com's Instagram account as a throwback promotion encouraging girls to compete to be cover models. Contemporary cultural entrepreneurs see the value in creating legacies, and rather than linking back to individualized iterations of traditional practice, they refer back to the industry's ur-style moment.

This transnational televisual representation of the quinceañera would set the stage for the intersection of popular culture and folkloric practice. The externalization of the tradition, its extrication from close family networks, means that girls can imagine their own quinceañeras regardless of the generations of the practice that did not exist in their family histories. Popular images come to set the stylistic tone for what will be remembered as a turning point in a woman's life story. In an interview at her best friend's home, Griselda Cervantes explained to me the effect Thalía's quinceañera style had on her personal celebration. A social worker and mother who celebrated her quinceañera in 1996 in San Jose, California, Griselda remembers watching the telenovela and idolizing Thalía. She was so enamored by the role and representation that when she was planning her own quinceañera she asked her grandmother to make a quinceañera dress modeled after one worn on the TV show. It was not that of Thalía's character, who hailed from a wealthy family, but that of her co-protagonist, played by Adela Noriega, whose family was characterized as working-class. Griselda's dress was a cream-colored, full-length, A-line gown, modestly cut with a squared neckline, and long, flared, colonial-style sleeves. The engineering of her dress represents a realistic middle ground in the consumer turn of quinceañera practice in which popular creative influences affect familial production of the gown and change rather than destroy intergenerational bonding.

The consumer turn is not a wholesale replacement of familial and community networks, nor is it the earliest onset of consumerism in the practice. Externalization of resources has always been part of the celebration, as the component materials, fabric, needles, and thread were all purchased, as well as technologies such as sewing machine and fabric glue were all bought, not made by families. Suddenly, dresses intended for brides, an established market, could be bought or altered, still requiring trained hands to convert a bridal gown into a quinceañera dress. The prevalence of Chicanas in the United States wearing white for their quinceañeras may have been about the overlay of color symbolism that bolstered social narratives of chastity and obedience but also about a product already available in extant formal dress shops. This premade quinceañera dress would become more valuable as more and more women started careers outside of the home, limiting their time to hand-make clothes. Indeed, many tías and abuelas who made dresses as gifts were also trained *costureras*, seamstresses whose labor was professional, even if the connection to the product was fundamentally affective. It is this connection between labor and product within Latinx communities that has not simply changed but has been elaborated. A consumerist model can be integrated into a homespun, do-it-yourself celebration in graduated ways. The most commercially saturated event—completely replacing familial labor with financial investment—and other options are based on families' own unique social and economic circumstances. The consumer turn refers to the onset of a specific body of quinceañera-inspired and -themed industries and the emergence of professionals whose work is devoted to the exclusive purview of quinceañera practice across inter-American cultural channels, however dominated by the influences of the United States and Greater Mexico.[3] This developing web of industries is rooted in the sale of formal gowns that establish the platform from which the wider event is planned.

The integration of US Latinas into wider realms of consumer culture rooted in notions of a mainstream American identity did not begin in the twenty-first century and certainly not with the making and marketing of quinceañera goods. The quinceañera as a cultural practice exhibits its enduring relevance as a flexible reflection of the lived experiences of Latinx communities, not simply the vacant insertion of romantic materialism. Vicki Ruiz discusses the complex relationship young Mexican American women had with American consumer culture as a resource for "circumventing traditional standards" ("Star Struck" 118), a relation recapitulated in the emergent quinceañera marketplace. Mexican American women in the 1930s were finding their own voices as they began creating lives for themselves outside of their family homes, taking work and using income not relinquished to elders in the "family wage economy" to purchase goods for themselves (Ruiz, "Star Struck" 112). Cosmetics and celebrity magazines helped them imagine hybrid lives that were not exclusively guided by the cultural expectations of conservative Mexican-origin families. Media influences became a key way in which young Mexican American women reimagined their own working lives. Ruiz notes that "movies and romance magazines . . . enabled adolescents to experience vicariously the middle-class and affluent lifestyles heralded in these publications and thus could nurture a desire for consumer goods" ("Star Struck" 113).

The power of consumer integration to reimagine one's social condition is a fundamental characteristic of life in the United States and has been a pattern of practice among Mexican American women since in the early twentieth century. Similarly, in "Silent Dancing," Judith Ortiz Cofer writes about not just products but the important role of Latinx-owned businesses in her native Patterson, New Jersey, in the 1950s:

> These establishments were located not downtown but in the blocks around our street, and they were referred to generically as La Tienda, El Bazar, La Bodega, La Botánica. Everyone knew what they meant. These were the stores where your face did not turn a clerk to stone, where your money was as green as anyone else's. (182–183)

Latinx-owned business construct culturally familiar places in public spaces that were particularly important to women, as they were some of the few spaces young and old women alike could be seen alone in public without fear of scorn. Ortiz Cofer reminisces that *tiendas* were public spaces her own mother could traverse without being accompanied by her father. They offered women a respite from unceasing domestic confinement. Marilyn Halter uses Ortiz Cofer's words to show the earliest history of multiethnic marketing in the United States to what Halter terms a "rainbow coalition of consumers" (Halter 138). Likewise, Ruiz spends time discussing how although Mexican American women in 1930s America were finding their independence through forms of consumer engagement, they did not do so without resistance from older generations, even as their efforts purchased "comfort" for their families ("Star Struck"). What becomes truly controversial then as well as now in Latina quinceañera practice is the star-struck desire for consumer goods that was interpreted as a desire for American assimilation. Such an understanding of the power of consumption begs a closer look at the relation between commerce and cultural forms. The quinceañera dress in particular, as its object life begins to include mass production, has been changed as the access to less expensive goods allows Latinas without clear generational ties to the celebration to craft experiences through the use of external professional industries.

Such industries have experienced monumental growth since the late 1990s, in part with the advent of Chinese-made quinceañera gowns that have become visible parts of the consumer landscape of barrio boutiques.

### HECHO EN CHINA/MADE IN CHINA

Planning begins with a dream and a dress. With the inception of professional industries guiding the staging of the celebration, the 1990s brought a new way to access the tradition without the benefit of a knowledgeable mother or seamstress grandmother and with the quinceañera dress "hecho en China." One aspect of the externalization of quinceañera culture from individual family-to-family networks is the way the tradition perpetuates spaces for women-owned small businesses in Latinx communities. According to the National Women's Business Council, between 2007 and 2016 "Hispanic women entrepreneurs have grown at a faster rate than any other group—137 percent," reaching 1.9 million Hispanic women-owned firms, employing more than 500,000 workers, and generating $97 billion in revenues. Their earning potential is still underrealized, and the report asserts that "targeting the untapped potential of Hispanic women entrepreneurs can accelerate U.S. economic growth" ("Understanding Diversity").

The statistics may not reflect businesses that depend on Latina labor and knowledge but are owned by male family members. Angelica's Designs in Des Moines, Iowa, is a family-owned formal-wear boutique with merchandise that is predominantly quinceañera-themed, including dresses, tiaras, cake toppers, and church accessories such as kneeling pillows. Angelica, in her seventies in 2015, had been the primary contact for girls seeking quinceañera gowns in Des Moines. When I visited the shop that March while in town attending a Quinceañeras Magazine Inc. expo at the Val Air ballroom, Angelica was fitting a young woman into a neon-pink ball gown to make alterations. The business side of Angelica's Designs was now handled by her son; a sense of authentic feminine knowledge was maintained in keeping the business in her name. The business offers a variety of quinceañera gowns to local customers in West Des Moines, but they are not custom made. They can be found on racks wrapped in plastic dress bags. Only a few are displayed to their full potential for quinceañeras, as only half the store is dedicated to the sale of quinceañera goods; the other half features a wide variety of women's general formal wear. The day of my visit the glass counters were piled with dress catalogues from overseas distribution companies.

In small, locally owned boutique contexts one can see the experience of buying a quinceañera dress developing. Small businesses run by Latinx entrepreneurs cater to local, co-ethnic clienteles and use their personal life experiences to market traditional knowledge as they tell young Latinas what a quinceañera dress could look like. Rather than being spaces of explicit creativity where dresses are designed, local boutiques that order from catalogues depend on the creativity of external companies.

At an early moment in my research, I walked into a small shop in San Jose, California, that I will call Jean's Bridal. I was astonished at the layer of dust that covered the shop. The glass cases holding piles of tiaras were cloudy, and the dresses were packed tightly into the small shop. It was an unattractive space, not by a failing of the management, but because this shop was a work space first, a display space second. The clerk at the counter, who was chatting away on her cell phone, was also hand-tying *capias*, the small ribbons printed with information of a formal event, the name of the girl, the date, and the type of event, in this case "mis quince años." She was attaching them to a tiny army of plastic containers that held bubble solution, a common keepsake at quinceañera events in the 1990s. But this was 2010, and I had seen the newest digital and Etsy-inspired artful keepsakes that were being marketed to a new generation of quinceañera celebrants and realized that this space was not competitive in creating quinceañera experiences. It was really helping manufacture a style of event that belonged to a previous generation and aligned with a particular working-class perspective of seeking inexpensive products for quinceañera events rather than paying for holistic staging of premium personalized experiences. When I asked the sales clerk where they kept their quinceañera dresses, she handed me a white three-ring binder. Each page inside a plastic cover featured a Design by Mary, referencing the corporate entity Mary's Bridal, an assortment of dresses for quinceañera girls, their *damas* (attendants), and their mothers. I sat for an hour on a small, gray folding chair at the back of the showroom leafing through the binder, trying to imagine how a young woman would need to have a color, style, and theme in mind to make entering this consumer space useful to her planning process. I soon realized it would be unlikely that a young women would enter such a space unprepared; more likely she would have searched the internet for potential brands and styles that she might then find in binders like this one of dresses by Mary's Bridal, among the most recognizable names in quinceañera fashion across the United States.

### P. C. MARY'S INC./MARY'S BRIDAL

Christina tossed me the small, slightly tattered look book for Mary's 2009 collection of quinceañera dresses, specifically from the company's Beloving line, the collection being featured at a local dress shop in Sanger, California, a small town just outside of Fresno. At the time, Christina was living there to be near her mother, Lupe, who has significant health issues. Christina was a do-it-yourself quinceañera mom. She was extremely interested in creating a polished look for her daughter Jazmin's quinceañera but was also highly protective of her budget. She explained to me how they were browsing gowns and that Jazmin liked the one on the back cover. The dress was bright pink with black piping. Christina was certain Jazmin's grandmother would not like this choice, and as Lupe was helping pay for the event, dress negotiations would need to continue until consensus was met. While the look book was used as a reference obtained for free when she and Jazmin went in to browse dresses in person, their search was digital. They spent hours looking online for the right look at the right price. Later Christina and I would run into the clerk of the local dress shop at a quinceañera expo in Fresno that she had patronized in her small town; at the store the clerk had treated Christina poorly, and she felt disrespected by how the clerk had assumed her family's price point. It was after that encounter at the store that Christina began traveling to expos and other boutiques outside of Sanger to get a wider view of her consumer options. In the end, Jazmin and the family compromised and purchased Mary's #F084183, in light pink.

P. C. Mary's Inc., known through the business moniker Mary's Bridal, was established in 1983 and is based in Houston. It won twenty-three awards in thirty years for "exquisite designs, impeccable reputation and excellent services" ("Mary's Bridal"). Mary's business mantra is distilled "in the concept of one stop shopping," a narrative later repeated in the work of quinceañera-themed consumer exhibitions. Mary's Bridal boasts three thousand full-service dress salons across the United States and around the world, and the service end of the business is the idiosyncratic production of the small-business owners whose shops offer Mary's various dress-collection catalogues from which clients can select and order "form fitting handmade gowns [that] make you look fabulous!" ("Mary's Quinceañera"). What is not advertised is that the hands making these gowns are those of laborers working in factories in China before they are imported by Mary's business partner Abundmer Inc. It is described in a business directory as a business of the "importing of woman's formal dresses importing bridal gowns, quinceañera dresses, prom dresses, bridesmaid dresses, flow girl dresse [sic]" (Abundmer). The company president, Sisin Chang, in a sparse LinkedIn profile was listed as the financial "controller" of Mary's Bridal for nearly twenty-six years, the exact time frame listed for the inception of Abundmer Inc. Such a narrative removes the dress from its fantasy provenance and centralizes it in the commodity flow of cheaply made goods from China.

Mary's dresses open up a new conversation around the production of the quinceañera celebration in the United States, one that focuses on the political economy of dress. As a consumer product central to the production of an ethnocultural rite of passage, the effects of the global political economy can be seen in the enactment of this inter-American experience. The reality becomes that quinceañera events are Latinx cultural experiences made possible by global markets, international importers, and cheap Chinese labor. In 2013, 43 percent of global clothing exports came from China ("Made in China?"). Like other Chinese-made goods, particularly textiles available in the United States, quinceañera fashions made in China are cheaper than American-made or Mexican-made options. Mary's Bridal options lead the way in affordable quinceañera gowns available to Latina shoppers in the United States. Moreover, Chinese-made "quinceañera" dresses were available as early as the mid-1990s, before other national retail brands like David's Bridal, which started a "quinceañera" gown line in 2009. David's Bridal is a ubiquitous brand in formal wear and the largest American bridal store chain. The creation of a quinceañera line marks the tradition's coming out front and center on the USAmerican cultural stage.

Mary's Bridal offers three lines of a quinceañera gown fashions: Princess Quinceañera, Beloving Quinceañera, and Alta Couture.[4] Each line has a distinct body of dresses designed along inspirational themes or stylized gowns that share color palates or design flourishes as well as advertising campaigns. Each of Mary's Bridal quinceañera dress lines offers an extensive range of styles and sizes. Each of these lines offers dresses in the plus size range, up to size 30. The lines gradually increase in price point, with the Princess line averaging dresses starting around $600 and the Alta Couture at $1,000. In the *pasillos* of el Mercado de la Lagunilla, my neon-coral purchase was extremely inexpensive, but the inventory from which I chose was significantly limited compared to the hundreds of offerings available to consumers at Marys.com, and the size range was narrow. The bodice and elastic-waist skirt that a size 2 mannequin now wears is unlikely to be altered beyond a women's size 10. That would leave a young woman in the nominally plus size range out of luck without extensive alterations that would increase the price considerably, thus bypassing one of the most prominent strengths of online shopping from chain retailers—lower prices. Mary's offers options and does so at a price point at or below custom-made couture gowns from ateliers in the United States or Mexican design houses that market specifically to US audiences, often drawing on a narrative of provenance to sell their gowns.

The Chinese-made quinceañera gowns and an infrastructure to import them into the United States creates a paradox of cultural performance in the production of the quinceañera event as a marker of ethnic identification. Dresses made overseas do work in the context of quinceañera cultural production. Chinese-made dresses and the boutiques that carry them are gradually moving toward an experience-centric economic model around the quinceañera celebration. Mary's Bridal invests in multiple generations of Latinx consumers through the simple act of naming. The naming of dress lines as exclusively "quinceañera" differentiates the practice of quinceañera as a stand-alone entity in the US public culture that is separate from sweet-sixteen celebrations, prom dances, and weddings. This consumer variation appeals to Latinx consumers and courts them as a distinctive audience with specialized needs to be catered to. From the distinction a wider marketplace has evolved for the consumer-based intervention into the celebration as a marker of consumer presencing, that is, being seen as valid and real through integration into mainstream consumer practice.

At the same time as this process of consumer presencing is acknowledged and appreciated by Latinx consumers, it becomes a signal to other entrepreneurs of the market in the quinceañera, spurring entrepreneurial activity in a specific professional industry around the celebration. Latinx consumers can shop on boutique racks for an identity and find themselves. The ability to find oneself is not romantic. Finding oneself amid the spectacle in the public sphere is a privilege that signals socioeconomic inclusion in a world where representation is reality. It is a sign that one's community has brokered a relation with mainstream structures of social power in which material objects come to define how people are seen by others and how they see themselves. And yet as Chinese vendors facilitate Latinx coming of age in the continental United States, how much longer can the celebration be considered "ethnic" and not part of a larger national and transnational stream of culture, goods, and knowledge that spills out beyond the confines of singular ethnic or national identifications?

Although it is an unromantic story, the mass manufacturing of Chinese-made quinceañera dresses does cultural work. It establishes a pipeline of available and relatively affordable styles of specialty gowns to a market of second- and third-generation Latina consumers who may be the first in their families celebrating quinceañeras. First-generation quinceañera girls do not have the luxury of sage female elders surrounding them. These young women are part of the growing Latinx population who may not speak Spanish and find their lives defined by a cultural process of "retro-acculturation," a marketing term established in the 1990s by the marketing executive Carlos E. Garcia that highlights the consumer tendencies of predominantly second-, third-, and fourth-generation Latinxs who are described as feeling like they "have lost their cultural identity." However, revisiting the idea in 2017, Garcia explains that the phenomenon is about recognizing individuals who are consciously pushing back on a sensation of loss and "making a conscious decision to go back and re-discover the culture of their parents and grandparents" (*Hispanic Marketers' Guide* 142). Garcia notes that re-adoption of traditions is part of this process, and yet, our understanding of changes in cultural practice needs deepening if we are to understand how Latinx subjectivities supported by consumer practices reimagine Latinx futurity on a national scale.

Consumption in this context becomes an exercise in autobiographic salvage labor, a recovery mission that mirrors quinceañera style as a function of both memory and desire. I will illustrate later how digital contexts of consumption complicate this process even further by invoking the notion of digital reculturation through the availabilities of online cultural influencers. Retro-acculturation is a cultural process in which ethnoracial identity is enacted through consumer agency and bolstered by the lure of conspicuous consumption, relatively understood as luxury, that is procured for the "comfort of the consumer" (Veblen 35). As such, consumer goods increase in quality, so the purchases also begin to indicate wealth and social status, therefore supporting the growth of specialized skilled labor of cultural entrepreneurs.

The marketplace thus becomes responsible for driving ethnic and heritage industries to provide goods of cultural formation to communities that do not encounter them organically through their own familial experiences. Cultural practice becomes a product to be sold. Such an outlook might seem grim and toxic to audiences who view the saturation of economic metaphors in everyday interactions as part of a neoliberal takeover of cultural life, but one must consider for a moment that not all Latinx individuals experience the luxury of long-term, stable residence in the United States with clearly documented family histories. Cultural entrepreneurs thrive as retro-acculturative marketing strategies appeal to Latinx communities precisely because they form a link between individual memory and ethnic heritage practices.

Latinx populations, rhetorically situated within the boundaries of the United States, have highly variable migratory and settlement histories. These populations have endured waves of destructive sociocultural policies that have affected their ability to maintain heritage forms such as language and folk practice. Yet, within those experiences and even within ethnic national communities, those experiences vary dramatically, and cultural rooting will be shallow for some and multiple generations deep for others. In Texas the practice of quinceañera is generations strong. This is perhaps bolstered by a thriving ongoing southern debutante culture. Commercial expositions sponsored by Quinceañeras Magazine Inc. in Austin, Houston, San Antonio, and

Dallas pale in comparison to those hosted in other states because Texans simply do not need as much help planning quinceañeras. But newer immigrants do. Latina youth whose families are recent migrants to the United States and have only vague connections to the celebration lean into consumer industries that open opportunities to engage in widely accepted Latinx culture, materializing their ethnic identity. Such desire to participate is supported by commercial industries that profit from providing an affective connection between families and heritage traditions. In this twenty-first-century position, how marketing tradition affects the signification of the celebratory process that for a rite of social and biological passage stems from a relation with dress and the body becomes an important consideration.

Chinese dresses give access to the cultural form of the quinceañera but not without changing the affective quality of the event in wider society. Look-alike mass-produced dresses from outsourced labor insert quinceañera practice into global economic streams while also contributing to a consumer narrative around the event that did not exist as intensely in previous generations. Some critics share my distaste for the consumerized quinceañera, and it has become a consistent off-the-record comment at academic conferences that the increased visibility of the celebration conjured through an assemblage of commercial goods has spurred the growth of the celebratory event across the United States. Julia Alvarez narrates her astonishment at the industry that has grown up around the event while also expressing her concern at the way the industry is growing a new kind of Latina, comfortable and eager to integrate socially through the consumer process. She notes the loss of intergenerational relationships made through the planning and execution of quince años parties but fails to recognize that for contemporary youth generations, such relationships may not be present to lose. The notion of loss is an imposed narrative that contemporary Latina teens simply do not experience. In their experiences, the quinceañera event is born from themed magazines, advice websites, consumer expositions, and the support of peers. Their desire for consumer experiences that are transferable and shareable with their non-Latinx networks become sublimated middle-class desires that are not rooted in an authentic or traditional past but a successful future that begins with the fulfillment of a dream quinceañera. Such dream fulfillment is being visualized and staged by consumer industries riding a lucrative quinceañera wave through the mass marketing of gowns from China. Quinceañeras are but one piece of a type of ethnoracial class-conscious social branding now in the hands of professionals who by staging luxury experiences integrate diverse forms of quinceañera style into the experience economy of upscale Latinx marketing.

The economics around the quinceañera have shifted. Once a mother or grandmother might have purchased the fabric, thread, and accent material required to make a quinceañera dress at home. Gradually, as the distance between families has grown and more women entered the workforce while also maintaining domestic responsibilities, dresses were purchased from local seamstresses or boutiques from China that might cost ten times more than homemade garments.

### MORI LEE

Mary's Bridal is not the only company that sells Chinese-made quinceañera dresses, although it is one of the most widely known brands, and its gowns can be found at retailers from coast to coast. Not far behind Mary's in popularity and visibility is Mori Lee, like Mary's also known for its formal wear more broadly. Mori Lee's Vizcaya line, designed by Madeline Gardner, a New York-based designer, offers new quinceañera designs season to season. Mori Lee designs offer an augmented frame to the Chinese-dress experience that obscures the mass-produced quality of the dresses. Terms like "taffeta" replace "polyester blend," and the naming of a particular designer adds a humanistic quality that denotes an elite and idiosyncratic provenance to dresses that is not part of Mary's advertising narrative. Mary's Bridal shelters its quinceañera dress lines under its trusted brand moniker, leaving out any mention of an individual designer. Upon closer inspection, a famous name is just that, a name. While Madeline Gardner "proudly puts her name on beautiful Mori Lee collections," there is no mention of her design influence ("Madeline Gardner"). At one boutique I visited in Southern California, a clerk quietly explained to a customer how Mori Lee dresses "are cheap and made in China" and that she could not guarantee the customer's desired dress would be delivered in time for her party. Despite these realities, Mori Lee's corporate voice claims to understand the brand's dresses in terms of the quinceañera rite:

> The dress you choose for your Quinceañera is much more than a beautiful piece of clothing; it is the symbol of your transformation to young womanhood. In our Vizcaya Collection you will find an array of stunning dresses worthy of this meaningful task.

> In our Vizcaya collection, our inspirational designer, Madeline Gardner, stayed true to the long-established and beloved spirit of Quinceañera gowns with skirts that are long, full and flowing.

> Choosing a Quinceañera dress is a big decision. Take your time.
> We know you'll find the perfect dress that bridges the girlhood
> that you're leaving behind and the womanhood that stands before
> you. How excited are you?! ("Turning Fifteen")[5]

This frame of ethnic marketing, which is generic enough to appeal to the
wide range of Latinx ethnic nationalisms, draws not on the product but on
the experience of the product acquisition and the potential efficacy of the
product in use. The Vizcaya line is marketing genius, as it appeals to the exact
implications of the celebration, putting consumers at ease that they are buying the correct product by acknowledging a reference to a traditional past
but not enough to alienate young consumers. The line is meant to help the
wearer's transition in this moment in time through consumer choice. The use
of the second-person form engages the consumer directly, as an individual,
rhetorically marking a personal experience of shared marketing. Mori Lee
does not just want a shopper to buy a dress; it wants her to feel good about
her purchase by accepting a personalized, American Latinx narrative around
it that is digitally savvy, English-speaking, and socially affluent. Mary's gowns
and Mori Lee designs appear on the pages of *Quinceañeras Magazine*. The
brands' placement within the covers of this industry magazine is strategic, as
the magazine's space is racialized as Latinx. Brands whose ads appear here are
able to reach Latina consumers and their parents directly while being considered part of the magazine corporate *familia*.

QUINCEAÑERAS MAGAZINE INC.

Established in 2005 in Las Vegas, Nevada, by the entrepreneur and former
professional photographer Rafael Aguayo, *Quinceañeras Magazine* has become a model for quinceañera professionals in the experience economy.
What began as a way to bring together industry professionals with Latinx
consumers in Nevada and California now has franchisees across the contigu-
ous United States. In September 2017 its website, quinceanerasmagazine.
com, touted the publication as

> the fastest growing magazine of its kind, serving primarily the His-
> panic community in the US. Founded and operated by Latinos,
> we have created a unique concept based on the knowledge of our
> traditions and a full experience in the industry.

In a 2018 overhaul of its website the company shifted the message. At the bottom left of each page on the site is this statement, verbatim:

> We, the team at Quinceaneras Magazine, proudly present to all
> of the beautiful Quinceanera to be girls a website tailored to their
> needs. We, believe in the fantasy created around the celebration
> of a Quinceanera—the most important event in a Latinas [*sic*]
> woman's life, because a quinceanera happens only once in a life-
> time. It is a unique event for the quinceanera and her family.

Since 2005 Quinceañeras Magazine Inc. has grown geographically and in
specializations, adding Miss Cover Girl beauty pageants to the event calendar
on top of twice-yearly product expositions. Regional pageant winners earn a
spot on the cover of the subsequent season's magazine cover and the opportunity to compete for college scholarships in the National Miss Cover Girl
competition. Neli Hernández, Miss Cover Girl Nebraska, was the inaugural
winner of the competition, held in Las Vegas in 2015. Regional expositions
give area businesses the opportunity to meet with prospective clients; the national competition establishes a hierarchy among regional franchises seeking
to take the crown home as a sign of their possession of superior quinceañera
professional services. Such awards cause a buzz around the regional expositions, where girls can meet national pageant winners and align their planning
experience with related social success and affirmation of their own beauty.
The crux of quinceañera-oriented businesses lies in the success of the regional
expos that generate an exciting, customized environment around the commercial culture around quinceañeras. Unlike the lure of purchasing online,
where consumers may find the best, lowest-cost, big-chain dresses from the
convenience of home, they cannot feel the texture of the fabric or hear the
sweeping sounds a ball skirt makes as the wearer twirls around a room. At
expos, girls can try on tiaras and see how the four-inch crowns look on them.
But more than anything, attendees can witness the centrality of the spectacle of Latinx femininity on display at every booth. Expos offer a temporary
staging location where communities of practice become real. In an era when
digitally mediated experiences are prized, regional brick-and-mortar small
businesses rely on "the absolute power of live events" that are staged through
*Quinceañeras Magazine*–branded expos ("Are You a Vendor?").

### THE QUINCE EXPO

It was my first *Quinceañeras Magazine* expo, and it was moving fast. The
Double Tree Hotel in Sacramento was much larger and fuller than I had
anticipated. I parked what seemed like a football field away. As I approached
the hotel entrance I realized I had no room number or reference to guide
me. I decided to follow a Latinx-looking family toward some pink signage.

The arrow directed us to Ballroom A on the upper level, and so we went. They were excited. The young woman was with her father and her mother, who was pushing a baby in a stroller. The young Latina had a small Coach purse on her shoulder and clutched a cell phone. She was ready. We turned a corner directly into a long line that snaked around the ballroom vestibule. All the girls blended together, with their knee-high boots, smartphones, and designer purses. They giggled and quietly discussed their ideal dresses as the doors remained closed, even after the clock struck noon. This scene would repeat itself at each *Quinceañeras Magazine* expo I would attend between 2009 and 2016 in California, Illinois, Texas, Iowa, and Nebraska. Each group waited outside the expo for the first time as they were planning their events that year or season. The doors opened and closed as harried staff perfected last-minute details. Each time the doors opened I could feel a wall of sound that energized the crowd anticipating the party within. I was excited. Not having had my own quinceañera, I never had a chance to shop for the dress, let alone attend an expo. My anticipation of the event was as if I were in line for a concert or to see some superstar celebrity; in reality I was in line to see the latest developments in quinceañera style. Just as my thoughts coalesced into a smile, though, I realized this kind of event did not exist when I was fifteen. This event was a product of strategic marketing in the twenty-first-century experience economy.

"El vestido es la protagonista de su quince" is the title of a 2010 editorial spread in the Bay Area *Quinceañeras Magazine* that features vendors from the east side of the bay in Oakland to the south in San Jose. The short Spanish-language article briefly discusses how choosing the correct dress is a vital step in planning an ideal quinceañera. The writer elaborates on how young women need to consider their own body shapes when choosing a dress style for their events, implying that a less than ideal choice can ruin a special day. The article is a subtle nod to the commercialization of the celebration and the externalization of creative controls to designated industry professionals. On the surface, expos offer families planning quinceañera events the opportunity to see multiple dedicated vendors in one place and one afternoon. In the early years, entry was five dollars; in 2011 the price rose to ten dollars, and children under ten were admitted for free. In our interview on April 20, 2010, in Union City, California, the Bay Area regional director Juan Medina said the expos started as more diversely framed events that catered to markets for quinceañeras and Latina weddings. But as organizers staged the events in their early years, they realized that the market for quinceañeras was stronger, and they decided to shift all their efforts to focusing on quinceañera girls and their families. The events, held twice a year, typically last for six hours on a

Sunday afternoon. The goal is to reach churchgoers and families with parents who work six days a week, with only Sundays to spare. According to a Pew Research Center report in 2014 from its national survey of Latinos and religion, 82 percent of Latinxs polled had some religious affiliation, predominantly Catholic and Protestant and only 1 percent identifying as other than Christian ("Shifting Religious Identity"). As the quinceañera has a parallel religious history with Hispanic cultural Catholicism, marketing the expos to avoid potential church conflicts allows the events to garner the maximum number of guests.

Joseph Pine and James Gilmore's "Welcome to the Experience Economy" in a 1998 issue of *Harvard Business Review* outlines the characteristic of this "next battleground" in competitive marketing in the global economy. In that pre-Y2K moment, the authors explain how businesses could no longer depend on goods and services to be competitive in their markets. To maximize success, savvy cultural entrepreneurs would need to internalize the message that experiences are "distinct economic offerings." Pine and Gilmore assert that designing and staging a sellable experience would depend on five key principles: theme, harmonized impressions with positive cues, the elimination of negative cues, memorabilia, and an engagement with all five senses. Quinceañeras Magazine Inc. employs the logic of experience economics not only to bring local vendors and potential clients together but also to transcend the need for material goods, to offer an ideal quinceañera experience before they have even purchased the dresses.

The expo stages a preview experience in which customers are treated like guests, offered free samples of cake and catered meals, and are provided with hours of stage shows of choreographed dance and live music. At the center of the event is the fashion show, when the curated gown displays are brought to life by young models who imbue a sense of commodity desire through their own objectified bodies. Chinese dresses are not part of the fashion show despite their ubiquity in practice and relatively accessible price points. The expo fashion show features original dresses designed and sold by local vendors or specially invited national designers.

## THE FASHION SHOW

It was 5:45 p.m. at the main ballroom of the Double Tree Hotel in downtown Omaha. *Quinceañeras Magazine* Nebraska's elegant and well-attended winter 2015 event was supposed to be coming to a close, but the room was still packed with people waiting for the surprise guest to appear on the fashion-show runway. The emcee was trying to keep the crowd organized and present. It was clear the surprise would be imminently revealed, and the crowd stood with outstretched phone cameras ready to capture, post, and tweet whatever lay ahead. What emerged was a series of models with hair and makeup exclusively styled by the Kansas City brand LB Styling and wearing one-of-a-kind quinceañera gowns designed by Adán Terriquez. Terriquez is a Los Angeles–based designer who hails from Mexico. He was invited onto the fashion show runway to feature his 2015 line of original, high-fashion quinceañera designs thematically titled "Mexicanisimo." The designs drew on familiar and romantic images of Mexican national imaginary through such details as silver and gold charro-inspired accenting and eagle and serpent motifs. Terriquez, formerly a dress designer for the singer and actor Jenni Rivera, "la reina de banda," mobilizes his professional cache as designer to the stars to capitalize on trends in quinceañera culture that highlight the desire for innovative textures and colors and a continuous connection to cultural heritage. While his dresses appeared on the runway at the last moments of the expo afternoon— a tactic used to keep consumers present at the expo as long as possible—he intimated to me that he does not sell his gowns in Omaha, San Antonio, or Las Vegas, where he had been traveling earlier in the week. He sells his gowns exclusively to one high-end dress shop in New York City, and all other potential buyers must visit his studio in Los Angeles. "You have to keep the designs exclusive," he said. "Once it's online it's gone, easy to copy. I don't offer discounts. It keeps demand high." Value in this market of high-end gowns is rooted in notions of exclusivity and a kind of cultural gatekeeping that frames events differently depending on the provenance of their material artifacts. Off-the-rack boutique dresses or custom local designs are distinguished from couture one-of-a-kind designs by professionals with name recognition in the larger US Latinx consumer system.

Expos strategically promote dresses that are available through the vendors patronizing the events. That is to say, organizers choose vendors who offer specific types of goods that will contribute to the most enticing and enthralling consumer experience. Expos are unique consumer environments, as few goods can actually be purchased there. An expo is a space of potential. Christina had attended multiple expos as she planned Jazmin's celebration but never with the intent to purchase. She paid to enter to have access to the newest iterations of quinceañera style so she could be up to date as she did the labor of constructing the event without the help of a professional planner. She spent much time honing her skills of observation and coordination; she even entertained the possibility of going back to school for hospitality management to become a quinceañera planner herself. Her intense focus on the labor of the event meant that most of her quinceañera memories revolve around the trials of planning and execution and less on the enjoyment of watching her daughter debut. The time-consuming and emotionally drain-ing process of staging their daughters' and their own desires becomes the core of the transitional ritual for which an ethos that appears to buckle to the pres-sures of hedonistic individualism affects the reception of a larger consuming public. The expos provide a space to dream big, a space of fantasy. They fur-nish a legible luxury ideology mediated through commitments to family and to communities accustomed to being degraded in popular media; they turn potential consumers into honored guests.

Expo events offer idealized consumer experiences as part of selling the quinceañera tradition as a familial investment. The events feature young women in gowns and young men in tuxedos roaming among the crowd, handing out various promotional materials in English and Spanish. Vendors stage their booths to present unending visual stimuli, akin to the décor of a themed restaurant. In 2014 at the *Quinceañeras Magazine* Chicago expo, dresses were displayed on elevated, slowly spinning platforms. Such staging made the dresses more visible from full 360-degree angles but also drew view-ers to booths with sparkling accents reflecting the lights against the rainbow-stained glass and sparkling disco ball hanging above the runway in the Sabre Room. Space in the room was itself another product for sale. Families by attending the expo were offered a sense of what their quinceañera events might smell like, sound like, feel like in such a ballroom. The space itself is a living advertisement for this particular venue. Tuxedo-clad greeters wel-comed guests at the San Jose expo, where guests were free to roam and ex-perience the expo at their own pace and on their own terms. Each future quinceañera girl is given a keepsake bag and magazine alongside regionally specific token gifts as part of the entry fee. As families enter the space, their senses are immediately primed to feel an affinity with the space. The scent of Mexican dishes wafted, reggaeton and Katy Perry music blared between com-peting DJs, and there was a constant voice-over stream of the emcee intro-ducing vendors first in Spanish and then in English.

The marketing principles Pine and Gilmore set forth would be met by *Quinceañeras Magazine* expos to stage and sell experience to a Latinx con-sumer base. Now, in the twenty-first-century USAmerican life characterized by the immediate exchange of information on digital media, style is a form of currency in the visual economy. As such, families prioritize the purchasing of quinceañera gowns but outsource the staging of the entire event to profes-sional service providers who promise transformation and dream fulfillment through the facilitation of memorable experiences.

In 2016 the business of the quinceañera expo appeared to be charging cus-tomers to sell to them. The reality is much more complicated, as expos sell the desirability of enacting tradition that makes Latinx families attractive and powerful consumers. Expos are selling the experience of market centrality and relevance. *Quinceañeras Magazine* is selling majoritarian experiences to minoritized communities. The expo space becomes a place where social capital is forged through shared practice rather than through kinship ties. It also inspires a competitive desire, that of purchasing such connections through the consumption of Chinese-made dresses.

### HECHO EN MEXICO

Adán Terriquez's dresses sell for at least twice the price of Chinese-made dresses. They are often custom-made in the United States. Their cost is not just for the gown but the attendant expense that comes with remote purchases. Terriquez gowns are commissioned. When I inquired after who buys his dresses, he told me a story of one of his most recent clients, who was not from New York or Los Angeles, but a Mexicana from Indianapolis. This family found his Mexicanisimo designs enthralling enough to commission a dress from him in Los Angeles and have him and the dress come to the daughter's quinceañera in the Midwest. Terriquez's designs proactively draw on nationalist nostalgia of Mexican immigrants with money on the occasion of their daughters' coming of age. The dress becomes a way to mark borders on the body and family history and nostalgia in a garment made by a Mexican designer and recalling a narrative of a romantic past. Terriquez's designs are hard to access and expressly harder than those of larger companies with prominent internet presence and ads in *Quinceañeras Magazine*. Mary's and Mori Lee are selling Mexican-made dresses as authentic quinceañera dresses.

### BELLA SERÁ

The "hecho en México" movement was a direct response to the market loss faced by Mexican companies that could not compete with the low cost of Chinese-made goods. The logo bearing an image of the characteristic Mexican eagle represents a form of consumer nationalism in which "consumer culture is treated as a by-product of the creation of nation states" (Gerth 279). Among migrant communities in the United States, consumer nationalism takes a complicated turn as ethnic nationalism and geographic nationalism blur boundaries in economic loyalties. Such a combination is further muddled by the reality of cost of living in the United States, and Chinese goods still trump other purchases based on their lower prices. Quinceañera dresses are not everyday purchases; as many parents and professionals -claim, they are essential elements of a once-in-a-lifetime experience. Therefore, spending on the dresses takes on a singular importance, distinct from expenditures on other, more banal goods, and becomes part of a network of strategic purchases.

Strategic purchases are those that have a greater impact on one's publicly visible class profile. In ethnic marketing, they also have a cultural aspect, making spending on traditional celebrations part of a dual public profile in which class performance and ethnocultural performance intersect. Such purchases gain currency in their role in retro-acculturation in the service of conspicuous consumption in Latinx marketing practice and the profitability of selling culture back to heritage communities that have been marked as suffering a kind of cultural loss recuperable through consumer agency. The process of imagined recuperation is materialized through the utilization of economic circuits and personal consumption in a shared cultural context. The shared interactive environment is national and regional and marked by a kind of ethnic specialization designated by the items purchased and the identities of the buyers as well as the sellers. In an assessment of anthropological perspectives on dress and culture, Karen Tranberg Hansen asserts a need for anthropological studies to move beyond semiotic explanations in the assessment of dress and begin to examine cultural production as a process "created through agency, practice, and performance" (370). Such a perspective allows scholars of dress to contextualize the specificities of space and place into a larger, globalized economic framework and consider the ways individuals consume material goods in myriad contexts. The engagement with quinceañera goods, in particular the purchased quinceañera dress, can thus be understood as part of a process of consumption that is "conceived not only as markets and economic actors but as cultural processes that construct identity" (Hansen 370).

One might ask what identity factors are at play in the consumption of the quinceañera dress. While the larger decision to celebrate a quinceañera might more easily be linked to a desire to reinforce ethnic identity and bolster community memories of practice, the purchase of the dress functions as a way to visualize affluence and the potential of an upscale Latinx consumer. One way that this narrative is reinforced in the expo is through the incorporation of luxury branding that lends a sense of exclusivity to the expo browsing environment.

Bella Será is a luxury quinceañera-dress design house that exclusively advertises to a US market with *Quinceañeras Magazine*. It has one US shop, in Las Vegas. Unlike Mary's or Mori Lee, Bella Será promotes some of its dresses as "100% Handmade in Mexico," and it claims to be the first company to have introduced Mexican-made dresses into the quinceañera consumer market in the United States as a national brand and in a local shop. Recently the narrative has shifted from Mexican-made dresses to those imported from

Mexico or designed in Mexico, which obscures the manufacturing process. The company's website, bella-sera-dresses.com, calls "conscious consumers" to the brand characterized by "luxury" and "innovation"—terms that are heard frequently from various vendors at expos. At the same time, Bella Será promotes a technologically advanced dress that is made of imported (Chinese), high-quality fabric and bold embellishments and still is lightweight and easy to wear—feeding a consumer desire to be visibly extravagant yet materially comfortable. The hecho en México model appeals to a nationalist nostalgia among Mexican-origin consumers who are already attuned to the cultural marketplace as they shop for quinceañera products; the label places a premium on consumer nationalism when clients' binational loyalty as residents or citizens of the United States is coupled with fierce devotion to *la madre patria* even in absentia. At the same time, Latinx consumers who have internalized the cultural history of the event in Mexico can claim a sense of authenticity from a quinceañera dress made in Mexico. Just as the expo provides an exclusive and memorable quinceañera planning experience to consumers who may or may not leave the event with any new products or reservations, Bella Será offers the quinceañera dress purchasing experience as one of fantasy fulfillment.

In its 2010 dress campaign advertised through *Quinceañeras Magazine*, Bella Será wove fairytale narratives to accompany its signature dress of the season, featuring layer upon layer of tulle ruffles in alternating colors. The narratives, published exclusively in Spanish, targeted Spanish-speaking, Latina teen consumers in a globalized campaign around their prospective coming-of-age moment:

> Once Upon a Time. . . . Una princesa que vivía en cualquier lugar y su nombre era siempre diferente. Era una Quinceañera, y como tal le encantaban las flores, la música, hacer nuevas amistades, sentirse querida y admirada, y lo era. Pues tenía con ella una familia que le amaba profundamente. Y aunque a veces pensaba que nadie la comprendía, sabía en su interior que jamás estaría sola.

> Once Upon a Time . . . [There was a] princess who lived anywhere, and whose name was always different. She was a Quinceañera and as such, she was enchanted by flowers, music, making new friends, feeling loved and admired, and she was. Because she had her family that loved her deeply. And although sometimes she thought that no one understood her, she knew deep inside that she would never be alone.

The text appears under the photograph of a model wearing a blue and pink organza couture quinceañera dress with a taffeta bodice, jeweled mid-section, and elaborate central flower bow image just underneath the bust line. Although the advertisement appears in Spanish, its content reflects common themes of American teenage angst, a desire to be loved, understood, and surrounded by affection. The characteristic fairytale introduction "Once upon a time" draws in English and bilingual speakers who understand that the story is a familiar artifact of childhood in US popular culture influenced by European-origin tales. In the advertisement, the quinceañera is an American teenage consumer. This bicultural representation illustrates that the quinceañera celebration is as much a product of American consumer culture as it is of cultural forms informed by ethnocultural discourses of practice.

Innovations in advertising and marketing are helping set apart competitive products and become increasingly important in quinceañera expos, where vendors are in close proximity to one another selling similar products to a finite client base. In the example of the marketplace in Mexico City I emphasize space or the lack thereof; in el Mercado, it is the concentration of vendors that attracts consumers across the city. The narrow aisles and ceiling-high product displays index variety. Consumers enter, and the physical structuring of space creates a near impossibility of finding what they are looking for. Such a consumer landscape does not index luxury. The expo space, a temporary agglomeration, represents a special kind of innovation in the quinceañera professional industry that broadly resembles other trade shows and particularly bridal fairs. In Latinx-specific marketing, agglomeration—the clustering of similar industries near each other—fosters an ethnocultural business landscape in an otherwise multicultural and multiracial space. Such consumer islands in large urban settings provide cultural refuges for new and legacy immigrants alike. Latinx neighborhoods around the country often feature quinceañera-oriented businesses. Teresa Gonzales, a sociology professor at Knox College, notes that on Twenty-Sixth Street in Chicago's Little Village, quinceañera "dress shops increase awareness of the area in the popular consciousness" (qtd. in Huggins).

Quinceañera expos constitute a temporary agglomeration of businesses unified under the flag of quinceañera practice. They become curated business environments where Latinx consumers are unquestionably targeted and courted. During the fashion show, the dress becomes the consumer focal point as local designers feature their product lines, ideally presenting one-of-a-kind dresses. It is rare to find a Mary's or Mori Lee dress on the runway. The temporary status of the expo evokes a sense of collaboration that Gonzales contends is inevitable when competing businesses are working in close proximity. Even temporary closeness can furnish a creative space from which businesses, particularly those invested in the quinceañera gown, are able to assess how to differentiate their products, the key to surviving in the quinceañera dress industry. Access to competitors keeps isomorphism at bay while also balancing variability of product by designer and price point. It is through consumer acquisition that value and worth are negotiated and filtered back into performance and play.

The quinceañera dress, as symbol of the celebration and a material object, has been the subject of controversy as a symbol and a material good. A "traje colonial," a colonial dress, as the quinceañera gown has been referred to in postrevolution Cuba, is interpreted as a vestige of colonial influences on Mexican-origin communities and Latin American and Latinx communities across the Western Hemisphere (Härkönen 90). The dress is a visualization of colonial powers directly imprinting on the female body politic. With the late-twentieth-century consumer turn in the production of quinceañera culture in the United States, the connection to colonialism has waned among participants. The celebration has taken on a consumer character that while not ideal does shift the discourse around the celebration as a performance of class aspiration in a neoliberal social environment. Spending practices help foster a materialized self, the product of a consumer process that within quinceañera practice is controlled by young Latinas and their mothers. While the consumer turn has shifted the primacy of family and socioreligious discourse of the celebration, consumption becomes a resource of many Latinxs whose lives do not and cannot fit into narrow narratives of idealized Latinx citizen-revolutionaries. Julia Alvarez has registered her sentiments of discomfort with the expo as a place where manufacturing identity is as disturbing as it is inorganic. That type of discourse emerges in other popular forms as a kind of ethnic moralization in which consumerism among Latinx communities is misguided and irresponsible rather than an assertion of consumer agency. Whether perceived as positive or negative, the consumerist turn in quinceañera practice has opened up the tradition to community members who may feel alienated from well documented versions of Latinx lives yet still desire to assert their cultural presence.

SUCCESS THEATER

Christina and her family spent a year planning Jazmin's quinceañera. One of the few objects they did not make on their own was Jazmin's gown. Comparison shopping and online availability of the dress made buying the Mary's brand dress possible and practical for their budget. The shopping labor that

Christina invested in Jazmin's quinceañera transcended their economic experience to emphasize a sense of self-worth and self-determination.

Quinceañera style represents a mode of cultural expression of an image of the future by mobilizing social capital of the past. The uses of elaborate ball gowns, ranging in price from hundreds to many thousands of dollars, become part of a system of seemingly magical thinking. Over and over again, young women represent their quinceañera events as dreams come true. In the creative space between aspiration and reality, families mirror principles of magic discussed by James George Frazer in *The Golden Bough*. Drawing on the Law of Similarity, practitioners enact a manner of sympathetic magic whereby a desired result can be attained by imitating it (Frazer 11). In this case, a quinceañera's elaborate consumer participation represents a ritual of similarity in which a performance of luxury will lead to the realization of such luxury later in life. It is an invocation through sacred assemblage facilitated by faith not in a god but in their daughter's capacity. The purchasing of a custom couture gown and fanciful adult high heels, arriving in an exotic limousine, dancing and dining with a court of attendants all index a socioeconomic status that few could maintain beyond the limited engagement of the quinceañera event. Therefore, it becomes important to understand what social value is encapsulated in the quinceañera event beyond its capacity to promote personal branding in a visual-social economy. The celebration is a way for parents to teach their children to dream; in doing so the parents instrumentalize confidence and creativity as a form of inherited capital.

The last formal interview I had with Christina took place one month after Jazmin's quinceañera. Finally having a chance to relax, we talked about what a great success it was, the photos beautiful, the dance with minimal mistakes, and Christina and her partner Louie beaming with pride. Christina told me she realized the shopping and planning were not just for Jazmin. The celebration had a wider significance.

> We got to show people that we can be creative too. Just because we aren't educated doesn't mean we aren't creative or smart. We brought the whole family together, that never happens, and everyone told us it was beautiful, like no other quince they'd ever seen.

The consumer turn in quinceañera practice is neither positive nor negative but simply one of many developments of a living cultural form. While some might continue to think of the dress as a manifestation of a European colonialism's forceful imprint on Latina bodies, they might be better served to look at the twenty-first-century gown centralized in a social and economic system of trade as a "traje popular," a manifestation of the will and desires of communities of practice and reflective of the influences lived experiences of US Latinxs have on the coming-of-age drama of an American quinceañera. The dress is a focal point of the celebration and a form of autotopographic control, in which quinceañera girls and their families are re-creating the space around their community starting with the intimate boundaries of the body. Dress becomes a collaboratively constructed "social skin" that is "two-sided" and "touches the body" while simultaneously "facing outward" (Turner). Quinceañera performance is a temporary reconfiguration of public and private spaces. What emerges from this space in between public and private selves are contingent discourses about the economic and social worth of Latinx-identifying communities and their traditions as they speak to the lingering potency of the American Dream but do so using tradition as a symbolic register.

Quinceañera celebrations are rich traditions that in the United States cannot be fully understood without acknowledging their relation to manufacturing and global economics. Contemporary quinceañera dresses are the product of innovative cultural entrepreneurship eager to bring premium experiences to the pan-Latinx market while also creating social value around upscale Latinx consumers and those who aspire toward upward social mobility that is the essence of the American Dream. The experience economy, which encompasses the selling of feeling and memory, extends into deterritorial contexts where quinceañera practice is digitized and curated on social media pages so that fantasy experiences take on a digital life as they are posted, shared, liked, and most importantly, envied in the visual economy. In the visual economy of digital spaces, representations take on a life that is generative, representing the subjects of photographs, blogs, vlogs, and other informational units in circulation on social media but also creating a publicly visible review process. This review process exposes new generations of practitioners to quinceañera style as it is unfolding live.

## CHAPTER 3

# COMING OF AGE IN THE DIGITAL BARRIO

## Quinceañera as a Product in Cultural Economies Online

We were seated at my kitchen table in Bloomington, Indiana, talking about what classes she wanted to take in the fall semester of her first year of high school. Muriel was fourteen at the time, in 2008, and hers was one of the first interviews I conducted around quinceañera traditions. I was acquainted with Muriel's family, and they allowed me to chat with her about her desires to have a quinceañera celebration. In my few earlier interviews, participants had narrated tales of organizing quinceañeras over months if not years. Muriel struck me as behind the generally expected quinceañera timeline. Muriel was being raised mostly by her father, an immigrant from central Mexico naturalized under the Immigration Reform and Control Act in 1986, and her mother, who suffered from severe alcoholism and caused more harm than good to their family structure when she was living with them. As we were talking, I asked Muriel if she could help me by explaining what a quinceañera was. She looked a bit confused and paused to pull together her thoughts. "It's a big party. . . . It's how you know a girl can start having sex." I waited for her to complete her thought. I was eager to jump in and assure her that was not what she should take away from the celebration, but I did not want to interfere by expressing my own socially gleaned interpretations of the event. After all, I had not had a quinceañera of my own. I asked her if that was all that she thought the event was for, and she replied, "Yeah, I think so. You can always Google it if you want to know why people do it." I had not meant to embarrass Muriel, but with her enthusiasm for the tradition I assumed she had been inspired by the practice of her older sister or peers. Her desire for the celebration was not about spiritual affirmation or the deepening of some ethnic-cultural narrative; it was strictly about age-based sexual freedom.

Her response gave me pause as I realized how little its origins mattered to her and that her generation felt empowered by the knowledge that was potentially and directly available to them at their fingertips at any given moment. Her response made me wonder where her ideas came from. Her family was devout fundamentalist Christian, and I knew her understanding had not stemmed from their beliefs. I had come to realize that the ideas were shared by her friends, who themselves were still figuring out the significance of the celebration as Mexican American teens. Muriel would not celebrate her quinceañera at fifteen; on a family trip to Mexico she would celebrate her sixteenth birthday among her father's family. She didn't get a gown but a T-shirt with a corset image printed on it and a vase of fresh flowers. The photo was shared with me through Facebook, where her father proudly posted it.

Quinceañera culture is all around. In Austin, San Jose, Omaha, Des Moines, anywhere enclaves of Latinxs gather and live, an emergent quinceañera consumer landscape can be found. Often dotted with *carnicerias* and *panaderias*, these areas reflect the establishment of barrios, communities of Latinxs collectively customizing geographic and consumer spaces. Like Latinxs, quinceañera cultural production is not confined to territorial locations but is also part of wider digitally networked communities of innovation and practice. Online, one need only search the word "quinceañera" (with or without the tilde) to encounter all manner of verbal and visual culture related to the celebration. Many will be advertisements promoting quinceañera goods and services, elaborate hairstyles, couture gowns, makeup, and more. In *Latina/os and the Media* Angharad Valdivia discusses how these spaces of media production are often taken for granted as the ease of their accessibility increases.

> You listen to some reggaeton, or read *Latina* magazine, or run into a website on quinceañeras, or watch Ugly Betty on prime-time television, or read about Latina/os in the news and you enjoy and/ or learn from their content without thinking what it took to produce them. (30)

At the same time, it will be difficult to divide culture-specific advertisements from self-presentations of Latina young women sharing their quinceañera journeys, the planning and review, through social media. Their micro performances of self vary dramatically from simple questions posted on Yahoo! such as "What is a quinceañera and should I have one?" to more elaborately staged YouTube videos documenting the quinceañeras' self-preparation process and often professional videography that has become an expected addition in US quinceañera practice. I explore the presence of quinceañera culture online as a new frontier in quinceañera planning and knowledge brokering. Rather than simply being a space to show off nostalgic photographs of past parties, online quinceañera culture resides at the center of quinceañera planning for celebrants who follow an indirect path to the tradition, one that is bound to ethnic and racial identity but where local, family narratives are actively supplemented by discourses mediated by internet resources. Indeed, it is common to find quinceañera planning services that are predominantly online. While they might offer direct service to area residents, they also simultaneously serve a growing body of national and international Latina consumers who look to vlogs (video blogs), blogs, and other forms of digital cultural entrepreneurship to help them plan and make meaning in their quests to come of age. These productions fit seamlessly into the wider visible/viewed social media venue for digital signifying practices that especially feature the visual cultural production and circulation.

Involvement in cultural production driven by ideas and images rather than things also means "expanding participation of consumers, and the possibility of reshaping those concepts" that were previously limited and exclusionary (Banet-Weiser 45). In social media, productions linked expressly to quinceañera consumer culture become integrated into a process of curating a public self through digital autotopographies, collections of personal objects that reflect the inner self physically mapped onto one's everyday environment (J. González 133; Petrelli et al. 53). Autotopographies may feature photographic and textual means to customize social media profiles in the curation of an online presence; visual references to quinceañera practice reflect a class identification process in which access to new media technologies becomes representative of upward social mobility.

Before my conversation with Muriel I had not thought about what role online resources played in shaping quinceañera practice among the newest generation of practitioners. As my research broadened I realized that part of the consumer turn in quinceañera practice was a vibrant online presence that spanned beyond the realm of retail sites for the purchase of wholesale goods or discount designer gowns. In online space it becomes apparent that rather than simply trafficking in goods and mediated knowledge, quinceañera practice becomes a product of digital consumption. The development around digital consumption has developed in tandem with the primacy of social media, where daily happenings get punctuated, critiqued, and shared often in real time. Social media platforms like Facebook, YouTube, Instagram, and Twitter are locations through which quinceañera culture is curated online. In an unregulated digital environment, "the economic nature of information and its content as a public, non-rivaled and non-excludable good becomes clear" (Pina 1357).

The internet plays a part in the continued circulation of quinceañera culture outside of purely economic participation, and yet it also opens a space through which the mass cultural interpretation of the celebration is available to individuals in wider consumer structures that are in the business of selling culture. Social media outlets become key players in cultural economics online, where individuals mobilize their connection to cultural practice as a way of differentiating themselves in the immeasurable sea of social media posts, while companies use the tradition as a way of accessing consumers who are drawn into recognizable group identities. Quinceañera culture is produced and recirculated online and cannot be separated from materialized traditions as social media permeate everyday activities, choices, and preferences. In previous generations, intergenerational influences on individual practice seemed to pass unilaterally from one generation to the next, from mothers to daughters, in contemporary social conditions, webs of influence both face to face and digital in origin affect how the tradition is developing in the twenty-first century.

Webs of influence implicitly function to open up but also restrict the social narrative built around contemporary quinceañera practice. I investigate discursive productions from sources on Facebook and YouTube. The examples I use fall into three broad categories: those invested in promoting a consumerist imaginary, those that criticize the cultural productions of quinceañeras, and those that are invested in practical creation. Symbolic digital artifacts that have connections to extradigital aspects of practice illustrate each category. Employing the user commentary reacting to digital content from quinceañera entrepreneurs, posts by Latinx-focused content producers, and the videos of an individual quinceañera vlogger, I illustrate the way quinceañera practice has become less focused on the acquisition of goods and services and more on the accumulation of feelings and experiences that become social currency in social media, where life is curated through the accumulation of readable signs of social success. Among multicultural and multiracial users in the digital sphere, the quinceañera becomes a branded product of US Latinidad that through its provenance online is fundamentally classed based on the patterns and limitations of accessibility of digital technology. The economic anthropologist Grant McCracken notes, "Branding serves as a mode of meaning management that draws on both a body of meanings that have come to surround the brand over time" and new meanings forged through digital recirculation (*Culture and Consumption* 179).

## QUINCEAÑERA AS CULTURAL PRODUCT

Before diving into the body of digital exemplars of quinceañera life online, I will sketch out how the quinceañera serves as a cultural product that exceeds its traditional context as a rhetorical artifact in discussions of US Latinx culture. An examination of the quinceañera as a product is an assessment of the value it generates and the value it circulates within and between communities of practice. The digital quince is a cultural production that contributes to ethnocultural "social goods," in particular "national identity and social cohesion" (Dayton-Johnson 16). Through material engagement with quinceañera practice, such ephemeral and intangible concepts become identifiable, yet online they are remediated as ideas and images rather than as physical, material manifestations. Quinceañeras come with a dual set of values, the intrinsic and the instrumental (Dayton-Johnson 15). Quinceañeras have little intrinsic value; they are not in and of themselves worth more than the cumulative expense of the goods that define them. Once purchased, they depreciate in value. Their lack of intrinsic value flies below the perception of participants who attempt to sell their used quinceañera goods after their events. A search of the online classified advertisement platform Craigslist will turn up a regularly replenished stream of posts by individuals attempting to sell used quinceañera dresses and material accessories. The goods are often priced at nearly their original costs, and the ads use phrases such as "only used once" and "only worn for a few hours." Many families invest a great deal of capital into these celebratory events, especially in communities where self-sacrifice is a way to exhibit love to one's children, but the monetary value of the objects depreciates fast, as the temporality of fashion and a demand for the newest gowns collide. In a similar way, the desire for an original look precludes added value onto a used gown or accessory. The only gowns that appreciate in value do so by virtue of social value. The inheritance of a handmade dress from an earlier generation may increase the instrumental value of the object, but that value is specifically confined to family groups or community networks invested in the conservative principle of tradition.

Tradition has a market value. Market value is how much a product can be sold for. In the case of the quinceañera as product, its value lies in the social value of the tradition in varying ethnic households and communities and the digital network that has come to value culture as a lucrative product for appealing to niche consumer markets. The relation between these two types of value, intrinsic and instrumental, is relative to circumstance; the greater value of the quinceañera is instrumental, in that value lies in the event's capacity to generate social value. In digital marketing, where the self becomes a commodity, a sense of value can be monetized by the capacity to draw consumer audiences to desired products. In the realm of social media, knowledge becomes a product for sale. The intrinsic value of the quinceañera-as-product is hotly debated by observers of the tradition and its consumer growth, many of whom find voice on social media outlets. Cultural entrepreneurs invested in the tradition are committed to sell the experience of the quinceañera and in doing so have helped transform the celebration into a product with a distinct brand profile. The cultivation of a brand profile produces extraritual meaning in the celebration beyond the public acknowledgement of girls' social and biological development. The branding process generates a metadiscourse of quinceañera practice that is meant to serve not as a marker of coming of age but as a rhetorical device to tap into the buying power of Latinx consumers.

## QUINCEAÑERA CONSUMER STRUCTURES ONLINE

The quinceañera can be found in a variety of digital venues. In our conversation Muriel alluded half-jokingly, half-sincerely to entering the word "quinceañera" into Google or other online search engines to recover tens of millions of references. The sites retrieved range from reference pages such as a Wikipedia entry, online planning guides like quinceanera.com, and hundreds of thousands of video links to YouTube, where young women broadcast their event preparation and performance through professional videography. The next most common autocompleted search terms beginning with "quinceañera" are "theme" and "gift ideas"; both refer to a larger consumer structure surrounding the tradition online. What a Google search does not cover is the body of social media streams dedicated to promoting and drawing from quinceañera culture in deterritorialized spaces and circulating ideas and practices from Austin to Des Moines, from Los Angeles to Indianapolis. Online, the quinceañera becomes a deterritorialized and translocalized practice, one that is a direct function of its place in a globalized cultural and economic system (Hernández i Martí). Translocality is defined in its simplest sense as "being identified with more than one location," which requires attention to movement and circulation (Oakes and Schein xiii). In this in-between position, interpretations bound to fixed territorial identities can be misleading. Deterritorialization disrupts the assumed "natural" relation between culture and social geographies (Hernández i Martí 93). This disruption recontextualizes symbolic productions, using frames such as mass media and commerce. Gil-Manuel Hernández i Martí notes that rather than framing these contextual shifts as a road toward the "impoverishment of cultural interaction" (94), one can view deterritorialization as creating an interstitial ground for transformation that shifts the gaze from Latinx culture as local to culture as inescapably transnational.

Anyone in the world, of any ethnic background or racial formation, could, if desired, access and draw on the tradition, its symbols, and its material artifacts. A fetishized version of Chicano cultural identity has a life in Japan;[1] similarly, quinceañera practices may be seen not as an ethnic identifier but as an expression of solidarity through shared experiences of class-based racialization that become embedded in a Latinx-identified tradition. This wider view of cultural practice does not erase local, geographically bounded iterations claimed by regions and peoples with deep connections to their social geographies. Those who claim connections to the practices have not hermetically sealed the traditions off from nonlocal influences, regardless of how insider-outsider boundaries are framed. In a contemporary constant state of mediatization (Tomlinson), boundaries between the digital and material, the local and the translocal need to be investigated as part of the critical cultural formation in the twenty-first century.

Quinceañera practices exist in a kind of translocality that implicates the lived experiences of their practitioners and the entrepreneurs who guide the practice development as a cultural product. They live at the intersection of dialectics of "homogenization and "heterogenization" where corporate Americanization meets a marketable ethnic Latinx. The quinceañeras become a cultural asset, a mechanism through which a new cultural identity manifests, and the pathways of traditional knowledge acquisition shift to reflect the dialectics between perceptions of the "traditional/modern, real/virtual, or urban/rural" (Hernández i Martí 95). It is the divide between the "real" and the "virtual" under discussion here, where the quinceañera tradition is in a state of ongoing cultural revisioning through its continuous circulation in globally networked digital (inter)space. The quinceañera becomes part of an ethnic heritage of Latinx-identifying populations but also national expression of cultural heritage, as national folklore. Quinces as social construction of the twenty-first century have been "revitalized . . . in a context of modernity by means of mechanisms of mediation, conflict, dialogue, and negotiation in which social agents participate" (Hernández i Martí 95). American folkloristics has been resistant to acknowledging the diverse range of potential social agents who participate in the life of folklore and reluctant to investigate the market mechanism reproduced through the bolstering of heritage traditions to truly recognize the lived experiences of cultural actors, especially those who live outside of the structures of idealized memory making and familial structures of tradition making. We must investigate cultural entrepreneurs, corporate entities whose investment in tradition comes with a price tag and a profit margin. These entities activate tradition through consumer activities; those working in digital cultural economies impact practice through narratives circulated through digital media online.

## SOCIAL LISTENING IN SOCIAL MEDIA:
### *Quinceañeras Magazine* IOWA

Investigating meaning management in cultural marketing online requires the qualitative interoperation of social media practices of key social actors. Rather than depending on quantitative data, social listening involves the fundamental understanding that social media data are "inherently qualitative," and a single quote, comment, or post "can spark an idea with profound implications" (Fournier et al.). Such information is fundamentally linked to the interactive social moment, and so analysis of it must also be framed with understanding of the relations between consumers, consumption, culture, and patterns in marketing. Social listening is a method being formalized and refined by economic anthropologists and marketing professionals, and it has great methodological implications for folkloristics as the discipline incorporates the digital field into its purview of essential contexts of social action in everyday life (Blank). Digital ethnographic practices have the potential to yield insights into populations whose lives are described in digital space.

*Quinceañeras Magazine* Iowa is a regional franchise of Quinceañeras Magazine Inc. The regional director Jackye Camargo manages and edits the print publication and organizes biannual expos out of her Des Moines office. In addition to working the Iowa market she oversees the magazine and expo production for Kansas City, Missouri. When we met in 2015 Jackye was twenty-nine years old; she had come to the United States from Mexico to take university courses to learn English. Although she had not initially planned to stay, she eventually found herself gaining permanent residency and living as a Latina in the Midwest. Raising her daughter alone, she had to make strategic employment choices so that her family could thrive. Directing *Quinceañeras Magazine* offered her the independence and flexibility to network with area Latinx-owned businesses while allowing her to raise her daughter with little outside help. She is the only franchisee I have found who directs more than one magazine and expo circuit in a given region. Other franchisees cover larger geographic areas under single magazines; *Quinceañeras Magazine* Tri-State covers New York, New Jersey, and Connecticut through one central publication and promotion network through a singular social media presence—shared accounts on Facebook, Twitter, and Instagram. Jackye publishes regional magazines for Iowa and Missouri and coordinates their four expos each, two in the spring and two in the fall, as well as four Miss Cover Girl beauty pageants and four Little Miss Cover Girl pageants each year. She also manages digital promotions through two Facebook pages, keeping her linked but discrete networks informed about the magazines' creative vision and networking opportunities. Her tenacity has helped network a midwestern circuit of quinceañera industries whose professional identities and successes have become entrenched in the *Quinceañeras Magazine* brand. She works closely with Claudia Ceja and Rita Rodriguez as well as Rocio Aguayo, who manage magazine and promotions from Omaha and Chicago, respectively. The group has organized a network of midwestern entrepreneurs who have capitalized on deterritorialized and translocal quinceañeras by blending digital marketing with their regional expositions and allied seasonal ethnic pageants. With the material presence of the company being seasonal, the daylong expo events in spring and fall coalesce into a larger network of regional cultural economics year-round through their individual franchisees' presence in social mediascapes.

Consumption as a cultural practice, and consuming online culture is a daily practice that is normalized in media-saturated lives. Social media platforms are ideal venues to reach a wide range of social and professional consumers. *Quinceañeras Magazine* franchisees use social media platforms to connect with their professional networks and potential clients between their coordinated regional exposition events. *Quinceañeras Magazine* Iowa's online profile is managed by Jackye, one of thousands of cultural entrepreneurs whose professional marketing affects the public character of quinceañera practice. While her work is centered on the event-planning process, her work as a regional magazine director is not as a direct event planner but as someone who stages the options of shoppers in the regional quinceañera marketplace by organizing other invested entrepreneurs. Her role takes on a metadiscursive function as she arranges for physical spaces to make manifest the power and potential of Latina youth consumers. In doing so, she modulates the social value of traditional practice alongside its market potential.

*Quinceañeras Magazine* online Facebook profiles, much like the magazines, share national content and region-specific content. Similar brand profiling appears in their "About" pages that links the regional page with some aspect of the national brand, either through a link to the national page or a narrative on that same page. The following narrative comes from a post on the *Quinceañeras Magazine* national Facebook page in 2017 specifically targeting potential advertisers:

> Quinceañera Magazine is more than just a print it is the most innovative concept to our hispanic/latino [sic] young audience in the United States, fresh content with valuable information for planning the most biggest [sic] event in your live [sic]. Our main events: Miss Cover Girl and Quinceañera Expo, Enjoy!!! :) . . . "Influence Starts Here."

The final statement, "Influence Starts Here," expresses the wider function of internet tools in marketing quinceañera practice to industry specialists. This sentiment expresses the company's intent to have an impact on Latinx and Hispanic youth audiences, mediated through those who directly access quinceañera clients, buy advertising space in the print magazine, and populate vendor booths at expos. The page is a way to cultivate business relations, highlighting the vibrancy of the marketplace and the lucrative potential of the consumer base reached. The end result is digital access to an upscale Latina consumer.

The page hosts an endless stream of digital visual marketing that frames what might be considered advertising "after shots"—visual testimonials after businesses have worked with *Quinceañeras Magazine*. The photos posted to the page help instantiate a curated vision of retail success facilitated through the connections that advertising with *Quinceañeras Magazine* Iowa could bring. The validity of the connections is bolstered through photographic posts. Streams of photos of recent pageant winners and runway models index youthfulness, ableism, and heteronormative beauty standards. Glossy glamour shots of young women clad in elaborate, multihued gowns are actual advertisements for local photographers. Sumptuously decorated tables and perfectly lit ballrooms promote venues, and photos of artisan sweets and colorful cakes indexing fare of locales that transcend local place and real time invoke a sense of fantasy desire that is accessible to quinceañera clients but is actually directed at industry professionals who are being convinced that their businesses will thrive if they can access the lucrative quinceañera marketplace more directly. Such a curated, immersive, fantasy narrative cultivated by industry specialists is a creative flourish intended for adults as much as youth communities of practice. The quinceañera as an attractive product of Latina youth consumer practice is sold to small businesses.

*Quinceañeras Magazine* online social media profiles present images of upscale Latina consumers who have money to spend in their industries. Jackye understands the quinceañera marketplace as lucrative when leveraged on the consumer potential of Latinas. On March 22, 2016, she posted a promotional photo aimed directly at advertisers for the magazine's upcoming issue.

The image is organized around the winner of the Little Miss Cover Girl pageant hosted by *Quinceañeras Magazine* Iowa and held at the Courtyard by Marriot in Ankeny, Iowa, in April 2015. The girl is in the center of the frame, lying on her stomach with her hands supporting her chin, smiling. She is wearing a bright-pink T-shirt, black cropped pants, and black shoes. The image is superimposed over a sketch of a city skyline; the girl is at the center, the sketch presumably her notes for planning her upcoming quinceañera celebration. Cartoonish thought bubbles emanating from the smiling girl represent different industries a quinceañera girl might be searching as she plans her celebration: limo, dress, ballroom, decoration, and cake. More affluent families shop to buy; others browse for creative inspiration. In the top right corner is a sketched heart, reinforcing the youthful and girlish tone of the advertisement that is being directed at adult professionals. The black and white sketch and list of desired goods are offset by bright-pink lettering at the top and bottom of the photo that reads,

(top)         QUINCEAÑERAS
              with DINERO

(bottom)      Are looking for
              SERVICES LIKE YOURS!

The interpretation is that *Quinceañeras Magazine* Iowa understands the desires of Latina youth audience and how to speak with a youthful register. It does this through cultivating a social media site that is visually enticing to youth audiences and captures a visual register that is interpreted as being capable and successful in reaching youth consumers and their parents. The advertisement, first posted in 2015, then again unedited in 2016, is entirely in English except for one word, "DINERO." This is a simple yet provocative linguistic shift that characterizes the larger quinceañera marketplace of both consumers and producers as bilingual and bicultural but conveys that the money is somehow ethnic, Latinx. The money, possibly earmarked from birth or newly acquired from a private loan, is meant to be spent on a heritage tradition linked to a self-selecting ethnic identity in the United States. The meta-advertisement not only lists the industries that should feel compelled to advertise with the magazine (limousine services, caterers, planners, designers, and hotels) but also markets a tradition driven by youth desires. The image depicts a daydreaming preteen girl imagining a celebration that can only be completed through a process of consumer engagement. Another advertisement in this sketch series, also released in 2015, has a young, casually dressed Latina midstep walking through a sketched cityscape as if she is looking for something. The same type of thought-bubble art appears with the words "dress," "cake," and "makeup" in bold pink letters; across the top is the line "SHE IS LOOKING FOR YOU," and a bottom line reads, "YOUR AD SHOULD BE HERE."

The two ads are compelling as a series, as they show the refinement of ideas of the quinceañera girl outside of her public performance, in the role of cultural consumer; it is a role born of a traditional space that places women as passive receivers of heteronormative beauty patterning, a Latinx "girling" process despite the claims of coming into adulthood (Butler). The ad with the girl walking is posted with a Spanish-language message encouraging advertisers to utilize the magazine; the girl is seeking out businesses, and it is implied that if those businesses were working with the magazine, they would be found by this agentive youth consumer. The other ad shows development in the structure of power around the perception of Latina youth consumers and sophistication in artistic form. The former version, depicting the girl walking, is a generic companywide image, while the other iteration is a more professional digital production, with Jackye's contact information and name embedded in a pink banner within the image itself rather than appearing as separate text. The implication is that Jackye spent more time and presumably money to refine the ad campaign.

More than artistic refinement, the message also shifted. No longer is the prospective quinceañera girl walking in search of consumer outlets; instead, she is at rest, waiting for those outlets to come to her. Second, the desires springing from her thought bubbles have increased, making her an even more lucrative consumer but also potentially more demanding as a client. Lastly, where the one ad features a girl walking in a sketched, street-level scene, the other ad has the reclining girl seemingly perched atop the skyline and taking up more space. With her increased expectations and less harried demeanor, the ad depicts her in a position of power rather than of need. The need in fact is reversed; she is a resource to be tapped rather than a customer in need of service. She represents the demands of a market that is modulated by ethnic identity, age, and a desire for personal recognition and social visibility—two social valuations that are central in the creation of the quinceañera product in online spaces.

## QUINCEAÑERA: THE COMMENTS SECTION

While courting advertisers is one key function of *Quinceañeras Magazine* regional promotional Facebook pages, social media also feature the quinceañera as a cultural product in the work of online content producers eager to define the "Latinternet" by ethnically and racially diverse original media content directed at digital Latinx audiences. Two content producers, the newer Pero Like and more established Remezcla, are only two of a variety of online publishers and digital strategists courting Latinx consumers with quinceañera-themed content. Here the quinceañera is an ethnic product circulated to elicit the participation and viewership of Latinx audiences through age-based cultural nostalgia regardless of actual participatory history. The memory of quinceañera practice living in audiences becomes a motivation to click through and watch thematically similar online content that generates a stream of online commentary reflecting the review process that the quinceañera as a cultural practice is undergoing all the time. The quinceañera, as an extension of identifiable Latinx cultural heritage in the United States, is a tool of marketing strategists eager to claim a Latinx millennial market share in the twenty-first century.

On February 24, 2016, a three-minute, nine-second video was released simultaneously on YouTube, Facebook, and BuzzFeed, three online platforms for the circulation and remixing of digital cultural artifacts. The video, titled "Women Try [on] Their Old Quinceañera Dresses," received more than 2,000 comments on YouTube and 1,700 on Facebook in its first twenty-four hours online. It has since been viewed more than 5 million times on YouTube (10 of those views by the author) and 916,000 times on Facebook with an accompanying 17,000 likes.

The video is the creative work of Norberto Briceño and Jazmin Ontiveros, of BuzzFeed staff and BuzzFeed Motion Pictures staff, respectively. Briceño is also a key staff member at Pero Like, mobilized as part of BuzzFeed's distributed content strategy aimed at diversifying both its staff and its web audiences to include "English-speaking Latinxs" (Wang). In Pero Like producers' formal launch memo, distributed through a tweet on February 11, 2016, Briceño and his colleague Alex Alvarez describe the new project:

> We're launching as a Facebook and YouTube channel, making content that resonates with English-speaking Latinxs (who are, to put it mildly, kind of a big deal). We're a group that's historically been under- and misrepresented in media, and we're here to change that. The purpose of this initiative is to feature the best, funniest, smartest, and most in-depth look at the myriad identities under the "Latinx" umbrella. This is for blaxicans in LA, Tejanos in Corpus Christi, Cubans in Miami (and their abuelitas), and everyone who's been told they don't "look Latina." It's for the bold, the proud, the creative, and even the hopelessly awkward. We're here for you too, man.

Their promise of Latin inclusivity is matched by the creation and distribution of hundreds of online videos designed to draw in Latinx youth audiences. While the currency of the moniker "Latinx" resonates with contemporary, progressive-minded digital Latinx audiences, the media do little to feature specifically queer-inclusive content. Instead, the term is mobilized as a marker of generational values—"Latinx" is queer-friendly, unlike terms used in premillennial generations of parents or grandparents. Much like the mobilization of Latinx culture as a marketable product, the essence of tapping into retro-acculturative nostalgia, queer inclusivity appears more as another marketing strategy in a welcoming umbrella of potential consumer participation. The business of Pero Like, like that of other digital content creators, is not selling the digital product but gaining a following and monetizing the brand's worth as a trusted entity capable of influencing loyal viewers. Pero Like is selling a rebranded, inclusive, Latinx cultural heritage back to a pan-Latinx audience of online viewers across multiple interactive social media platforms, and one product it has circulated is quinceañera motifs.

Pero Like's ideal product is tongue-in-cheek reinterpretations of Latinx cultural practices. Its content leans into notions of exoticized Latinx cultural products that have been recontextualized in the United States among mixed ethnic and racial audiences—foods, languages, and behaviors that have in the past been used to criticize and marginalize communities. Pero Like produces videos with such titles as "What Does Conflei Mean?" and "People Try Salvadoran Food for the First Time." These humorous but telling reinterpretations take on tensions of growing up in multilingual homes where English is deprioritized in relation to the speaking and retention of Spanish—here "cornflakes," an all-American breakfast, is called "conflei" as an interpretation of how bilingual parents might pronounce the word. The representation is not a diatribe against Spanish but a public acknowledgement of shared experiences of bicultural tension manifest through socially determined nonnormative linguistic variability. The videos simultaneously draw on nostalgic ties to childhood experiences that become laughable and light-hearted, as children grew into technologically savvy and English-speaking American adults. The latter video features a multicultural cast in order to take control over cultural stereotypes and ignorance that it reworks from a new generational perspective of Latinxs in the United States who are always in the process of proving their worth and value in an Anglicized socioconsumer system and proving their authentic Latinxness in intergenerational social contexts.

The videos' approach to the lived experiences of Latinx subjectivities in the United States flouts narratives of a fantasy of ethnic-national authenticity in exchange for self-determined Latinx hybridity based on class standing and market prominence, luxuries not experienced by their parents' generations. In this socioconsumer realm, to be represented is to have products that reflect one's cultural identities, to find oneself on the shelf, in public qualified by opportunistic marketing. Quinceañera culture represents one instrumentalization of Latinx cultural production in the digital marketplace. The marketplace of ideas produces and reproduce itself as it informs cultural practice that manifests as constantly updated user comment streams. These comments are the digital communities cultural critique, and a by-product of drawing on cultural narratives as marketable consumer products and advertising tropes.

"Women Try [on] Their Old Quinceañera Dresses" did more than garner views and likes; it started a comment stream in which Latinx women and some men developed a forum around the practice of quinceañeras in the twenty-first century. The video itself is made in a common style used by BuzzFeed to appeal to a youth market attracted by quick, witty, and culturally relevant social media. The video is one in a series with similar formats of mostly women trying on old clothes such as Catholic school uniforms or wedding dresses and commenting on the objects but also their reflections on the experiences of initially wearing the ritual garbs. The participants are staff actors, akin to a sketch comedy troupe, and are repeatedly seen in other Pero Like and BuzzFeed Motion Pictures productions actively circulating on social media. The quinceañera-dress video documents five Latinas trying on their old dresses. While details are scarce and no ethnographic timelines are provided, it is clear that participants are at least eighteen years old, and their quinceañera celebrations were likely staged in the early 2000s. The timeline is less relevant than the contribution of each woman whose engagement with the dress as a *recuerdo*, a memento of her event, offers candid albeit brief commentary about her individual experience. The comments are offered in jest and are often reflections of how much their bodies have or haven't changed since they were fifteen, but the responses to the video content from viewers form an organic commentary in decidedly inorganic space. Several intertextual practices emerged in specifically the Facebook comment stream after the video was posted. The most interesting was a process of tagging.

Some of the first Facebook-based responses to the video were in comment tagging, in which viewers would identify other registered Facebook users who they thought would find value in the post. This process is how I found the video, as a friend tagged me as part of an identifiable network of online users who would appreciate the content, in my case both for its humor and the quinceañera's primacy in my research agenda. Others were tagged by friends who had shared in their mutual quinceañera performances as teens and used the video as a site of nostalgia, marking the usefulness of folklore as a tool of consumer marketing online. The very first comment that still appears in Pero Like's Facebook comment feed for the video is from a collaborator of mine, Luis Hernández. Luis's comment is brief, to his sister Diana Kassandra, about their need to re-create it based on their own quinceañera experiences of their youth. Luis and Diana are now quinceañera professionals, styling quinceañera girls and brides in Kansas City, Missouri, and training runway models for *Quinceañeras Magazine* Iowa and Kansas City expo fashion shows. The appeal of the video is not lost even on those who work in the industry and face demanding youth consumers regularly. Branding online outpaces traditional forms of marketing, as intangible realities are malleable and can change functionality on a dime. Grant McCracken notes that "e-commerce" has the capacity to respond to a kind of market urgency that traditional modes of print media cannot (*Culture and Consumption* 185).

The desire to share and spread the content around relevant circles not only promotes Pero Like's brand but acknowledges a cultural connectivity in deterritorial space. Some post only names, which also appear later as commenters developed a chain of associations. Others use the comment space not to reference the video's content, even when most commenters are actually discussing the video's content, but instead find open space to share their own quinceañera experiences or lack of experiences. Some of the two thousand posts on this page are only tagged references to other users or emojis, such as hearts of smiley faces. Several commenters go so far as to include photographs, creating visual and textual logs of quinceañera practice in digital public space. The photographic responses accompany what I label "appreciation narratives," posts of various lengths that actively support the practice of quince años celebrations. Such comments often include details of personal experiences and sentiments during and reflecting back on their personal events.

> *Evelyn Desoreé Salazar*: My sister & I were very lucky and are so grateful to our parents for our Quince. Even though it stressed my mom out she wanted us to have one so bad and we wanted it. I loved feeling like a queen for a day. I had a full court—15 guys & 14 girls. My sister had 9 & 9. It was beautiful and it was back to back. Mine in 2011 hers in 2012. And both on our actual birthdays! What a beautiful day with months of work put into it and the waltz. Mine alone was over $15,000 & I'm pretty sure my sisters was too. By no means is my family rich and we didn't have Padrinos to help pay but we just had amazing parents who worked hard to give us an amazing birthday when we became young women.

> *Lucero Chavez*: My sisters and I were lucky . . . we each had one
> and we have such a big family the parties were pretty big . . . we
> didn't have padrinos or anything like that. . . . My daughter just
> had one in Mexico two years ago. . . . I think it's a beautiful tradi-
> tion . . . but it's not for everyone . . .

> *Yesenia Castro*: This is great! I have amazing memories from my
> Quinces—complete with 3 photo albums and a 2 hour video, lol.
> My mom/abuela had been saving for literally 15 years for it, haha.
> They were so happy that day, as was I. Such a blast, poofy dress
> and all!

The only comments more prevalent that those that express gratitude are
those that express an inability to practice the celebration due to financial
constraints. Thirty-seven narrative comments directly cite the prohibitive
cost of the event as the only element that kept them from performing the
ritualized celebration. Such comments show the way communities have
bought into consumer narratives of quinceañeras that stage fantasy events as
the ideal celebrations. Outpourings of support, some coupled with posted
photographs of past quinceañera events, and family and individual portraiture are met at times with counternarratives, Latina life stories in which the
quinceañera motif exists as a narrative of absence or alternative supplementa-
tion. Some user commentary can even be described as offensive, as the video
stirs up feelings about the correct way to retain cultural identities among
co-ethnic strangers.

> *Eugenia Salinas*: I wanted to have a quinceañera really bad when
> I was younger, mostly to wear a poofy dress. My parents decided
> to give me a trip to Orlando instead. I was angry at them for not
> giving me what I wanted when I left, by the time I came back
> from the trip all I could think was "I was so wrong, this was the
> best choice." I love my parents so much.

> *Karla O'Rourke*: Don't feel bad girl! For my mine I got $300 and
> got dropped off at the mall, but that's because that's how I wanted
> it. I saw how stressful and expensive it was on my parents and I
> was like "man, fuck this! Give me some $$ and let's keep it rolling"

> *Madian Tovar*: Im sorry but who does she think she is judging
> females about not having a quince? She doesnt know why we

chose not to and to say we were just throwing away a tradition. My family is very traditional, but i chose not to because i decided it was the fiscally responsible thing to do even though my parents said they wanted to. That shit is expensive as hell, im sorry i worried about finances at 15 and didnt want my parent to not be able to pay their bills for a party. We had a good old fashioned barbecue instead.

These posts, more than simply their individual value, demonstrate the "one post could start a revolution" mantra of social-listening experts. The comments about quinceañera practice and perceptions of meaning within quinceañera culture speak to the power of collectivity, for the purposes of branding but also as intellectual documentation of communities at large. Together posts following a viral video capture a cross-section of Latina perspectives on the quinceañera as a cultural phenomenon. The life-logged commentaries, though brief, likely represent group cultural perspectives not found in print elsewhere—a new archive of cultural knowledge representing the digitally savvy and technologically literate. What needs to be understood is the motivation for entering the discourse to claim digital space through the inclusion of personal narratives for or against quinceañera practice among relative strangers bound by a three-minute, nine-second video about trying on old dresses. As archives of perspectives referencing past events in the present moment, this archive of digital commentary—open to continuing additions—represents how quinceañera narratives are caught up in alternate temporality where multicultural marketing practices in the present moment provide opportunities for documenting shared memories. The memories implicate traditional practice; the sentiments around cost and family responsibilities are the most prominent, as girls reference the exorbitant cost of staging luxury events particular to the US communities as the primary reason for the lack of celebration. Such commentary draws on an organically manifesting discourse of racialized economics in which spending, especially luxury spending, becomes a contentious factor in the personal experience narratives of Latinxs authenticating their lived experiences and celebratory spending choices online.

One of the most prominent criticisms in this ongoing online review is the lack of temporal progression—the quinceañera as anachronistic or outdated and only really appropriate as a subject of memory but not a laudable choice for contemporary Latina youth. The continued existence of a quinceañera in a critical framework of user commentary becomes a marker that instantiates a pan-Latinx community of practice but at the same time leads to a discourse around the limited intra-Latinx potential for economic diversity and class performativity. Unlike the content of Jackye's regional magazine Facebook page, this online quinceañera product was not invested in enticing cultural entrepreneurs or inspiring young practitioners; it allowed a sense of belonging, evoking a stream of content more interesting to view than the original video itself.

In Latin America, the cost of events has also played a major role in online criticism. In particular, disdain for the production of quinceañeras among those identified as living in circumstances of poverty adds a new, more complicated dimension to the cultural practice. User commentaries on a photo exhibit circulated through the online Latinx-oriented content producer Remezcla offer a distinct critique of consumer pressure attributed to what is deemed ignorant and "criminal" luxury spending.

Remezcla, similar to Pero Like, is a digital publisher and marketing agency that documents and circulates news about emergent "Latin music, events and culture." Its physical headquarters are in Brooklyn, New York, and Mexico City, emphasizing the media brand's goal to be the most valued cultural influencer outside of a purely American Latinx market. It claims an avid audience of "Latino Millennials with national and international audience in the US, Latin America, and Spain" (Herrera).

On August 12, 2016, Remezcla covered a 2014 photo exhibition series by a French photographer, Delphine Blast, that features images of contemporary teens in Bogota, Colombia, posing in lavish and colorful quinceañera gowns in front of their homes and in their neighborhoods. The piece is titled "This Quinceañera Photo Series Highlights the Sacrifices Parents Make for This Rite of Passage." Its author, Carolina Dalia Gonzalez, writes, "Some may see the images and think these parents made unwise financial decisions, but Delphine gives them room to share their own stories." Young Colombian women were photographed; captions explain the circumstances of their families, and many reveal the cost of the gowns with respect to family circumstances. The photos are staged and tinged with exotic poverty, creating dramatic disjunction between the opulent dresses and impoverished physical environments.

The collection of photographs draws on the fantasy images that readily circulate in glossy, staged images of girls posing in their dresses in fabricated, idyllic environments. Those perfected images are fabricated by using high-quality digital cameras and professional editing and by literally cropping away the unsightly bits of reality. One example posted from Blast's series through Remezcla's Facebook page is of the photo and brief story of Laura. She is photographed in a bright-red and white ball gown with elaborate bodice accents and a *pañuelo*-style skirt that gains its fullness from strips of different-colored organza and tulle cut into even squares that look like handkerchiefs sewn together.[2] Laura is seated on an old loveseat positioned on a dingy rooftop patio with discarded wooden boards to one side and plants on the other. The scene is the antithesis of the curated, professional photographs solicited by quinceañeras and their families. The photo of Laura Cristina Zarta in her dress and tiara is paired with a caption in the photographer's narration:[3]

> Laura's father is a fruit seller, and her mother is unemployed. Laura loves playing football [soccer] and will join the female youth Colombian football team in 2015. Her parents saved money for six months to organize her quinceañera. 200 people were invited. Laura wants to become a criminologist.

The visual narrative is meant to serve as its own register for communicating experience that is seemingly in conflict with the social circumstances of the dress's acquisition—in particular the employment status of Laura's parents. These visual narratives implicate an underlying deceptive register in the production of quinceañera culture and event portraiture that would stage luxury as a kind of visual lie. It implies class mobility, although never outwardly, and the private financial circumstances of families that a quinceañera celebration potentially renders public.

Gonzalez's article and the seven photos from Blast's collection soon received hundreds of comments from around the world on Remezcla's webpage and hundreds more on social media postings. The key theme that emerged, much like in the case of Pero Like's video, was money. Latinx families are framed as economically illiterate and irresponsible for the continued practice of quince años celebrations. One user went so far as to call the continued "waste" of family funds "criminal." Users commenting on the article itself (not Facebook posts or reposts) established a social narrative that was divided three ways: direct criticism of spending, support of quinceañera practice as a cultural event that has lost currency among second- and third-generation Latinxs, and acknowledgment of modest quinceañeras. Unlike Pero Like's video, the Remezcla story had a more pronounced mixed-gender audience of commenters. Men and women alike were apt to attack not the photographer or the subjects specifically but the entire Latinx community as complicit in the continuation of the celebration.

> *Melissa Castillo Nuñez (Dallas, Texas):* Maybe I'm wrong but I feel like Hispanic parents have their priorities really messed up sometimes. But it's just our culture.

*Eliezer Montanez*: Priorities need to be rethought of, $3,000 can help pay for a semester, I'm sure that would cover a lot more over there. At times, tradition can be a burden. People forget we're in times where having some form of education beyond high school is beyond important. There should be articles for spanish speakers describing how much better it would be if they reinvested that money towards their kids trade school or regular college education.

*Daniel Coriati*: Is only a big deal because people have make it a big deal. Its not written in the bible, it has nothing to do with religion. Is just a simbolic ceremony. And the peole who spend the most on these Quinceañera parties are the ones who can't really afford it.

This shared and ever-developing discourse around the intersection of economic practices and Latinx communities is problematic in its shallow interpretation of the social intention of the event from a practitioner's perspective, but it also assumes a sense of a sociocultural solidarity, that simply by identifying as "Latino" or "Hispanic," populations are thought to share values. This is a dangerous assumption that often falls along lines of resource accessibility among those who have had the opportunity and the desire to attend institutions of higher education and save in a way that is satisfying to cultural elites. Such criticism only serves to illuminate the diversity of US Latinx experiences. It also demonstrates that intracultural paternalism is not a matter of community development as much as it is self-serving rhetoric that would presume a singular route to social success in the United States—the one guided by a class-blind Latinx intelligentsia. This narrative is reinforced in social mediascapes that would minimize the choices of those whose behaviors have been deemed socially debilitating from using mainstream cultural rhetorics of idealized spending and saving practices. Those individuals are not being judged by logics of behavioral economics or the psychology of economic decision making that would frame choice—even limited choice—among personal survival strategies of those living in the realm of interstitial social (and consumer) spaces.

In examining quinceañera practice through the lens of social media commentary, the perceived value of quinceañera practice collapses upon notions of its social worth. Extracultural discourses stemming from non-Latinxs who observe the traditional practice in their regional localities frame the event as interesting or exotic, while the rhetoric of intracultural narratives identifies the tradition and the associating spending as pathological. Behavioral economists contend that there is no perfectly rational economic subject and that all economic agents are bound to distinct social conditions, and thus their decision making must make way for nonstandard economic logics—those that assume the normalcy of imperfect decision making. Using that framework reveals a tension between social subject formation and narratives of class mobility that in Latinx cultural contexts have come into direct conflict. Online spaces become the informal repositories for in-group perceptions of culturally inflected economic logics that affect the practice of quinceañeras in the material world. Criticism and review become an ongoing process made possible by the assumed anonymity of online commenting, offering critics the freedom to be honest or even hyperaggressive in "trolling." Taken together, the user commentaries on Blast's provocative photos, Gonzalez's essay, and Pero Like's posted video illustrate the ways the quinceañera is perceived as an economic decision through the expressions of nostalgia and personal responsibility in the context of a Latinx cultural exchange. The tension produced is fundamentally a battle between the tradition's worth and the monetary value placed on its materialization. What bridges these two ideological standpoints is the notion of moralized poverty.

The body of commentary on quinceañera practice as critiqued in online environments and promoted by online cultural entrepreneurs is fundamentally as an affective expenditure based expressly on sentiment rather than practicality. Couched in collective statements about economic responsibility, online users imply that Latinxs who practice quinceañeras do so irrationally. Such a discourse aims to shame and punish those presumed to be spending beyond their means. In her essay "Poor People Deserve to Taste Something Other than Shame," the journalist Ijeoma Oluo asserts that class-based shaming is a product of popular media and conservative publications alike. Oluo contends that as

> a relic of the "Welfare Queen" stories of the '80s, the fear of poor
> people squandering the charity of hard-working American tax
> dollars leads to countless classist memes, reactionary petitions,
> and tighter restrictions on the ways in which poor Americans are
> allowed to live.

In her own life, Oluo notes, reprehensible poverty manifested symbolically as a Boston cream pie brought home by her mother, who Oluo knew could not afford to indulge. The pie became the material manifestation of her contempt for her mother, a feeling she internalized as she accepted a social narrative that would classify her single mother's "luxury" spending as a product of poor life decisions and her mother as a single black woman who was socially defective. Oluo writes,

> We had no phone, often no electricity, and if there was a package of ramen in our cupboard, it was a very good day. I wasn't quite sure why, but I knew that this was all my mom's fault. She had married the wrong man, she had gotten the wrong job, she hadn't saved enough or scraped enough or worked hard enough. But we had no food in our fridge and I was pretty sure this Boston cream pie was why.

Similar discourse in user comments on Remezcla's spread of Blast's photos and Gonzalez's essay reinforce a relation between Latinxs and presumed working-class social status, as the gown explicitly indexes any supposedly superfluous, luxury good in impoverished surroundings. The ease with which cursory viewers linked Colombian (Latin American) quinceañeras with all Latinxs in the United States is quite a leap and yet is a product of the globalizing framework of online interactions—where Colombian girls in lavish gowns must be synonymous with Chicanas in California, Cubanas in Miami, and Latinas in Indiana. The ease with which the correlation is made illustrates the way narratives of racialized poverty among US Latinxs are normalized and even expected in a larger intracultural romance of working-class experiences that validate a connection between self-determinative strategies defined by struggle and opposition to dominant society. Quinceañera practices that engage in consumerist knowledge economies, indeed making Latinx culture part of mainstream narratives of being American, disrupt ethnicized narratives that would link Latinx communities in solidarity through shared anti-establishmentarianism. While user comments were shaming those presumed to be in poverty by criticizing how their earnings were spent, I assert that they are also critiquing a desire to embody middle-class performativity.

The visible practice of quinceañeras among co-ethnic and non-Latinx social actors becomes a Boston cream pie. As read from its online critique in the public space of global social media, the event becomes a categorically irrational economic decision that serves a larger, affective purpose in the lives of individuals, families, and communities. This assertion also holds in engaging with families who are in fact middle or upper class and whose class status is part of the social production, as well as the affective qualities that lend the tradition to widespread popularity as a nostalgic artifact of collective coming-of-age commemorations. What is lacking from the social media environments is a youth-based perspective. Facebook sources are designed to draw in consumers who have already celebrated by using nostalgia as a cultural marketing tool. What is left to examine here is how Latinx teen cultural producers are using the product of the quinceañera to self-brand and using online space to enact a postfeminist quinceañera production that interjects itself into the online knowledge economy based on the demands of youth consumption.

## TAKINGONGISELLE: YOUTH CULTURAL ENTREPRENEURSHIP ONLINE

By late 2018 Giselle Guerra had nearly 114,000 subscribers to her YouTube vlog TakingOnGiselle. With the vlog, established in January 2015, Giselle has made a name for herself among Latina teens across the United States, specifically as an online quinceañera vlogger who not only authors autoethnographic online content but also has had her videos and ideas featured on the popular quinceañera planning guide site, Quinceanera.com. Her vlog, a classic beauty and fashion page targeting English-speaking youth audiences, also takes up space on what has been termed the "Latinternet" as Giselle actively features her Latina life through video diaries. She hosts a special-topic series titled "Quinceañera Help and Tips" in which Giselle tells quinceañera stories—of her own event and those she has attended—and uses her know-how as a teen fashion and beauty vlogger to help Latinas plan and budget for their perfect quinces. Giselle manages her videos with the occasional accompaniment of friends or her boyfriend and seemingly without adult intervention into the creative content. Her work adds to the growing body of social media outcroppings changing the racialized consumer landscape of the digisphere, the collective body of internet, digital media, and computers, that many have taken for granted as a white, male creative space. While young digital-native creatives like Giselle are folding their lives and interests into digital spheres, their online practices are actively influencing narratives of traditional cultural practice in heritage communities in the material and territorial world. Innovations such as Giselle's quinceañera vlog are not alien deformations of cultural practice; rather, they are the expected next step in traditional practices that continue to find relevance in the daily lives of heritage communities that exist in the interstitial reality between "real" and "virtual."

TakingOnGiselle's video posted on June 18, 2016, is titled "Rhinoplasty Reveal." While some viewers might frown upon the decision of a sixteen-year-old girl to undergo elective, cosmetic surgery, it was one Texas Latina vlogger Giselle Guerra did not undertake lightly, as she explains her motivations and process to her viewers. Giselle is articulate, warm, and extremely gracious. Guerra discusses her life as a teenager living in the Dallas-Fort Worth area, mostly focusing on providing fashion and beauty tips to what appear to be adoring fans. The majority of comments on her videos include the grammatically questionable but perfectly sincere professions "ILY" or "ily," meaning "I love you." Many are accompanied by emoji smiling faces or multicolored hearts. Whatever knowledge she is disseminating, it was clear, Giselle has a way of making her subscribers feel welcome and affirmed in the digital milieu of her bubbly and colorful vlog posts.

Giselle's lifestyle vlog features playlists; an early one was dedicated to sharing tips for planning and executing a quinceañera celebration. It was titled "Quince Planning Helping Videos! :)."[4] The entries represented collective creativity and ingenuity, as most of the videos originated from user requests. Three videos in particular illustrate the dialogic nature of her vlog, coordinated in specific question-and-answer style, a common addition in professional how-to blogs. Giselle started her blog at age fifteen, approximately six months after she celebrated her own quinceañera. Her expert perspective is supported by her own experience as a proactive planner of her quinceañera, her willingness to share visual documentation of her event, and her capacity as an articulate, English-dominant, Spanish-competent Latina to explain her process and the motivation behind her event. Her status as a teenager invites a peer-to-peer network that despite her lack of formal business expertise attracts Latina subscribers eager to hear Giselle's story and find connections to themselves within it.

Three illustrative posts of Giselle's vlog are not necessarily the most visually compelling or the most innovative in content, but they depict the relations being built through quinceañera narratives between Giselle and her digital Latinx YouTube community. These three Q&A videos came about from a call posted through Giselle's equally highly followed Instagram account of the same title. Her mixed methods of promotion link her Instagram, YouTube, Snapchat, Poshmark, Depop, and other accounts in a multiplatform mobile barrio system that allows Giselle to reach her Latinx subscribers and them to reach her without the limitations of territorial space and place.[5] Common ground is forged in deterritorial, creative space.

Giselle's video posts on her vlog are organized into playlists for her viewers. All of the playlists feature original content filmed by and starring Giselle herself along with occasional guests. One category is composed of "liked" videos, the original content of others including many fellow vloggers whom she follows. In 2017 the quinceañera theme dominated her channel. But the 2019 version of her site shifted the focus to reflect her changing social identity. In this iteration of her channel, Giselle has consolidated her quinceañera advice videos in a single playlist as her larger channel shifts focus to health and beauty tips as well as promotion of her brand and her online boutique,

Risueña. As a beauty and lifestyle blogger she composes her videos from layers of consumption of her presence and beauty, which are often commented on by her viewers in video comment feeds, but also from vicarious experiences of consumer culture. The videos in her quinceañera-themed playlist emphasize this dual concept of consumption through thematically linked content. At the same time, the updates to her channel serve as a microcosm of Latinx social development in which the quinceañera, though an important stepping stone, is meant to mature into different expressive forms.

The videos in the collection of quinceañera-themed content have reflective commentaries on why and how Giselle planned and executed aspects of her celebration. The longest video (15:40) is titled "How To Plan Your Quinceañera! Tips, Advice, DIY's, & Personal Experience." Other videos have curated videography and photography clips mined from her own personal quinceañera collection. The memory videos are presented as teaching tools to an eager audience of quinceañeras-to-be, and they serve as Giselle's credentials in the subject. Videos such as "My Quinceañera Vals" and "My Quinceañera Slideshow/Presentación de Fotos!" recirculate Giselle's personal memories as part of asserting her authority to help guide others through their planning processes. In their titling and use of Spanish and English code switching, they actively racialize Giselle's blog but only in her quinceañera-themed content. "Vals" stands for "waltz" as a named traditional element of the quinceañera celebration, with particular expectations in form, content, and audience, and not just any dance routine.

Her direct translation of the latter title is in keeping with the development of her blog to be Spanish-speaker inclusive. This changing pattern is visible in her comments sections, which have gradually become a blend of Spanish and English since the earliest, which were wholly in English. Both titles speak to the audience Giselle reaches and those she is eager to attract. In the realm of social media vlogging, such images, both still and video, affirm Giselle's self-objectification of a product in and of her own social media sharing. Yet at the same time, she chooses to use her curated self as a product for creating her own social media brand but also in the service of her followers, who are grateful for her willingness to share her insights about the Latina coming-of-age experience.

TakingOnGiselle featured three "Q&A: Quinceañera Edition!" videos. Each vlog post drew its content from questions asked through Giselle's Instagram account. The first, in the fall of 2015, one year after Giselle's own quinceañera, was so popular that she decided to create more of the same, posting a new answer session in February 2016 and another the next month. The average length of each session is around nine minutes.

Her third question-and-answer vlog in the series begins with a summary preamble that reads like a quinceañera resume. The description of the video assumes what her viewers already know from the body of quince videos on her channel, that Giselle herself had a quinceañera celebration and that much of the celebration was constructed and co-constructed through DIY methods. This is affirmed through the videos about making one's own quinceañera centerpieces and party favors. The actual listed credentials include links to the two previous Q&A videos, a link to her page as a "quinceañera ambassador" to the online quinceañera planning website Quinceanera.com, links to articles she has published on the planning site in English and Spanish, links to videos that feature moments from her own quinceañera, and her social media tags.

The three videos do more than reinforce Giselle's place as a teen quince guru on social media; they also establish the capacity of self-objectification in quinceañera culture to build community through internet branding and self-promotion. The questions are gleaned from Instagram, another promotional tool used to triangulate Giselle's presence on social media, but they also brought viewers and subscribers together, especially as questioners were eager to see if their questions were asked and answered. The responses of girls looking for recognition on social media are among the most profound I found in Giselle's vlog posts. Expressions of gratitude and appreciation are found in most of the video viewers' comments. Unlike other spaces, this digital space had no sign of trolling or criticism and appeared to be a place of relief. The user Phantom at My Chemical Day posts, "Hey Giselle, Your videos are so helpful for my quince! I love you!" User Aritzy Rios comments, "OMG your videos are so helpful my quince is in March of 2016 and I'm so stressed but videos are helping me so much so THANK YOUU I LOVE YOU." A comment by the user It's Just Alondra hints at the tension that arises when young Latinas try to plan quinceañeras in families that lack their own direct experiences: "Thanks this helped so much I'm 13 Turning 14 in February and my family is driving me crazy!!" Even beyond planning, users return to the site to share how Giselle's advice affected their celebrations. Perla Espinoza writes, "my sister's quince wad [*sic*] the nineteenth of September, and thx to ur advice her party was perfect." The fleet of Latina and openly mixed-race young women asking questions about their prospective quinceañeras underscores a desire for cultural knowledge that is not readily available in their immediate home networks or that such knowledge is more easily accessed through social media and online interfaces than personal communication.

User responses to the three question-and-answer videos were overwhelmingly positive, in some cases bordering on obsessive. One observation about

Giselle's channel as well as other vloggers' is the fierce loyalty of their audiences. Giselle's quinceañera followers are no different. Unlike her other more general entries, though, her quinceañera-themed vlogs had decidedly more views per post. In her general categories, the most popular posts such as fashion hauls and challenges had fewer views, and the top five videos on her channel in May 2018 were from her quinceañera playlist, which at the time had up to a half-million views. Giselle's creative work is nothing if not a popular place to seek out quinceañera tips but also a digital space in which to connect to a like-minded community of peers. In her three Q&A video posts, the questions often bring up repeated content that is available in previous posts. Rather than simply referring viewers to previous vlog entries, Giselle gives fleshed-out responses to a waiting audience of her Latina teen peers, endearing her to them.

Comments reflect that this space is not just about getting answers but, like the quinceañera itself, is a space of recognition. The vast majority of posted user comments were those expressing gratitude and appreciation for making and posting videos that are so relevant to the young female audience's needs. Another subset of these gracious notes specifically reflect on girls simply having their questions and names revealed through the video. The user karla hernandez submitted a question on Instagram and later commented on the video: "Thank you so much for answering my question! I love watching your videos, you're such an inspiration!" More intense was the response of user stacy flores, who responded to the video with greater, revealing intensity, "When I hear my name in this video, I almost cried [crying emojis], I love you so much [heart]." Such emotional or at least textually expressive responses illustrate that the internet is both an information acquisition tool for Latina youth, specifically of cultural knowledge, but also a place of communion, of solidarity, and of visibility. Being referenced by name lends a sense of inclusivity and affirmation that young people are seeking among their peers. Quinceañera culture offers a platform that is distinctly crafted to give Latina preteens and teens an authoritative cultural voice reinforced by networks of cultural knowledge that lead back to one another, not to parents or adult cultural entrepreneurs.

The digital Latina space cultivated by Giselle and indeed her parents and others who supplied the technology to document her vlog, the funds to draw on consumer products, and the middle-class Latinx cultural space in a Texas community formed an implicitly racialized niche in cyberspace. It emphasizes unification through a community of practice rather than a narrative of ethnic or racial solidarity. One young user recalls that Giselle's posts helped her feel comfortable having a quinceañera even though she was only half

Mexican. Such a comment is not surprising, as Giselle's posts focus on practice rather than ethnic identification. Her videos are punctuated with cultural markers that subtly draw boundaries around the networks of viewers.

Her quinceañera-themed titles use Spanish-language terms in a normalized way, without reference to translation. The only translation appearing in titles is the reformulation of a Spanglish title to one wholly in Spanish. Within her videos Spanish language is used to establish and reinforce specialized quinceañera cultural terms. Giselle speaks perfect English, and her videos are in English, although she practices single-term code-switching by using quinceañera-specific terms as she explains projects and practices. She uses "quinceañera" but also "quince" and "your fifteen" to refer to the event itself, making reference to phonetic breakdowns to appeal to completely non-Spanish speakers. She makes the assumption that her viewers are competent in the terms of the celebration, using them as specialty vocabulary rather than translatable verbal references. Escorts are referred to as "chambelanes," party favors as "recuerdos," and waltz as "vals." Her linguistic practice affirms that these elements, while having English translations, belong to the cultural practice that sets them apart from a separate, decontextualized use.

As she mobilizes these terms, she also teaches them to her varied followers, who may or may not be Spanish-language competent but who also use code switching in a similar fashion, inserting quinceañera vocabulary terms into their English-dominant questions and comments. This subtle linguistic practice adds a deeper layer to understanding how the celebration is understood among a new generation of Latina youth. Rather than being a product of individual families in distinct localities, the quinceañera accessed through YouTube channels, brokering knowledge between peer networks, is placeless, existing outside the strictures of geographically limited experiences.

Geographically nonspecific quinceañeras reinforce the way the internet is networking communities of practice and shifting the way scholars enter the tradition not just of small, intimate practice but one that can be and is experienced as a national and hemispheric phenomenon mediated by digital networks. The growing peer networks reflect new sources of intergenerational cultural knowledge. Giselle's videos and online how-to articles are the product of her own experiences. But as she shares them in digital space, her experiences join new circuits of cultural knowledge that are rooted in cultural entrepreneurial motivators particularly cultivating desire through practices of consumption. No longer can quinceañera practice solely be said to be the work of family histories or even local experiences of community; instead they represent just one way that US Latinx communities exist outside of personal boundedness as the product of a hermeneutic spiral of consumption practices. Place, territorial space, is a now a less reliable indicator of how and why quinceañeras are celebrated. At the same time, the structure around personal branding through a vlog persona and performance, reinforced by Giselle's followers, indicates that the young woman's entrepreneurial gumption has wider implications in the marketplace of cultural practice online.

Giselle's vlog is a commodity unto itself and mobilizes her own quinceañera experiences as a product to sell herself as a culture influencer capable of reaching Latinx youth while drawing on the familiarity of traditional practice to lure in viewers, the same strategy used by market strategists at Pero Like and Remezcla. Giselle's vlog reflects Sarah Banet-Weiser's assertion of the capacities of interactive user interfaces online to "animate strategies of self-branding" (54). Unlike Banet-Weiser's subjects, I am not discussing the online auctions of virginity, but the mobilization of quinceañera practice by youth entrepreneurs also reflects a "quest for visibility" through self-promotion that links the visibility of the individual to the product; in this case, quinceañera practice is implicated in a branding process. Giselle's self-branding process is made possible through a normalized framework of post-feminism. Banet-Weiser describes a theoretical and practical way traditional feminist ideologies are incorporated into a consumer field. In this framework, concepts of freedom, independence, and choice are distinctly animated by neoliberal capitalism and participatory culture that structure much online activity (Banet-Weiser 55, 61). As a strategy for engaging with the world, Banet-Weiser finds, self-discourse has "been almost seamlessly incorporated into consumer culture" and serves as a "particularly rich context for girls and young women to build a self-brand" (56). The branding process for a Latina cultural entrepreneur online is built into Giselle's attention to the quinceañera as a brand structure of its own.

## CREATING AND CAPTURING VALUE: QUINCEAÑERA AS A BRAND

As social texts, quinceañera celebrations manifest the problematic social value of ethnicity and by extension race as a commodity (Valdivia 21). In terms of acculturation through consumption, a quinceañera can be examined as an assemblage of goods that contains a meaning greater than the sum of individual parts. That summation represents a brand profile that is legible and meaningful to Latinx-identifying audiences and increasingly interesting to non-Latinx communities. Elsewhere I have explored how digital cultural economies function such as those of social media postings with quinceañera motifs (González-Martin). They develop into online networks of cultural knowledge that remake the quinceañera for a new generation of digital natives eager to focus on the event's futurity and innovative potential rather than on narratives of the past. A narrative of futurity is an innovation and a necessity to those who cannot look back to their own intimate experiences to stage a quinceañera celebration. Such outwardly focused planning results in new cultural patterns of practice that I deem "unhomey" to a desire for a defamiliarized coming-of-age event. The unfamiliar event, though recognizable, fails to index the same collective nostalgia and instead elicits a web of reviews and critiques around the material celebration. The critiques are illustrated in user commentary toward the Pero Like video and the Remezcla coverage of Blast's photographic presentation of fantasy dresses in reality backdrops. Such reviews bolster the idea that "quinceañera" is a brand in production in social media and beyond.

As a field of practice, social media use of the quinceañera motif to entice Latinx consumers of a range of ages to reinvest in the tradition is part of a process of online meaning making. It is produced through social media as a marketing tool constantly promoting cultural products to consumers whose lives inevitably become the real, valued product generated for the consumption of advertisements. Marked by intangibility, the quinceañera is mobilized as an idea that generates value through a body of controlled and uncontrolled "cultural domains" and "delivery devices" (G. McCracken, *Culture and Consumption* 178). As social media posts illustrate, the controlled elements are represented by formally organized entities that have cultivated a distinct identity profile for the quinceañera as a cultural product; such a narrative is potentially disrupted by the uncontrollable contributions of user comments.

Branding relies on affective connections to effect consumer participation. As a brand, the quinceañera derives from a variety of cultural domains that supply the tradition's meaning, even when it is alienated from its material production such as age meaning, gender meaning, time and place meaning, and class and status meaning (G. McCracken, *Culture and Consumption* 177). Goods in the service of producing the quinceañera event, although varying by geographic region, are brought together in digital space and reinforce an ideological connectivity among communities of practice that emphasizes the social value of the event as a class marker. Individual performance arises from intimate narratives such as of family ethnic histories and patterns of migration, while patterns of practice linked to identity industries "are vital to the self-invention or self-completion of the individual" in collectivity (G. McCracken, "Living in the Material World" 26). Consumer practice is accepted as full participation in a national culture community in which regular consumption is a marker of deracialized social citizenship. As such, the quinceañera becomes an ideal location through which an established narrative of brand "heritage" can be manipulated successfully in a cultural economic context in which all manner of traditional practice can be mobilized as aggregations of meaning marketable to ethnically segmented consumers (G. McCracken, *Culture and Consumption* 179).

Meaning management of the quinceañera brand exceeds the traditional boundaries of family and kin networks and has new connections in cyberspace, where consumption of and reactions to online cultural artifacts intervene into socially accepted narratives of quinceañera practice. Consumerist revisions of the quinceañera event have affected its social reception, yet the curation of visual and narrative topographies of cultural entrepreneurs in digital mediascapes demonstrates that the event continues to be a community-driven tradition built from innovative moments of circulation and recirculation. The voice of a new generation of Latina youth and intergenerational divergence begin with a native facility with and a temporal and emotional investment in online social media.

## RECULTURATION IN MAKING THE DIGITAL BARRIO

Quinceañera culture in digital space incorporates marketing rhetoric directly and indirectly, making the quinceañera a product of a branding process that capitalizes on consumer practices inflected with cultural nostalgia and a desire to belong. The online life of quinceañera practice in the digital barrio is just one example of a larger twenty-first-century marketing trend termed "digital reculturation" (Carrasco). Mario Carrasco, a cofounder of the Hispanic marketing firm ThinkNow Research, notes that acculturation remains a factor in the American marketing industry but has a new character as English-language, Hispanic-made, focused media continue to thrive. Alternate forms of acculturation, rather than being about integrating culturally through ethnic or racial means, are about social and consumer integration being nuanced by their platforms of dissemination. The marketing logic of acculturation is that the longer an individual resides in the United States the more acculturated or integrated into a hypothetical mainstream American identity the person becomes. However, as we are witnessing with the boom of ethnoracially marketed media platforms across communities, acculturation is no longer being framed as a linear process. Hispanic consumers of the twenty-first century respond to media and advertising differently than generations past did; with US Hispanic-identified births outpacing those of immigrants, fewer consumers have a culturally fluent relation to the Spanish language. This phenomenon also changes the way cross-generational relations are forged and maintained and how heritage traditions are circulated. Acculturation as an adaptation to the surrounding culture now also implicates digital spaces. "Digital reculturation is the process of rediscovering one's culture of origin/identification online through digital representations of culture" (Carrasco). In this space, the quinceañera tradition becomes memeified. At the same time, the tradition itself becomes part of a larger social phenomenon in which marketing precipitates communities' access to cultural knowledge and spurs genuine connections to heritage. The reacculturation process also changes the composition of digital spaces as Latinas use familiar images such as those of the quinceañera to self-brand through a process of digital autotopography.

Digital autotopography contributes a text form that indexes class performativity. A tendency to brand quinceañeras as luxury events through visual representations also reinforces a narrative of upscale Latina youth consumers who desire and have the financial means to invest in the quinceañera brand. Through enticing ads, Latina practitioners are ascribed an implicit social worth, and their consumer desires drive market practices in a niche arena. Although user commentary on social media posts by networked Latinx culture producers suggests that such social worth is hotly contested, value and worth are evaluated from a variety of community perspectives that frame folkloric practices like the quinceañera as social burdens. Class-based intracultural tensions are exacerbated when Latinxs are assumed to be living beyond their economic means. External criticisms of parentally controlled practices lose traction as the quinceañera is repackaged as a construction of entrepreneurs whose cultural influence builds intimacy and a sense of community through marketed meaning making in online video blogs.

The quinceañera as a tradition and as a brand is sensitive to shifts in the cultural economy surrounding US Latinidad and developments in digital technologies evolving the ways communities live and share experiences. Indeed, using the frame of digital reculturation, digital space is not simply where culture is shared but where communities intellectualize practice and reimagine its use-value in their lives. Reculturation does not replace retroacculturation as it affects dress branding in brick-and-mortar retailers; rather, the two dynamics work together to accentuate the layers of social consumer experiences within Latinx communities and how individuals curate their lives in material and digital space. In an examination of a single practitioner circulating her photos through one media profile, a simple digital conversion of face-to-face fieldwork interactions would also tell a compelling tale of how digital lives are curated and how the quinceañera becomes another strategy of visibility. An examination of online practices that affect multiple networks of entrepreneurs, practitioners, and influencers allows a wider frame through which to theorize the practices of individuals and to examine the phenomenon of quinceañera as one strand of a process of consumer marketing online. That marketing is transforming distinctions between cultural value and worth among Latinx populations and being instrumentalized by communities of practice as users implicitly realize that their choices to feature their ethnic heritage through quinceañera practice make visible a consumer narrative of aspirational class formation.

While Muriel did not get an elaborate ball gown or decorated ballroom, she did get her fifteen seconds in the digital spotlight. Her narrative of coming of age returned to its online source, where her ideas were originally formed and shared with her peers. In that moment she became visible as a young lady in her family and a cultural consumer to outside audiences. Her birthday photo with cake, flowers, and corset screen-printed on a T-shirt sent a distinct message of her family's connection to *la madre patria*. She celebrated in Mexico, and although it was not an elaborate event, her celebration drew on the intentions of the brand that benefits from a deterritorialized online profile and bridges the experiences of transnational cultural productions. An aunt had applied Muriel's makeup and straightened her hair. This image served as her quinceañera portrait in the online archive of cultural practice populated by posts, tweet, and comments that lives indefinitely in cyberspace. The process of documentation has been part of the quinceañera narrative, as portraiture is a key way young women are included in social histories of families and communities. The narratives of gender, class, and age become complicated as their production becomes entrenched in beauty industries employing professionals whose job it is to craft and circulate an ideal quinceañera look.

## CHAPTER 4

## MADE IN MEXICO, USA

Beauty Professionals and the Manufacturing of Quinceañera
Beauty Culture

When I walked toward one of the marked ballrooms at the Double Tree in Commerce, California, I wasn't sure what to expect. I was greeted initially by a doorman checking tickets, which made me feel as though I were entering an exclusive space, a sentiment I felt was intentional, as tickets were being sold to see and speak with cultural producers whose work would be otherwise free to browse outside the expo space. The doors were flanked by two six-foot-tall, roll-out, portable signs—each with a six-by-two-foot image of a *Quinceañeras Magazine* cover girl. Larger than life, these images displayed the aggressive visual styling of expo events as spaces of the production of the young Latina form and also one of exposure. I walked in and was greeted by a wall of sound with a heavy bass beat. It was difficult to hear anyone, but I could see everything. Lights from media vendor booths flashed and spun, and from the stage a swirl of multicolored spotlights added to a partylike atmosphere that supported the DJ's vigorous party sounds. Everything I was seeing was for sale in one form or another, all with customizable options. The lights on the stage reminded onlookers that there would soon be a quinceañera runway show featuring trends in quince style for the fall 2011 season. The vendor lights mirrored the energy of the stage lighting and implied that such a stage could also be re-created for personal use at a quinceañera event. Then I saw what I had yet to see at another expo in California. A life-size cardboard cutout of a quinceañera girl in her full formal gown, posing as though she was leaning against a tree, a stereotypical quinceañera photo pose in portraiture posted online and seen in photo albums. As I stared at it, attempting to take a picture around the crowds that were forming for the promotional goodie bags from the same table, the expo staffer Armando asked if

I wanted to "take a picture with the quinceañera" and laughed. In that moment I realized that the image of the quinceañera was circulating and doing work in the community long after the event was over.

The future orientation of the quinceañera experience is manifest through the changes a young woman undergoes in a physically transformative process romantically expressed in narratives of coming of age or implications of social maturation through an idealized sense of responsibility for family and community. In reality, such transformation is made material through the manipulation of the female form through beauty technologies. The practice of the quinceañera event recasts spaces as ritual locations where social evolution becomes a ballroom's or church vestibule's central focus of a given day, but it is the intimate location of the body that undergoes the most striking visible changes for the sake of presenting the possibility of a successful future. The Latina teenage body thus becomes a site of cultural transition where the curves and points of a changing physical form are burdened with the psychological character of a larger, Latinx-identifying family and even wider national public. In the United States, hair design and cosmetic technologies are no longer simply lessons of impending womanhood but become creative industries in the business of brokering a highly visible and marketable commodity emerging from Greater Mexico.

The quinceañera event is a space where young women practice a form of personal branding characterized by aggressive visuality made possible by migrant Mexican entrepreneurs who have brought more than a sense of ethnic nostalgia from their home country; they are helping remake the tradition through a combination of "Mexican-made" personal determination and business acumen. The business of US-based quinceañeras is increasingly the product of the labor and creativity of Mexican-born cultural entrepreneurs whose geographic location, cultural knowledge and experiences, and ability to network with other Latinx professionals are driving innovations in the cultural practice of US Latina quinceañeras. Innovations in the celebrations are facilitated first by a culture of increased professionalization of quinceañera events; families fund rather than directly participate in aspects of event preparation such as dressmaking, hairstyling, and makeup application. Second, as professionalization increases, so does the marketplace for high-quality, professional photography and videography services. These services reinforce the acutely visual nature of the celebration; the young women rarely are heard in recordings, and thus visual narratives of intention and practice predominate. The industries of beauty and photography work hand in hand as together they create images of a single moment in time to document in Latina personal history as well as identify patterns of practice and traditional forms as the quinceañera portrait is a central memory object during and after a quinceañera event.

Quinceañera celebrations foreground visuality in their construction and presentation. Their impact plays out in a series of nested contexts, which manifest simultaneously as the personal self, the public Latinx, and the consumer-citizen. The event and its attendant processes bring to the fore the way bodies can be seen in sociopolitical spaces. The construction of contemporary quinces is not simply the production of familial narratives of practice and memory but an aggregation of material and digital realities, the affective and topographic that influence the creative arrangement of bodies in ritual performance space. Quinceañera production also alludes to the absence of visuality, the politics of the invisibility of certain classes of bodies and experiences in contemporary American society or, with similar contempt, the overvisualization of bodies outside of autonomous controls. "Poverty porn" is witnessed through social media posts of able-bodied, middle- and upper-income, western citizens spending their vacations among the rural and urban poor of developing nations. Likewise, the popular Netflix series *Orange Is the New Black* turns the experiences of incarcerated women of color into "trauma porn" for those whose lives will always be situated safely from the dangers of the prison industrial complex. Jillian Hernandez documents the aesthetic practices of chonga girls whose highly visible, raunchy personal style conveys unapologetic hypersexuality and a penchant for low-class consumerism. She shows how such self-conscious personal styling thumbs its nose at contemporary middle-class moralizations of poverty and female sexuality.

The connection to a Mexican-descent chuntara is uncanny. Chonga-style aesthetics are the basis of a regularized personal aesthetic, and the quinceañera is a once-in-a-lifetime experience, yet they share a symbolic system as the youth who claim their aesthetic systems as their own are eager to adopt modes of personal style that connect them to larger communities of practice but also challenge the stigmas associated with culturally coded systems of bodily adornment that would vilify young women who are not afraid to be seen.

Quinceañeras' essential visuality is based on vivid materiality, codes of colors and textures that participants understand as culture-specific visual narratives. In pieces taken out of their ritual provenance, dress and bodily portraiture are clearly central to the quinceañera celebration as markers in practice but also as tools of documentation and commemoration. In the celebratory ritual moment, the visual markers of dress allow onlookers to cross-reference spatial positioning relative to personal adornment; visual components such as dress design and color, parallel thematic composition among peers, and a tiara or diadem can help audiences classify a quinceañera event as the community ritual. The visual markers are normalized in certain spaces—church steps, for instance. The same markers, such as elaborate multicolored ball gowns, are then exoticized in different settings deemed inappropriate to quince celebration, such as the suburban mall. This visual betrayal of the quinceañera "out of context" has become a new way to document the celebration that acknowledges the waning primacy of the church in the ritual's social significance.

At the Houston Galleria mall on any given Saturday afternoon, but more often in the temperate spring months, dozens of quinceañera girls roam, eating and laughing with their courts and photographers as they are photographed in candid scenes in the wide-open space of the Galleria rotunda. Such public consumption of the quinceañera event becomes more acceptable and normalized as the demographics of Houston are increasingly Latinx. The US Census Bureau estimates Houston's Hispanic or Latinx population in 2018 at 44.5 percent ("QuickFacts"). The Latinx population largely affects a quince girl's reception in public. But even within Latinx communities, not all quinceañeras are equal. The reception of a quinceañera girl who is wearing her gown offstage or outside her quinceañera party largely depends on how class is read from her body. At times it is based on who accompanies her. A young woman posing by the side of the road in Central Texas on private property would not raise suspicion when maneuvering in her ball gown to avoid snagging the fence while accompanied by a professional photographer.[1]

The chuntara whose image was captured in the mall was berated and labeled low-class, a criticism more likely directed at her audacity to indulge in luxury rather than her found location. In these cases, different bodies are seen as differently deserving of respect. But the juxtaposition of a quinceañera girl and a mall does not inherently betray the ritual; it only exposes the observer's level of knowledge about contemporary trends in the traditional template of the celebration. Trends include sequined quince sneakers and off-beat photo shoots. Photographing the quince celebrant in myriad public places makes her unapologetically visible not just for herself as an individual; her visage is used as a market of the presence of Latinx culture more broadly. The quinceañera defies the logics and boundaries of assumed racialized and classed topographies. The quince girl can be seen on church steps and in rented *salones*, but she is also being photographed at her state capitol building, drinking a frappuccino in her local Starbucks, and roaming the mall in her city.

At the same time, her appearance in public places acknowledges that the tradition has become comfortably entrenched in consumer culture, so much so that a trip to the mall is an opportunity to take professional photographs but also a space to be consumed publicly. And yet, within such innovations in form, an intracultural class dynamic emerges in which practices are read differently based on assumption of class status. A chuntara's right to demand gaze at the mall is questioned, but the right of debutantes to appear at the Houston Galleria with elegantly coifed hair and impeccable makeup is not.

Dress is among the most commented-upon elements of quinceañera performativity. The young women with whom I spoke who said they did not have quinceañeras, although they may have celebrated their fifteenth birthdays in some fashion, often claimed that they lacked the dress. Despite its prominence, the dress is only one material manifestation of the bodily transformation being remarked upon through the ritual frame. Observers and participants making sense of the tradition often remark on how it signals a series of social and cultural firsts—while it is presumed that it marks the onset or at least the acknowledged onset of biological sexual maturity, it is the social marker of secondary sexual characteristics that are highlighted throughout the celebration.

Shifts in US social customs have impacts on dress style, permitting tailoring and dress customization that would leave much more of the female bodies exposed; face, hands, forearms, shoulders, neck, and décolletage are all potential areas of exposed skin and adorned for the celebration. Across embodied geography, innovations in jewelry and accessories help complete and reinforce the social efficacy of formal dress looks. The idea of the look circulates liberally around planning guides and quinceañera fashion networks. It is the job of a young woman to find and secure the right look by taking stock of the composition of her body—height, skin tone, shape, hair type—and determine what beauty profile suits her best. Suitability is often framed by popular western beauty standards. Young women are encouraged by planners to seek inspiration from mainstream beauty sources, often those featuring white, able-bodied Hollywood stars. The *Quinceañeras Magazine* New York area editor Diana Zavala advises readers in the January–June 2012 edition, "Para encontrar el look que te gusta busca en internet fotografías de actrices o artistas que te gusta como se ven. Siempre es bueno buscar fotografías de alfombra roja" (To find the look you want, look on the internet for photographs of actors or artists whose look you like. It's always good to look for red-carpet photos). Her advice reinforces the focus on embodied practice, in which a quinceañera is a spectacle that is more than hosting the young brown body—the show is the young brown body. The body becomes a site of direct racialized critique, where long, straight locks coifed into large curls and pale skin are the aesthetic ideals represented through industry marketing.

Such marketing establishes an implicit system of standards that young women aspire to meet. The creating of beauty norms in quinceañera industries reinforces the tradition's contextual frame as both nationally and internationally informed. When making her expert recommendations, the quinceañera blogger, consultant, and former editor at Quinceanera.com Hilda Gabriela Hernández informs quince girls about the "it" colors for 2016 quinceañeras: "rose quartz," also labeled the "color of 2016" by *Vogue* Italy, citing trends in use from Hollywood A-listers' birth announcements to New York Fashion Week runways. Connecting to global trends in couture fashion culture further links the event to standards of beautification and body modification that are rarely achievable without the intervention of professionals.

The public eye is drawn to this already politicized body through beauty technologies employed to communicate physical health, youth, economic standing, and personal creativity. In quinceañera performance, makeup artists employ a system of aesthetic communication that works in tandem with dress and hairstyling meant to transform the quinceañera girl's body into an idealized, readable beauty text. Young women rely on the work of professionals and culturally deemed experts to unify their personal preferences, style ideals, and physical presentations into their fantasy looks. In many ways, these professional aestheticians, stylists, hairdressers, and creatives are gatekeepers to idealized womanhood facilitated by the transformational power of makeup and other facets of style. While my experiences in expos have allowed me to observe that although the quinceañera professional industry focuses on appealing to young Latina consumers, the professional leadership is predominantly populated by men. In the hair and makeup industries, queer Mexican men dominate the marketplace as the cultural entrepreneurs responsible for the visible, bodily transformation of young Latina teens.

## MEXICAN BEAUTY ENTREPRENEURS

"They think we are magic or something," Elias Pérez said of some clients during our interview in January 2016. I was sitting in the chair next to Elias's station at his salon in Austin. I had asked Elias why he thought straight women might prefer gay male hairdressers. His response immediately put me on edge, as I had not expected to be faced with a response that dehumanized queer creatives as the objects or tools of heteronormative beauty technologies. I responded that I thought the idea put undue pressure on him as a professional to make female clients feel good about him. Elias and other queer creatives working directly with people's bodies are made responsible for mediating heteronormative desire to and through them. "Isn't that a lot, like a lot of pressure on you?" He replied simply, "It really is."

As a regular patron of a stylist in his employ, I used the time between bleach and color to discuss quinces with Elias. He explained that he is not fond of constructing up-dos, and so he works with few quinceañera clients, preferring a "less dramatic" client base. Elias's Amethyst Salon is an Aveda Concept Salon that offers custom hair color and Aveda makeup consultations as well as the usual salon offerings of cuts and styles. In good researcher fashion I inquired about a promotional makeup cart that looked mostly unused, asking what they offered. "Girl," he said, "don't even. Those are white girl colors. . . . That's who they are really good for." I laughed even though I find it hard to pass for Latina at times, as my manner and education often mark me as culturally white. Elias brought me back, implying that my darker skin and hair would never benefit from cosmetics manufactured in the service of paler-hued populations. I realized that if Elias were a straight man, I would have taken offense at his comment and his familiar tone—after all, I was a paying customer. But my understanding of his manner as a longtime patron of his salon made me read his professional experience through a queer register that allows gay male hairdressers a modicum of extra respect with female clients as a recognition of their capacity for beauty "magic."

Elias is vocal about his lack of desire for quinceañera dramatics, opting not to serve the local youth community, but there are many other professional creatives of Mexican origin who devote their time and passion to innovating in the beauty culture associated with the traditional practice. They may also identify as gay Mexicanos,[2] forming a new intersection in the quinceañera professional industry as fostering migrant entrepreneurship but also a space for queer-identifying entrepreneurs to shape cultural practices that in the past have been framed as exclusively and even divisively heteronormative. Jonathan Gutierrez of La Pelu Salon and Luis Hernández at Royal Beauty Services are cultural entrepreneurs who spend much of their spring and summer months styling quinceañera girls in their respective regions. La Pelu Salon in San Antonio serves quinceañera girls in Central Texas. Royal Beauty Services has itinerant brick-and-mortar locations around Kansas City, Missouri, but specializes in "a domicilio" services, bringing beauty expertise directly to quinceañera girls' homes on the day of their events around Missouri, Kansas, and Iowa.

Jonathan and Luis had different paths to the current quinceañera marketplaces in their cities. In part, understanding their paths helps characterize the role of cultural producers cum entrepreneurs who sustain and innovate quinceañera culture in the United States. Their role has gone overlooked in studies of quinceañera practice that focus on the experiences of individual family identity politics and church in reinforcing gendered norms within larger ethnic enclaves.

Jonathan, who has worked in the quinceañera industry in the United States since 2005 began his career in his native Monterrey in the Mexican state of Nuevo León. As he shared with me in his salon, La Pelu on San Antonio's west side, he came to the United States "siguiendo el amor" (following love).[3] After a transnational relationship that ended only a few months into Jonathan's residence in San Antonio, he was offered employment in a San Antonio salon that gave him his first opportunity to materialize his professional profile in the United States. Jonathan had earned a degree in fashion marketing at the Universidad Technológico in Monterrery. He transformed his childhood fascination with fashion and dress into a thriving career first in Monterrey and later in San Antonio. "Mi pasión desde pequeno era ser diseñador" (My passion since I was a young child was to be a designer). His training sets him apart from many of his stylist peers in that he brings a studied, holistic approach to beauty practice, styling hair, doing professional makeup consultations, and making clothing including exclusive quinceañera gowns. His skills also include concept innovation for runway shows, a practice learned from university training in fashion marketing and modeling. His formal training and personal aspiration manifested in a number of business ventures tied to beauty culture in the United States.

Establishing himself as a business owner was natural for Jonathan, who said business and business aspirations ran in his family. In Monterrey he belonged to a core network of eight friends who were all entrenched as professionals in the beauty industry, and so embarking on a career as a stylist was both attractive and fulfilling. Five years after arriving in San Antonio in 2009, Jonathan opened his own dress shop, where he made exclusive dresses for clients, mostly quinceañeras, who could not find what they wanted on any rack or in any catalogue. He explained, "Vendío puros diseños exclusivos" (I only sold exclusive designs). He shared with me that the majority of his custom-dress clients were sent to him by friends who also owned shops or worked in the regional quinceañera industry but were unable to serve a client's particular needs because they were not dressmakers or designers; they worked with national dress wholesalers, ordering dresses from companies such as Mary's Bridal and were limited to the designs offered for retail sale for a given season.

One of Jonathan's most interesting designs was a quinceañera gown that thematically modeled the colors and emblems of the Liga México soccer team Club America. It is a completely off-beat and unique design, and I was immediately floored when I heard his description of this design, as I had seen the dress years before online in a photo collage of "unique quinceañera dress themes." Such an unlikely design, one that is not in any designer line, would

not have been possible without the collaboration of Jonathan with his particular collaborator cum soccer fan or the colleague who went out of his way
to recommend Jonathan's work. Jonathan's quinceañera industry networking predates the more organized methods of the quinceañera expo business
family, where expos bring together professionals for the purposes of networking as well as access to and convenience for the consumer.

Before La Pelu, Jonathan owned a smaller salon, and due in part to the
exposure offered to him through *Quinceañeras Magazine* expos, his clientele
has grown, and his visible reach in the community has expanded as his salon
has grown. He has space for four chairs in addition to his own. Despite the
increased visibility, with his creative work having appeared on four of six
consecutive *Quinceañeras Magazine* San Antonio covers, Jonathan still contends that word-of-mouth testimonials and direct observation remain the
best forms of advertising he has. Through those means he can assert a brand
of professional integrity that affirms that "su cara es mi tarjeta de negocio"
(her face is my business card) and "lo mal hecho" (poorly done work) reflects
on the stylist, not the individual client's "capacidad de ser bonita" (capacity
to be pretty). Nowhere but in quinceañera marketing could this be a truer
or more ambivalent statement, as quinceañera girls often find their faces and
bodies displayed on the backs of photographers' and videographers' business
cards as products of professional skill that continue to recirculate and influence the next generation of quinceañera girls that follows.

Jonathan explained that he did not find the magazine but rather, "La
*Quinceañera Magazine* ha encontrado a mi" (*Quinceañeras Magazine* found
me). Their professional relation was established in 2009. Its inception, a
process of professional courtship, is a point of pride for this hardworking
entrepreneur. The national magazine recognized his skills and place in the
quinceañera cultural marketplace as one of the best and most innovative
professionals to reach a growing contingent of Latinx millennials. Its readers
would be eager to see dramatically visible and uniquely affirming social portraits for their coming-of-age events.

Similarly to Jonathan, Luis is cultural entrepreneur working as a creative
professional in the quinceañera beauty industry and more than anything
is eager to establish trends in quinceañera fashion and beauty. Luis established Royal Beauty Services in the winter of 2015 in collaboration with his
sister, Diana Kassandra. A model, modeling coach, and former quinceañera
dress model, Diana works exclusively in makeup, while Luis's expertise lies in
hairstyling. Luis identifies as "Latino, Hispanic, or all the above! It's so con-
fusing."[4] He and his family migrated to the United States from Guanajuato,
Mexico, in 2001. Luis was still a teenager and claims now that Kansas City,

Missouri, is his hometown. He identifies as being from the Midwest, saying, "We've spent the majority of our lives here." His family's goal above all is not to blend into regional culture but "to stand out." That desire figures into the philosophy Luis and his sister bring to their profession, "to break people's concept of the Midwest." Stylization of the quinceañera event in the greater midwestern region centralized in Kansas City allows Royal Beauty Services to instrumentalize personal, cultural experiences with the tradition alongside professional training to reach out to wider beauty markets that centralize Latina consumers. Luis's ambivalence toward ethnoracial monikers allies him with his clients, who are often not overlaying an ethnic narrative onto their brand of quinceañera practice and instead focus on creating the best, "most glamorous" version of themselves as American teenagers. Luis asserts that his role in this larger production of self is really to help girls realize their beauty potential. He said, "Most girls come to us not really understanding what glamour is for them." Much of his labor occurs before the application of foundation or the teasing of hair, in helping young women craft ideas of style that suit their personalities but also their bone structures, skin tones, or desired themes. Royal Beauty is only one of the team's interventions in the midwestern quinceañera professional beauty scene.

Luis is a self-taught creative who started working in the quinceañera beauty industry in 2012 with his former business partner Bryan Aguirre and occasionally Diana Kassandra, whose modeling career was developing alongside theirs as a styling team. Even before then, Luis and Diana started working with smaller-scale local expos run by Kansas City–based business magazines that promoted area niche businesses. Quinceañera services were part of those broader industry expos, and Luis and his sister would conceptualize and manage runway fashion shows that featured seasonal quinceañera fashion. He explained, "We had creative control over everything, girls, dresses, the entire fashion show. Now we are just getting started with *Quinceañeras Magazine*." He said he and his sister got started in business because of shifts in Latinx cultural practices that directly affect the market potential of beauty industries. "It's the market," he said. "A lot of people aren't getting married any more, so quinceañeras are a big, big market here." Luis didn't share statistical background to substantiate his comments, as his perspective emerges from and is directed toward lived experiences among Latinx communities in Kansas City.

His perspective is echoed in comments made by Jonathan, whose career longevity allows him a perspective Luis has yet to acquire in observing clients' social milestones. Jonathan said that in his line of work one gains a sense of people over time, and in his years in San Antonio he noticed in doing women's hair and makeup for special life milestones that Latinas were often having children, cohabitating, starting careers, and only later having wedding ceremonies for which his services would be sought. Rather than being able to depend on Latina clients in their early twenties to fill out their business schedules, Luis and Diana see the increased frequency of quinceañeras in their area of the Midwest as the market in which to stake a claim to ensure their career success. This market is served in part through professional expos as anchor points for accessing future clients. As much as a chance to feature artistic skill and creative potential, expos are places to gain professional traction needed to turn passion into a career. Expos of *Quinceañeras Magazine* as well as the smaller citywide events organized by professionals reframe the quinceañera event as a practice of ethnic or racial nostalgia or familial history but also as a specialized cultural product manifesting the influence of accepted notions of American social success and Mexican migrant entrepreneurship.

## STYLIZATION: RENDERING THE NATURAL AS MANUFACTURED

The professionalization of the quinceañera industry across the United States, as in these examples from San Antonio and Kansas City, is furnished by the expertise of migrant Mexican entrepreneurs who work to attract clienteles eager to make the most of their quinceañera events as platforms of successful self-branding. Together the professionals and their clients collaboratively render the process of gendered social production transparent as they benefit from revealing the contrived nature of beauty industries.

When I asked Jonathan Gutierrez his beauty philosophy, he laughed heartily and shared this adage: "No hay mujeres feas, sino maridos pobres" (There are no ugly wives, only poor husbands). Knowing his career as a fashion designer and stylist spanned many years and crossed international borders, I thought it was logical to attempt to analyze the ideology that tied his creative experiences together. His response surprised me but also invited me to reflect on his craft and his professional training as well as the criticism of beauty, privilege, and politics that runs rampant in the United States as well as Mexico and globally. Beauty is not a natural state of being; it is not neutral or universal, but as a concept it represents a relative judgment of shared appeal. Through his comment Jonathan affirmed his role as a professional in an industry that profits from the manufacturing of beauty, both ideologically and in practice. Beauty, in his statement, is a function of personal or familial resources. Beauty being judged by white, western, heteronormative, ableist standards may be purchased by the bottle or the tube, by the pill or the needle. Beauty privilege reflects the capacity to fit into standards of beauty that are allied with wealth and social success, increasing one's social capital as an individual in a society obsessed with the visual. One function of the hair and makeup specialists in quinceañera celebrations is to help young women accentuate and capitalize on their physical attractiveness. As a culturally relative concept, beauty privilege in the United States is decidedly western, with the occasional dispensation for exotic ethnicized and racialized attributes becoming currency in beauty industries' marketing of distinction and difference as raceless accessories of globalization.

Beauty privilege among USAmericans is available to those who approximate a particular ideal public presentation: light-skinned, straight-haired, able-bodied, heteronormative, and thin. In recent years androgyny and gender-fluid models have become increasingly visible, yet their attractiveness is still a specialty item that lacks currency in everyday modes of being and seeing. Similarly, as models deemed "plus size" are finding greater visibility in professional modeling circles, the popular backlash to unapologetically visible fat bodies is aggressive and persistent. Jonathan claims to be able to professionally intervene into that social and economic system, creating for even just a day the appearance of an ideal self that is projected from an internal value rather than external traits.

Both Jonathan and Luis have styled *Quinceañeras Magazine* cover girls in their given regions. Luis and Diana were chosen to style the cover model for the 2016 national edition of *Quinceañeras Magazine* that features the first National Miss Cover Girl, Dusty Rodriguez from Omaha, Nebraska. The magazine and expos provide a platform from which artists can feature their talents while also pushing the limits of expected quinceañera fashion and style by, as Jonathan explained, "creando la 'imagen' de la portada" (creating the cover girl look). These published looks give stylists creative control over the patterns of practice, eliciting a desire for glamour among the Latina teen audiences in their regions, and the covers are conceptualized by Jonathan and Luis as places to feature creative potential. They concur that the real work is helping an individual girl locate and identify with her own personal style and then materialize it. In these cases, expected practices of beauty are subverted to help design a customized hair and makeup look that encourages personal acceptance and features professional credibility.

Jonathan was hesitant to generalize at all about quinceañera girls or the professional culture surrounding the event. He assumed them to be in a state of constant becoming in which malleability is the key to personal development and professional success: "Each girl who comes into my salon is different. I have to do an individual assessment of each before we commit to a look." Potential looks are mediated by a variety of factors including personality of the girl, selected theme and dress style, and parental preferences. However, Jonathan was very clear that when a client trusts him they give over a credit card and their daughter and simply let him work uninterrupted. Jonathan shared that he has never encountered an irate parent who has disapproved of his work, "¡gracias a Dios!" (thank God!). He did share that he made an all-black gown with dark purple accents for a quinceañera "rockera" (rocker girl) that nearly gave her grandmother a heart attack: "Se parece que queria tener un infarto." His connection to dress, although seemingly appropriate as he is a fashion designer as well as hair and makeup artist, reveals the way the styling of dress, makeup, and hair are all fundamentally interdependent if one wants to assemble a cohesive look.

The construction of a quinceañera look is itself a contemporary one fueled by professional industries that benefit from inciting a sense of panic among young women who may look upon their quinceañeras as deconstructed events with isolated parts. Among professional styling teams, Jonathan and his staff as well as Luis and Diana, hair and makeup are facets of a style complex that is anchored by a choice in dress. Jonathan's rocker-girl black gown that stunned a quince girl's grandmother was accompanied by a stylized, feminine mohawk hairstyle. As neither mother nor daughter wanted an actual cut, Jonathan had to work extra hard to turn long strands into a centralized swoop of dark, loose curls brought to the center of her head by tight, cornrow-like braids that vertically lined the sides of her head. The vision of "la rockera" was what the girl brought with her to the salon. It was his job to use cosmetic techniques to bring her vision of beauty to life. This, he said, was one of his favorite events to style because it offered him wholesale control over dress, hair, and makeup so that the end result was a masterpiece of his own creation.

Many girls do not come with such creative or unique ideas regarding their events. Jonathan shared that most of the girls he works with are fairly "plano." He quickly corrected himself, restating in English that they were "plain," with less personal style. He remarked that this was of course not surprising, as they already had the most important beauty accessory, "la juventud" (youth). I took his initial turn of phrase as particularly insightful, noting that the quinceañera event in many cases takes girls with flat personalities, at a stage of great personal malleability, and offers them a dramatic space through which to show off their potential multidimensionality. The quinceañera offers one avenue through which girls can test the waters of a dramatic version of heterosexually defined "womanhood" and through it gain personal insight. Such insight is a product of the process of planning and negotiating elements of personal style that are aspects of a quest for social definition. It is a process of becoming that long precedes a final reveal in rented ballrooms and public halls. Many times, such a process of becoming is furnished through a personal encounter with a creative professional who offers not only the expertise to wield comb and brush like a magic wand but who also bears a brand of *confianza*, trust, that shapes their labor as they guide clients through a symbolic process of self-revelation.

Confianza comes in the form of honesty. Jonathan asserted, "Yo soy muy honesto" (I am very honest). While Jonathan admitted that he rarely tells people "No" to their ideas, he does urge his clients to think deeply about their style choices and whether those fit into their own personalities or are simply popular trends of the moment. He sees the quinceañera as an unrepeatable realm of possibility when for a day a young women can "lucir de adentro" (shine from within) while testing out different aspects of her personality than seen in daily life and turning the event into a dramatic stage. The process of becoming a quinceañera girl, the part that focuses on restyling her into a young woman, is not finite nor static but a sociocultural proposal, a staged potential, that a girl can develop, modify, or discard. Such is the case with simply choosing to celebrate a quinceañera or not.

While some have viewed the quinceañera as a gendered trap or even a system of heteronormative oppression, in professional industries "es lo que quiere ella" (it's what she wants), Jonathan said. His perspective shifted from a professional stylist to an uncle of two beloved nieces who he explained could not have been more different in their quinceañera practice. His older niece, Frida, celebrated her quinceañera in 2015, but her younger sister rejected the tradition, claiming she instead wanted to celebrate a sweet-sixteen party. Frida, he shared, "tiene mas raices mexicanas" (has more Mexican roots), while his younger niece "tiene tradiciones de aquí" (holds traditions from here), the United States. His nieces' roots in Mexico run deep, he said, but he also finds value in being a professional stylist from Mexico who is presumed to have a cultural reference point that matches parental ideals of femininity and propriety. What he really understands, though, is the affective link between becoming a quinceañera girl and seeing a quinceañera event for the first time. Jonathan worked collaboratively with his niece Frida on making her a custom dress and styling her hair and makeup to match. His perspective on the quinceañera became deeply personal after their first dress fitting: "La primer prueba de vestido, yo lloré junto a ella" (During our first dress fitting, I cried with her). This he described as his primary motivation for styling quinceañera girls, that of being able to see the changes on their faces when his work is complete but also the moment when their parents see their little girls as women for the first time. Seeing the passage of time, cost and time no longer matter.

On the surface, Jonathan's work with quinceañera girls is based on surface, material transformation, but most of his labor is with clients' emotional and psychological aspirations. His work is to help foster the personal transformation implied by the ritual of coming of age. His ideal quinceañera girl is the *vanguardista*, a young woman with creative ideas and an interest in being "lo único" (the only one). She is a person with whom he can collaborate rather than guide through a process of personal production. Their collaboration involves using makeup and hairstyling to project her individual personality rather than replacing it with an empty, fashionable shell. This is why *Quinceañeras Magazine* has turned to Jonathan often, not because he does hair or makeup so much better than his regional competitors but because he knows how to use his material skills to evoke an image. Vanguardistas appear to be the most self-aware, self-assured, and able to articulate a version of themselves they desire to feature in their quinceañera events. These girls, Jonathan remarked, understand personality and presence as context-specific. He illustrated this point by sharing with me his work on *Quinceañeras Magazine* fashion runways, where he works with "niñas reales" (real girls) who are rarely model types but instead can rise as finalists because they understand how to "manejar el ecenario" (work the stage).

Jonathan's work in part is to help young women find the inner confidence to rise beyond the limited structures of surface beauty to learn the skill of self-conscious transformation. He offers girls a tutorial on the backstage structure of the quinceañera ritual as a practice of beauty technologies to illustrate the way women's social success is often predicated on their ability to be social chameleons, changing and modifying their manner as the stage shifts. Fashion in his estimation is about changing attitudes, moods, and outlooks on life outside the salon. "Cuando alguien llega y me dice, 'soy fea,' yo le digo 'da me chansa.' Si veo a diez personas, se hace diez personas feliz. Es rejuvenecedor" (When someone arrives at my salon and says "I'm ugly," I tell them "Give me a chance." If I see ten clients in a day, I make ten people happy. It's rejuvenating).

As he is a professional stylist, Jonathan's work in hair and makeup fuse and come to represent a broader structure of material transformation in sync with other stylistic elements as well as his personal attitude during the creative process. His clients depend on Jonathan to be confident in his work so they can find confidence in themselves. He claims to cultivate an honest and supportive relationship with clients when they arrive at his shop and that there is no better advertising than making one of their peers look beautiful. Girl-to-girl peer networks drive Jonathan's quinceañera business, much like that of Luis, who finds that girls see their friends' quinceañera styling and want an entirely new look but of the same quality. The peer networks depend on the circulation of professional portraiture in person and online for the businesses' success. Trust is more clearly engendered in new clients through viewing Jonathan's work on the cover of *Quinceañeras Magazine* San Antonio. Word-of-mouth recommendations, often after a friend's or cousin's quinceañera party, are the most common, followed by girls Jonathan says "me encontró como tú" (found me like you did). I found his work by attending the expo hosted by *Quinceañeras Magazine* in San Antonio, just like a large number of his teenage clients did. His skills as a quinceañera industry specialist are seen in the cover art he envisioned and the quinceañera as a product of Latinx entrepreneurs in the United States.

For the Royal Beauty team, Luis and Diana, the clientele is "70–80 percent quinceañeras." This huge percentage shows that their work and passion focus on engineering trends in quinceañera culture in the greater Midwest. The labor of the look is focused on creative collaborations, and the emotional labor of convincing a Latina mother that her daughter is in competent hands. "The girls trust us, but the moms, they take a while," Diana told me. She said Royal Beauty Services' goals lie in not only simple beautification but also the experimental capacity of makeup and hairstyling to transform perspectives on what constitutes acceptable beauty practice. Unlike Jonathan, who has an affective relation to his work, Luis and Diana are more removed and offer a different perspective on their role in the industry as creatives looking to impact the way quinceañeras look in the twenty-first century. Luis explained,

> We have to guide them. . . . The quinceañera industry has been
> revolutionized in the last couple of years, you know. It's not just
> the quinceañera [girl] and her white dress. Now they have themes
> and all these outrageous colors. I would say a lot of it has to do
> with social media. It makes them want to be really glamorous. Not
> everyone has the exact idea of what glamour is, so that's when we
> step in.

Luis shared that with regard to hair, girls require coaching and coaxing on specific styling rather than on generalized self-esteem. His intervention is best characterized as saving girls from bad ideas that make bad photographs. The professional photography industry works hand in hand with styling professionals who modulate their work with how and when a girl will be photographed.

Jonathan said that when a girl is going to get her portrait done two to three months prior to her actual celebration, the makeup must be impeccable, often more finely detailed than what is done on her actual quinceañera day. After the event, the portraiture will remain and serve as a memory of the coming-of-age drama, but also the timeless and flawless skill of industry professionals. Jonathan narrated his extensive experience working closely with quinceañeras and their families, even the intimate disclosure of being himself an emotional uncle. His preference is giving individualized attention and stewardship for transitioning Latina bodies.

Luis's work in Kansas City and the Midwest is still primarily focused on developing characteristic style as a professional creative. His experiences have led his drive toward formalization of offered services and honing the craft. Luis's perspective is that of an entrepreneur who is also a Latinx millennial who came of age in the United Sates, and his creative work engenders a sense of self-definition in his own right rather than the promotion of affective experiences between generations. Our Skype conversation took place in the winter of 2016, just after the end of a busy quinceañera season, which he noted is extending further and further from spring and summer months into fall and early winter. He was quick to add that midwestern ice often keeps parties from being planned in the coldest months, January and February. He and Diana center their work on the basic premise of difference. They are eager to manipulate beauty technologies in innovative ways to guide the quinceañera market in new directions. Quinceañera girls seeking Royal Beauty Services bring in photographs printed from the internet that depict other girls' quinceañera events or formally styled celebrity hair and makeup. Rather than walking the girls through analyses of preference and theme, he often voices his discontent for their lack of creativity directly.

> They come to us with theme picked out and images from the internet. And I just have to tell them, "Do you really want something that someone's already done, or do you want something different?"

This notion of difference is often considered antithetical to the production of tradition in which change is often confused with distortion. These creatives are using difference as a stylistic tool to entice young women to infuse new life into traditional practice. Luis and Diana said they use their time doing hair and makeup at expos to show girls "what's trending." At a 2015 appearance at the *Quinceañeras Magazine* expo in Des Moines, Luis styled a model who wore a gown by guest designer Adán Terriquez. Luis said Terriquez designs "beautiful gowns that are classic and elegant," and yet this aesthetic is not the style that Luis or Diana wish to associate with the work of Royal Beauty. Luis recognized the opportunity, as the special 2015 Mexicanisimo collection of gowns was being featured as a surprise for expo attendees. The dresses portray romantic Mexican nationalism using mariachi accents, gold side clasps, and equestrian embroidery designs. The challenge for Luis was to construct a hairdo that would set his work apart from the classic traditional, or expected styles while capitalizing on its increased visibility on the expo stage. The style was a high, teased bouffant with extra-large accent curls and long braids that employed hair extensions for special drama and volume. The hairstyle was coupled with makeup set off by pale hues and bright-white lipstick.

Together the hair and makeup combination was otherworldly and in my estimation resembled what he and I later humorously deemed "Mexican Marie Antoinette." This three-part hair structure has become Luis's personal trademark since developing it further with Royal Beauty clients. It gained favor in his repertoire after he admitted to growing tired of doing the same style multiple times in the same season. While this pattern bores him as an artist, it is also detrimental to the business, as the advertising networks are generated through online postings of hair and makeup designs with the company profile tagged. Every tagged photo is a de facto business card and every comment stream a business review. "We don't ever try to do the same thing twice," Diana said. That particular runway design was not constructed to give young teens in the audience a style to admire and re-create locally; it was a point from which to imagine the possibilities of their own personal styles. The now trademark Luis style is constructed from drawing on three distinct styles and choosing parts from each to incorporate into unique amalgamations. It emerged when a young bride wanted a hair design that was "vintage" but "modern," and her husband insisted there also be a "braid" included. It was a risk, but the end result of 1940s-style pin curls in front, messy "bridal" curls in back, and asymmetrical braid not only were loved by the bride and her family but also led to a multitude of similar requests. Even Luis sounded a bit incredulous about the popularity of this tri-style do, and yet it reflects the capacity for innovation through collaboration. Rather than simply repeating past designs, he embraced innovation to ignite imagination.

Parallel experimental ideology characterizes Diana's makeup applications. Part of what Luis calls the "revolutionizing of the quinceañera industry" is characterized by the simple introduction of colored gowns. More than adding bright hues, it was the addition of choice, any color, any hue, any texture that can be found, made, or requested by quinceañera girls with money to spend. Diana Kassandra shared a very simple professional mantra with me—

unexpected combinations. When dresses used to be primarily white or pastel, a natural face or minimal makeup suited the tradition. With the inclusion of quinceañera style in wider fashion circles facilitated by industry professionals, color carries new weight in putting the image of the quinceañera together. Diana Kassandra explained:

> I like working with color, and putting together colors that they [clients] wouldn't think of together. They come with color ideas that look a lot like other people, so I suggest they do a pop of color here or glitter or sparkles there to give them ideas about how to stand out.

While standing out is important for girls in their peer networks who do not wish to share colors or party details with each other, young women are also differentiating themselves from their families' past. Luis said, "Moms have a vision for their daughters. . . . Many have ideas of what they wanted to look like for their quinceañera." But girls are eager to curate designs that suit their own personalities and US lives. The integration of styles that are outside the approval of ethnically or traditionally sanctioned practices in the quinceañera event create an outward trajectory letting external cultural influences replenish the celebration through innovations in hairstyles and makeup. Parents, in this case mothers, are no longer the primary force behind the event; parents are the sources of financial support who offer their credit cards and their trust to the professionals crafting their quinceañera girls' enduring styles. Royal Beauty's style ideology of "romantic, with an edge" has lasting effects as the stylists' work, like that of other creatives, becomes immortalized through quinceañera portraiture that captures the artistry of migrant Mexican entrepreneurs as representations of Latinx culture in the contemporary United States.

### PORTRAITS, HISTORY, RECUERDOS

Although the quinceañera is labeled a "Latina" tradition, the celebration's roots are obscure, in particular its connection to indigenous practices from Mexico. Even the event's ubiquitous gown, *el traje colonial*, uses aesthetic standards of continental fashion that was made popular during Mexico's colonial period. Such a dress does colonialize the body as it makes reference to the historical transition between precolonial and European influences on what is now modern Latin America. Across the Americas the narratives are unique to regions and countries but amalgamated in the United States under the moniker "Latinx"; the attendant cultural practices compress distinct Latin American histories into shared celebrations. Rather than considering the quinceañera a remnant of the past, it is more productive to examine it as a manifestation of the present. As an expression of culture and identity among its participants, the nature of beauty and privilege it embodies is western. Whatever the quinceañera might have been in earlier epochs, in the twenty-first century it is a westernized tradition that demonstrates a communal desire to maintain a through-line to cultural heritage but in a form that reflects a brand of successful social integration.

The process of westernization in quinceañera celebrations is visible in the beauty standards on display and required of its successful participants. Professional stylists are gatekeepers in efforts to westernize brown bodies, and yet the intimate labor of their trade engenders trust in clients who also see them as confidants. The impact of their work is as much emotional and psychological as it is physical. While patterns in innovative restyling of ritual adornments reflects a presumed westernization of community values, the moniker "westernization" is greatly limited and even false. A westernizing perspective might have had currency when one was examining quinceañera celebration in transition from a precolonial to colonial moment in Latin America, but no such relation to history exists among US Latinxs who are born directly into western culture. The quinceañera itself is a product of westernizing ideologies that spawned a need for national identity in a new Mexican nation. Its latest iteration is therefore not newly westernized but instead consumerized to the extent that the tradition takes on a brand of cosmopolitanism. Contemporary quinceañeras are not exclusively the product of public or private historical narratives that would root the traditions in local pasts. They are the product of consumer desire that looks outward to ethnic-specific narratives and welcomes external influences particularly from fashion and beauty industries.

One unassuming offshoot of beauty industries serving quinceañeras is professional photography and videography. Professional photographers are part of the quinceañera industry as they serve two main purposes. First, they often document the entire quinceañera event, from the morning wakeup through the hairstyling and makeup application to the mass and reception until the wee hours of the next morning. Second, they contribute to the materialization of a social history of quinceañeras in the United States through the staging of professional portraits. In other areas of the Hispanic Americas like Cuba, portraiture is the primary quinceañera production, as many practicing families cannot or choose not to hold large parties for their daughters; in the United States, portraiture is one branch of a the larger quinceañera consumer complex (Härkönen).

Quinceañera portraits can be understood as self-oriented recuerdos. The customary practice of offering guest recuerdos, memory objects, at quinceañeras, baptisms, and weddings among Latinx communities signals a desire to use collective events to piece together a community narrative of shared experience. In the 1990s, when I was coming of age, capias were the common memory objects. The small, colored, scalloped ribbons were embossed with the event name and date and the name of the celebrant. Such objects were keepsakes that families collected to remind them of family milestones while also representing an informal log of family life as reminders of the unrecorded memories or happenings that transpired between individuals. One woman I ran into while shadowing quinceañeras in California told me every time she looked at her daughter's quinceañera recuerdo she remembered how her daughter and her damas took off their shoes to dance after their formal waltz and how she was riddled with embarrassment that her own mother saw this. She even repeated her mother's wise words about women's shoe fashions: "If you can't wear them all night, you shouldn't wear them at all!"

Recuerdos serve myriad purposes, some collective and readable, others idiosyncratic and deeply personal. When one considers portraiture a form of recuerdo, the narrative that emerges is quite personal. While professional creatives are invested in styling in the present, they are also tasked to create images that will endure, aging well even when the subjects do not. By attempting to understand the relation between professionals and their quinceañera clients, memory and memorability emerge as key themes in styling and marketing quinceañera girls as artistic products. At the same time, it must be acknowledged that it is the young Latina woman whose body bears the burden of collective memory.

Returning the focus to the expo space with larger-than-life images of quinceañeras models and life-size cardboard photo cutouts of quinceañera girls, one can begin to see how more than simply documenting the present, the Latina body is made into a site of commemoration. Through materialized portraiture it becomes a material access point to family history, a US Latinx social historical narrative that is in part being constructed, in some cases, primarily through migrant Mexican queer entrepreneurs. Such an interpretation gently radicalizes these patterned portraits and allows observers to rethink the history and purpose of the quinceañera event beyond the strictures of heteronormativity as having been nuanced by the emotional and physical labor of queer hands. A discussion of professional beauty industries only lays bare the professional influences that are setting the tone and pace of the rapidly expanding quinceañera beauty industry. It is primarily queer men whose creative labor is being overlaid on a tradition that cannot wholly be classified as heteronormative any longer but rather a product of myriad social and economic influences. The role that queer creatives are playing and have likely played cannot be ignored in the construction of heterosexual desire in generations of quinceañera practice that now only exist in photographic memory. Those memories are integral to the social life of this feminine Latina spectacle that mobilizes the image of the adorned brown body across space and time.

The stylization of quinceañera beauty practice mirrors the dramatic shift in portraiture. I could walk into a family home and see a ten-by-twelve-inch framed formal head shot taken at a young woman's party, but portraiture has taken on a new life that leads into the celebration and endures long after it ends. It appears in tongue-in-check cardboard cutouts as a kind of quinceañera mascot, and yet these photos also appear in newspaper articles as tragic reminders of those lost before their time. Most dramatically, the images serve as ways to customize space and, I assert, Latinize spaces of public use.

The art historian and visual art critic Jennifer A. González defines "autotopography" as a "syntagmatic array of physical signs in a spatial representation of identity" (133). Objects organize an affective grammar through which an individual as artist can cultivate a space for self-representation. Moreover, it refers to "a spatial, local, and situational 'writing' of the self's life in visual art" (133). Javier Durán describes it as the materialization of a "psychic body," both individual and potentially shared (62). In the remapping of memory and nostalgia in space, these material assemblages offer a "'counter-site' to both resist and converse with mass-media images" (63). A political lens forms around what is made and what is seen as who is made and who is seen.

González's initial framing of the term applies it to the work of professionally trained artists and especially connects the creation of autotopographic art scenes as political acts in western museum spaces. An example is the work of Puerto Rican artist Pepón Osorio, whose dramatic and elaborate domestic scenes recall his complex relation to and longing for home. More recently, media studies scholars (Petrelli et al.) have used the concept to refer to the everyday objects as well as digital artifacts, photos, and video maintained by households to recall shared family histories. The artifacts, material and digital, recast home spaces as autotopographic zones of creativity—intimate spaces that tell a story and overlay authorship with ownership. This is particularly important as one can consider quinceañera practice as a product of Latinx youth occupying public spaces and claiming a right to be present beyond barrio spaces, whether materially or ideologically.

The quinceañera as a one-time event becomes space through which to stage material objects and preserve them in different stages of use and display. I will consider for a moment representations of the quinceañera material arts in digital space, namely the quinceañera trousseau. A trousseau is a traditional assemblage of goods designated for a bride in preparation for a wedding and includes home and personal goods in preparation for married life. For a quinceañera the assemblage of goods is the collection of material objects put together for her quinceañera day—dress, shoes, bouquet, religious objects as desired, tiara, and other jewelry. All carry mutually informative affective and consumer narratives with them, transforming what Durán terms "integral objects" into "autobiographical matter" (63) in the present to index a future status. They are also gathered as representations of feminine maturation, what Cantú calls a system of "feminine symbology" ("Chicana"). They form a material composition that documents the cultural practice as a consumer practice in which the same objects are linked to aspirational class narratives mediated by budgeting, branding, and buying infused with optimistic potential—that of an upscale Latinx consumer.

In reality, these objects are only ordered together in memorial photography and videography. They become part of online quinceañera representation as professional videos are posted online in digital portfolios, however contrived they may be. They are an intellectualization sending a marker of remembrance into the past, representational bread crumbs leading future quince girls to the situational self-portraiture of their quinceañera predecessors who wanted to be seen and now want to be remembered.

Portrait photography becomes a key locus for thinking about materiality and representation in quinceañera culture. While the material objects have but a short shelf life, often in use only once and then finding their way onto regional Craigslist resale pages or trash-the-dress photo shoots, their representations endure. Trousseau and images like them that distill the quinceañera event to a small body of material goods take autotopographic strategies into digital space, where material assemblages become digital photographic on social media. Quinceañera memory videos that include images of trousseau items as part of the preparation process are regularly posted to quinceañera-themed YouTube channels, yet it is the quinceañera herself that becomes the most potent ephemeral display. As the objects are integrated, the young brown body becomes the newest commodity manipulated in space.

Unlike popular assumptions, the day of the girl's quinceañera is not her first day in heels or with makeup. For some this reality is much more stark, as girls who regularly wear makeup allow their quinceañera makeup to be the work of another, a professional or family member. For others the professional makeup and hairstyling process is not new, as it is the custom that young women take portraits in their formal gowns and crowns that then grace their formal invitations and are often hung in dramatic fashion at the entrance or head table of the quinceañera reception.

Jonathan said his work, the labor for the portrait, is "mas detallado" (more detailed) because "es cuando la mas enfoque" (it is when one focuses the most). These photos are also the most likely to be uploaded to Facebook pages and Instagram accounts and become implicit advertising for professionals seeking to reach young clients through social media. Each portrait tells multiple stories. It narrates personal development of a young Latina and the affluence or ingenuity of her family to afford formal portraits and professional beauty services, but it also tells the story of a burgeoning Latinx professional class whose business acumen and advertising skills are a valid and inescapable part of cultural accommodation and integration of Latinxs in the United States.

## MAKING OVER THE COMMODITY FETISH

The commoditization of the quinceañera process has resulted in a bind in that turning the event into a cultural product has taken away its sociocultural sanctity but at the same time allowed it to thrive in changing Latinx communities. While it might seem that a discussion of quinceañera beauty professionals is a discussion of the dissolution of traditional value of the celebration, what truly emerges is a desire to make memories and document community experiences. Examining the experiences and ideologies of a body of beauty industry professionals highlights the consumer influence on the cultural logics of the celebration but also reveals the significance of the backstages of quinceañera performance that are rooted in teaching self-awareness and lauding originality while continuing a tradition that allows families to connect with their ethnoracial roots. The work of Jonathan, Luis, and Diana as stylists reveals the quinceañera tradition from the perspectives of cultural entrepreneurs who are not fixated on ideologies of race politics but live and experience their Latinx identities in the United State differently and translate those experiences into their professional lives in shaping traditional practice. Moreover, their work shows how the quinceañera, as a performance of a visible self, becomes an affective visual narrative communicating social transformation above all else. This is evident in the fundamentally contrived nature of modern beauty schema that can be purchased one tube at a time. But also, economic privilege enables a new visible legacy for Latinx consumers. Part of this social transformation is the work of a Latinx entrepreneurial class of those who have drawn from their personal experiences and formal professional training to revamp the cultural tradition as a cultural product in a new sociocultural frame. And while critics might scoff and claim that his entire professional enterprise is a waste of money, I offer Jonathan's words to me speaking of his relation to his nieces: "La alegria, para ver un ser humano que mas lo amas—un hijo—transformado, sin precedentes, increíble" (The joy in seeing a person you love the most—a child—transformed, it's unprecedented, incredible).

## CHAPTER 5

# AMBIVALENT EMBODIMENT

## Reconstituting Quinceañera Performance Space

*Empiezes a ser visible. No solamente se trata de irrumpir con otra propuesta de otra corporalidad en el espacio público, sino de entender a los otros que son parte de ti, saber que hay otras realidades, otros estilos de vida y otras formas de estar, de poner el cuerpo en el espacio.*

*(You begin to be visible. The goal is not only to try to interject another approach from another corporality into public space, but rather to understand that others are part of you, to know that there are other realities, other lifestyles, and other forms of being, of placing the body in space.)*

LÍA LA NOVIA SIRENA

I had to catch my breath. We had been running to get out of the rain and took cover under the awning of a bistro. I was staying at the edge of Roma Norte and Doctores, two very different socioeconomic areas of central Mexico City.[1] We were headed deeper into Roma, leaving Doctores behind us, and the houses were historic and stately, not dingy or crumbling as they had been only blocks before. We briefly stopped to catch our breath and wait out the downpour. Lía assured me that this, the unexpected torrential downpour, was normal for Mexico City in the summer. I admit, it added to the romantic traveler quality of the first evening of my first visit to the impressive labyrinth of a city. Young adolescent girls begged our attention from a bench in front of the restaurant as if to ask for the time, only to try and sell us chocolates. Lía politely passed, and we went on our way. The rain was gentler now, and it was easy to find brief respite as we walked close to buildings as the center strips of the uneven sidewalks pooled with runoff. Following closely on Lía's heels, hoping not to fall behind, I realized I had not traversed a big city in many years. The streets smelled like sewage and moisture mixed with the wafting scent of street cuisine. Lía was eager for me to connect with the city, to feel it as she does. Our schedule was so packed with locations to visit and experience and the city so magnificently large, I wouldn't have any time to simply wander the streets. No one seemed to wander here. Everyone had a look of intention and exhaustion on their faces. We seemed to be scurrying around people back and forth, making our way through commuter foot traffic and bus lines, through the maze of downtown, through the Zona Rosa, and finally coming up for air at the Paseo de la Reforma. In front of us looming over the bustling financial district was El Ángel. The Angel of Independence is a towering victory column in the center of a roundabout on Paseo de la Reforma in downtown Mexico City. It was commissioned during the presidency of Porfirio Diaz and designed by architect Antonio Rivas Mercado. It is considered one of the most recognizable monuments in the city and is a public gathering site. Lía nonchalantly mentioned that protests and community events like Mexico City's Pride Parade start here. It was commissioned to commemorate the centennial of the start of Mexico's War of Independence. Today, Lía said, it is *the* site to take quinceañera portraits.

We stood across the street, gazing upward, watching people photograph themselves into history. I realized that this site, like capitol buildings and city halls in Austin, Des Moines, Lincoln, and San Francisco, is a space of quinceañera performance. These are settings where young Latina women place themselves in larger social and political narratives of rightful belonging. This story is one where rightful representation is contested, as bodies and feelings fail to sync, and where public representations can be questioned and successful engagement with quinceañera style is interpreted as socially deceptive in the context of racialized capitalism. I refer to this phenomenon as "cultural *engaño*."

Through an examination of Mexican and American queer quinceañera performances I view the notion of engaño, deception, that is shared by the creative corpus of work by performance artist Lía García. The representations of the ritual invite a rethinking of the reception of youth performance as a cynical event of middle-class passing in which social perceptions of Latinx Americans harbor a disconnect between social performances of aspirational and realized class advancement. As such, they mark quinceañeras as cultural engaño, vicious deceptions of class standing. I assert that from both intra- and extracultural perspectives, quinceañera celebrations are critiqued as inappropriate or wasteful because they are assumed to be attempts at passing for middle-class status in US society and the internalized assumption that a strong Latinx middle class does not exist. The fantasy of the event extends far beyond courtly waltzes and fairytale themes and directly criticizes the dreams of young Latinxs and their families to be upwardly mobile in America, rendering intentionally inspirational events delusional and dishonest.

When most people think about quinceañeras they imagine bounded, private spaces—hotel ballrooms, rented historic houses, church halls, or even private backyards. But there are also many public zones in cities across the United States and Mexico, likely across greater Latin America as well, that hold quinceañera memory and with it the presenting of gendered derivative youth culture that might not be seen as socially integrated or important otherwise. While the image of young women in platform wedges or stiletto heels climbing the steps of important civic sites and historic monuments is not interesting, what is interesting is the way other, unexpected public places come to hold the memory of quinceañera occupation and with it a new sense of signification for the event and its representative forms.

Lía's corpus of quinceañera-themed performance art, which she broadly terms "encuentros afectivos" (affective encounters), represents a strategy for self-representation that rejects the inscription of tradition, and instead authors an unstable and ambivalent narrative of potential and possibility that belies the reality of comfortable repetition of form and meaning (Bhabha 1). Her performances are both creative and destructive—engineering connections between histories of heteronormative performance and queer absence in the quinceañera's sociocultural narrative through affective performance while breaking down boundaries between heterosexual and transgender subjectivities as her encounters close the gaps in social and material bodies. Lía herself lives a border life; her trans body becomes a place of transition and a connection to "presencing," a performative mindset in which "the actions we perform originate in the coming-into-presence of the future" (Scharmer). Her embodied performances as a quinceañera celebrant reinforce her social role as an interstice, a physical location where domains of difference overlap and are displaced (Bhabha 1). In this space of quinceañera performance, Lía becomes more than a sum of biological parts of social relations; she is a subject in formation. Such being and becoming are grounded through performative practice in which Lía as an artist interjects the possibility of queer subjectivity and the reality of transgender subjectivity into the raced, classed, and gendered celebration of quince años in Mexico. Choosing to restage the past through the interjection of transgender subjectivity into quinceañera celebration in a variety of affective, public performances asserts Lía's "right to signify from the periphery of authorized power and privilege" (Bhabha 3), and it foregrounds her desire to claim her own public space as a mujer trans.[2] Lía's performance style and personal politics, while pushing toward the beyond, embody a return to the present of spatial intimacy, of emotional encounters, where through practice her individual body becomes a collective body.

The quinceañera not only occupies but also simultaneously changes social space. The event itself is a physical space materialized through a combination of inanimate objects and people who together diversely and at times obliquely manifest senses of intimacy connected to family, historicity, nationalism, and social mores. Such overlapping experiences can be disarticulated to see the quinceañera conceptually as an intellectual space, gendered space, cultural space, and sociohistorical space through which individual lives are refracted at a particular moment.

Through an analysis of three quinceañera performance texts, I use a framework of engaño to examine how the artist uses variable quinceañera performance spaces to disclose her contested trans Mexican feminine body in public, a practice that puts her life at risk, as violence against trans bodies is often directly preceded by interpretations of unexpected discovery. Such revealing performances center on tenderness, compassion, and honesty and refract tensions around hostile public interpretations of quinceañera celebrations in the United States as consumerist, wasteful, and deceptive. Lía's performances, which use the quinceañera as a gender-queer and intellectual space, contrast the event's defamation as a economic-consumerist space, where hostile interpretations of the celebrations emanate not from genuine engagement with the tradition or its social significance but a sense of engaño, of malicious deception. In this space, quinceañera practice is a costly expenditure that is assumed to be out of sync with the financial resources of Latinx communities of practice and is therefore interpreted as a pattern of deception. Such extracultural and extrasocial interpretations minimize and even negate the existence of a thriving Latinx middle class in the United States.

## QUINCEAÑERA SPACE

A discussion of space with regard to quinceañera practice must be divided into two large initial categories, the quinceañera as a space and the space that the quinceañera can occupy. These two categories peer into the tradition from distinct vantage points, one from within and the other from without. The quinceañera as an independent space, a space of cultural and gendered performance, has been the subject of this work thus far. This perspective acknowledges the way culture is materialized and constituted through the manipulation of third-party spaces to annex zones of performance for an individual girl and her family. This quinceañera space is where decorations hang, tables hold elaborate centerpieces, and through the entrance of a young women in an elaborate gown, social and cultural transition occurs. Quinceañera space is a resignification of space, of ballrooms and backyards. This space is fixed, chosen, and marked by families and professional planners. At times this space has been one of ritual accumulation used multiple times over, gaining a reputation as an ideal space where quinceañeras regularly happen. These are places like the Val Air ballroom in Des Moines, a private venue that advertises specifically for prospective quinceañeras.

Private spaces of quinceañera performance can become inadvertently public, where members of the public contest notions of privacy. One young man who discussed attending quinceañera celebrations in his youth told me that where he lived in South Texas, quinceañera celebrations were never allowed to be private. He and his friends would hear about local parties on both sides of the border and attend, crashing the events without invitation or ticket and often bypassing private security. Indeed, these violations of quinceañera performance space are commonly reported in seasonal news stories of uninvited community members looking to party or seeking out attendees for undisclosed nefarious purposes to interrupt quinceañera events. Party crashers are the expected pushback to the privatization common among quinceañeras in the United States and those of upper-class practitioners in Mexico. In the US, such spatial tension is documented in reports of violence and other criminal activity that audiences often assume are a regular occurrence in Latinx barrios. Private space and private celebration are framed as a privilege of the upper classes and public street performance as the purview of the working class. The space of quinceañera performance becomes space where ambivalently gendered subjectivities appear in physical and at times public space.

In contrast, spaces quinceañeras can occupy are varied. They are characterized by the presence of quinceañera culture but are not simply performance spaces; they also are spaces of commerce. They are public locales like El Ángel that exist all over cities and towns where quinceañera traditions break into public culture. In San Jose, California, the bridge at the Japanese friendship garden is a common place to find quinceañera girls and their courts being photographed on Saturday mornings. In Austin, the Tejano Heritage Monument can have a line of quinceañeras in peak season waiting to be photographed alone or with their *chambelanes de honor*, inserting themselves in a narrative of Texas history, Tejano representation, and the Latinx future of the state while creating a temporary representative space that materially manifests their sociocultural liminality between Americanness and Tejanidad. Churches represent spaces where quinceañeras can be seen and where their social memory lingers. Carmen Lomas Garza's 2008 painting *Quinceañera* presents the image of family and court of honor in pink gowns lingering outside a Catholic church while the quinceañera girl waits in a car fixing her hair, an image that is unmistakable for a wedding or funeral, or other life-cycle ritual. One can tour any Latinx neighborhood in the country and see overdressed youth sweating in the summer sun, sometimes even waiting outside for the previous quinceañera to finish before they can take their ceremonial places. Such is the case at the Church of the Five Wounds in the Alum Rock district of San Jose. The beautiful historic church with glittering chandeliers and stained glass is booked solid for a year in advance of quinceañera celebrations.

Quinceañeras also exist in dress boutiques, in commercial expos, and on billboards, physical spaces where the tradition lives. These spaces are not places of transition but of consumer representation. The consumer space of quinceañeras has overtaken much of the public culture of the event in the United States. The consumer narrative dominates the representation of the event precisely because quinceañera spaces have developed as decidedly private, family-oriented events. The only public culture accessible to wider publics are those that focus on selling the diverse body of celebratory accessories, including the sale of space itself! In quinceañera spaces gender subjectivity is contextualized in zones that have multilayered signification and that at times are characterized as out of place or inappropriate.

A third category of quinceañera space, and this will allow thinking deeply about Lía's artistic productions dedicated to bringing the event into the public sphere in Mexico City, is the space of the body. Particularly visible in the other two spatial frames, the young brown body is a space where quinceañeras happen but also where quinceañera memory can linger in public space and in plain view. Adorning the body is a key way of claiming personal bodily space and defying or acquiescing to the expectations of others. Critiques of such frames of personal expression imply a kind of external ownership of the body—that an individual is beholden to external standards of raced and classed respectability politics. The body becomes a transitional space teetering between public and private subjectivities, from where the quinceañera is introduced into public, intracultural and extracultural space, spaces of family and friends, but out into the wider world beyond the geopolitical and digital barrios. It is at this interstitial zone that domains of difference affect the reception of the celebration or its representational allusions. Borders on the body become marked by material and ideological codes of social expectation. This is the spatial zone from which Lía's performances emerge. She uses quinceañera practice to publicly claim her transgender subjectivity while also interjecting queerness into quinceañera practice and layering upon that the interjection of quinceañeras into public spaces—displacing narratives in the quinceañera's social history as having a complete and impenetrable hetero-normative character. Lía's claiming of gender nonbinary space for mujeres trans in the quinceañera celebration is tinged with complications. To intro-duce a nonbinary possibility into the performance practice, she destroys the accepted premise of the event entirely. And by using her own body in tran-sition to hold space, she immediately faces the possibility of violent removal from space or the negation of her right to exist in space previously claimed as exclusively cis-gendered. The body of work, the tradition, must be transfig-ured to suit the needs of a new generation whose notions of gender presenta-tion are complex, dynamic, and generative.

Violation of space, particularly the quinceañera as gendered space, is pred-icated on a hierarchy of social expectation. Expectations are based on the repetition of traditional representations that socialize audiences to assume quinceañera bodies are biologically female. In Lía's case, this is where her street theater begins, through embracing this violated expectation. By begin-ning her encounters with this premise, she runs an intense performative risk, as her body in public space becomes a vulnerable and exposed text to be read and judged. At its riskiest, Lía's body, like any transgender body, may be read as a lie, as a betrayal of expectation. As such, she must balance her desire to claim queer space in public with the real chance that her very presence pushes back on an assumption that bodies deemed marginal or nonbinary cannot claim public space without the fear of rejection and dismissal. Here I would like to elaborate on a framework of engaño that pervades the lives of mujeres trans in Mexico and quinceañera girls in the United States. While not ex-perienced in the same way or with the same gravitas, the idea of deception plagues public performances of difference that fail to meet a social burden of proof expected by majoritarian culture groups.

Notions of engaño can only exist when the accusing party presumes to interpret social norms "correctly," leaving those culpable in need of justify-ing the existence of their subject position in the world. Lía's embodied pub-lic presentations fit in between and draw on aspects of the traditional expec-tations of quinceañera space and quinceañera representational space. Her works re-create in material form quinceañera space; the familiar material forms serve to recast public venues, plazas, street corners, metro stations, and hotel lobbies into intimate spaces of social transformation and bodily transition—the key symbolic frames of the ritual celebration shared by Lía as a mujer trans undergoing her own biological and social transition. Her choices of venue, public spaces around the city, are temporarily transfigured, but rather than for the purpose of coming of age, these open performances become investments in communities whose lived experiences have been explicitly absent, erased from quinceañera practice in Latin America and the United States. Her encounters therefore incite a process of queer-traditioning in quinceañera culture, a process of seeking to engage with the possibility of inclusion of queer and trans life experiences within the imaginations of nation through performativity in everyday life.

## LÍA THE ARTIVISTA

Born in 1989, Lía was an old soul even at twenty-six, her age when we met. She lived modestly as she finished her master's degree in visual arts at the Universidad Nacional Autónoma de México. Her rooftop studio apartment was one that could hardly be considered simply a room; it was her refuge. Lía's life was in upheaval beyond the space of her body as she was finishing her thesis and figuring out her next step in life, which was rocky given that she also was working to pay for transition. Her journey was slow, but Lía is patient.

She kept a small altar to Yemaya, the goddess of the sea, as an homage to her love of *sirenas*, mermaids, next to her bed along with academic books about gender and performance. In this tiny space, I asked her where she kept the dresses she uses during her public quinceañera presentations. She replied that they were in storage at her mother's house in Portales in the southern part of the city, not far when she needed them. Their absence offered relief in her tiny rooftop abode. Space in Mexico City comes at a premium, one that Lía could not indulge. She remarked that her mother struggled with Lía's decision to publicly become her daughter but still supported Lía when she needed help.

Her home overlooks the corner of Avenida Cuauhtémoc and Calle Durango in the district of Roma Norte. Avenida Cuauhtémoc is a major line dividing Roma Norte from the district of Doctores; she lived on the border of these two zones. This was fitting albeit temporary placement for Lía as she found that much of her life is conceptualized as intensely in between zones of understanding. But one would never guess that from her manner. She explained as we walked down Calle Durango that if we had left her apartment and headed in the opposite direction, the streets would have immediately taken on a different character, one that required much more caution especially after dark. Roma Norte was quite affluent, and the winding streets with quaint patisseries and fountained plazas with minimal traffic surrounded by historic architecture make the area a popular tourist destination in the evenings. Lía explained that she prefers the more "popular" areas of the city, those that are characteristically inhabited by the working class and poor. She said working-class men in particular are often more compassionate to her experiences of marginality, as they too find themselves on the margins of what is determined to be respectable society. When she goes out salsa dancing, she prefers to go to gay-friendly clubs nearest the Plaza Garibaldi frequented by men from Tepito and other outlying areas rather than patronizing the Zona Rosa, an upscale neighborhood known for its gay community and nightlife scene. Lía plainly stated that the Zona Rosa is "white." Although she occasionally goes there, she doesn't feel as welcome as she does in other area of the city. For one reason, she said it is harder to find a willing dance partner in the Zona Rosa. Lía is not dark, but in an urban hierarchy of race and class as an olive-skinned mujer trans and a poor graduate student, her status is marked as lower than it would be if any of those factors shifted.

She is optimistic to a fault, and even as a poor graduate student she devoted time to trans activism in the city as one of the co-founders of the Red de Juventudes Trans México (Trans Youth Network Mexico). She also spends time conceptualizing how she can use her passion for visual arts to reach out beyond her own familiar circles. She defines her work as creative and pedagogical. Her goal is to educate those around her of the realities of trans lives in Mexico and to be an ambassador of trans understanding. As a result she shares herself through her "encuentros afectivos y educativos" (affective and educational encounters). In those moments, Lía stages opportunities for people to unexpectedly experience tenderness and compassion from a complete stranger. In defining her public exhibitions as affective encounters prioritizes the realization of common "structures of feeling" that emerge through material engagement in space (Williams). In her artistic work Lía endeavors to use unconditional tenderness toward audiences to counter the violence and hatred hurled at trans communities. Her affective encounters centralize the public recognition of the right of trans lives to exist and thrive in Latin America and more specifically Mexico. Second only to Brazil, Mexico is one of the most dangerous places in the Western Hemisphere to be an openly transgender person, especially a mujer trans. In this way, Lía's desire to identify as a mujer trans is accurate but also fundamentally political as well as highly dangerous. In this intellectual space I will mirror Lía's self-identification and refer to her gender identification as a mujer trans because she is abundantly certain that her life as a mujer trans is materially and ideologically linked to her hometown of Mexico City. She said, "Mi cuerpo no solo es mío. Es una cuerpa collective" (My body is not only mine. It is a shared body). Her body becomes a collective site of artistic production and a tool in the service of trans "artivism."

## QUINCEAÑERA (TRANS)ARTIVISM

Lía self-identifies as working within the framework of "artivism." Her works are intellectual exercises that use familiar sociocultural images to draw audiences into conversations about gender expectations in Mexico City in the twenty-first century. She works with well-worn understandings of acceptable femininity by claiming a public space for her own brand of womanhood through the celebration of trans quinceañeras to publicly humanize the experiences of transgender Mexican youth who risk their lives daily just leaving their homes. Lía asks her audiences to see the quinceañera, culture, gender, and prejudice refracted through the intimate location and experiences of a trans body. By publicly introducing a trans body into the quinceañera rite, most certainly "made in Mexico," Lía's *artivismo*, artistic activism, dares to integrate trans lives into the everyday lives and consciousness of her Mexican and transnational audiences. "Artivismo" as conscious practice is defined by Chela Sandoval and Guisela Latorre as a "hybrid neologism that signifies the work created by individuals who see an organic relationship between art and activism" (82). Sandoval and Latorre use the term as it is allied with "*la conciencia de la mestiza*, that is the consciousness of the mixed-race woman" (82). Based on our shared experiences, I assert that Lía's artivist engagement is heavily practice-based, rooted in affective relationship building in order to humanize trans communities and condemn the regular violence inflicted upon trans bodies. Lía's methodology, using her transitioning body as a tool and a focal point to destabilize assumptions about gender identifications, draws more closely on Molefi K. Asante's definition of the artivist:

> The artivist (artist + activist) uses her artistic talents to fight and struggle against injustice and oppression—by any *medium* necessary. The artivist merges commitment to freedom and justice with the pen, the lens, the brush, the voice, the body, and the imagination. The artivist knows that to make an *observation* is to have an *obligation*. (203)

The connection between method and obligation becomes particularly important to Lía in her work as a quinceañera celebrant. Lía uses her body as a resource and in the process transforms objects of adornment from the private quinceañera ritual such as dress, gloves, and tiara into tools of artistic representation and transformation. Such objects in artistic practice become metaphors of an accessible kind of femininity that when adorning a trans body cease to be easily categorized or accurately identified without understanding the signification being asserted by the artist herself.

In engineered moments of unexpected but intense public connection, Lía said, she does not perform a character or a contrived persona. Instead, her public presentations are extensions of her everyday self, functioning as creative personal experience narratives. This narrative is intimately associated with and makes Lía's body metaphorically and literally accessible to the publics with whom she connects. The burden of the openly trans artist was revealed to me in passing when Lía noted that when she started her program at the university, she had a professor who aggressively insisted that she photograph her naked body to document her transition as a form of compelling auto-ethnographic art practice. This method that disallowed her right to privacy simply because she was a mujer trans forced Lía to find alternative critical ways to purposefully link visual art practice, her personal gender transition, and human rights advocacy. Her form of trans artivismo acknowledges that as she is a mujer trans advocating for her community, her body must be used as part of her artistic toolkit to foster understanding and spur transformation. One of myriad strategies Lía has found is a repurposing of the well-known and well-worn quinceañera ritual in Mexico.

Lía interprets the quinceañera celebration, the coming-of-age ritual, not to mark the metaphorical passage of a fifteen-year period, as many who use the quinceañera as a metaphor do, but as an extension of her own recognition of her gender transition in the public sphere. While she can acknowledge her choice, she turns her personal choice into political action by calling for compassion for not just herself but for mujeres and hombres trans across Latin America, particularly those who do not have the capacity or financial and community resources to safely speak on their own. Her use of the quinceañera is a metaphor of public gender transition, particularly the transition from masculine-identifying to feminine-identifying, coupled with instrumentalizing tradition as an experience of feeling.

## MIS XXY AÑOS, 2013–PRESENT

The quinceañera ritual has long excluded gender-nonbinary communities through a brand of implied rejection. It represents pageants of heteronormative living characterized by feminine female bodies in the service of cis-gendered male bodies connected through systematic interpretation of idealized desire. The quinceañera is a courtship game in which sensuality and sexuality become confounded amid the social strictures placed on Latina bodies in public and private space. While quinceañera apologists would deny that a narrative of desire exists, choosing to focus on the ritual as one of personal piety and family values even among contemporary quinceañera celebrations in the United States, desire is coded on young bodies but also more liberally as a desire for middle-class social mobility.

This notion of desire spills over into Lía's artistic practice surrounding the quinceañera as well. Here, the politics of desirability build a social hierarchy around acceptable and unacceptable bodies in space, both personal and private. The average quinceañera's body is styled toward acceptability as a reference of social worth, and cis-gendered quinceañeras are understood to transform back the following day from a fantasy that is unsustainable, reinforcing one grand deception in the ritual and celebratory process, the reality that actual womanhood is not living as a princess. In fact, such a reversal of the ritual moment, one that is invested in publicly declaring the presence of a functional and fecund reproductive system, only serves to reinforce the future labor that a young Latina woman will incur as she endeavors to prove that her life is defined by more than biological functionality. For Lía, themes of desirability and deception are also at play in the presentation of quinceañera encounters, especially as the initial draw of spectacle was not explicitly coded as queer or trans-identifying. The presentations require that onlookers close a physical gap and focus upon Lía's body adorned as a quinceañera, creating a moment of desire for a young brown body before they are informed of that same body's trans reality. Lía uses her public stage to momentarily objectify her trans body and intimate a sense of desire but also instability. It is a social space that has the potential for affection and connections and for rejection and violence. The rejection engenders a sense of engaño, of betrayal by deception, a theme that resonates beyond Lía's trans quinceañera encounters and has implications for intracultural and extracultural interpretations of quinceañera practice in the United States.

Lía explained to me that the quinceañera is not inherently a queer celebration, but it can be queered by filtering through *transfeminista* (transfeminist) artistic practice. On January 19, 2019, Lía performed an iteration of her "Mis XXY años" performance on Calle Doctor Atl 275 in the historic Colonia Santa María la Ribera in Mexico City. Dressed in a light pink taffeta gown, curls piled on her head, she ran into traffic, twirling as though it were her reception dance floor. She took her waltz to the street, spinning and carrying a five-foot-tall black and white poster of her image when she still presented as a young man. She ran up to cars on the busy street, forcing the drivers to stop in the middle of the street. Some let her ride on their hoods down the block. They were her escorts, ushering her through physical and affective space and time. As the cars slowed and stopped, passengers saw that the feminine quinceañera and the masculine portrait were two versions of the same self. In a video of the event posted on Facebook Lía proclaims,

> Yo voy a transitar mi vida con mis pies. . . . Firmes como la arena, la calle es nuestra! Para vivir dos o tres vidas una tiene que aventarse, a veces con los ojos bien abiertas a lo que puede ser tu propio fin. . . . Esta es la fiesta de todas mis caras, el dulce vals de todos los cuerpos que he tenido.

> (I am going to move my life forward with my own two feet. . . . Firm like the sand, the street is ours! To live two or three lives one has to get up, sometimes with eyes wide open to what can be your final end. . . . This is the celebration of all my selves, the sweet waltz of all the bodies I've had.)

She speaks to the power of action and reaction, in particular the tension between the quinceañera as a private cultural marker fetishizing cis-gendered heteronormalcy and public encounters that interject other, unexpected cultural markers into the public celebration.

In 2013 Lía presented the first of an ongoing series called "Mis XXY años," which featured her and other community members and trans youth in public performances as a quinceañera to share her gender transition on the streets of Mexico City. "Mis XXY años" is a series of public encounters presented with the goal to move people toward tenderness, compassion, and understanding through direct engagement. The title of the series plays on notions of very real biological transitions that are alluded to but often left out of heterosexual interpretations of the quinceañera celebration as a marker of social transition. "XXY" refers to the chromosome composition of sexed women and sexed men. Lía frames her experiences as quite literally in between the XX (female) and XY (male) designations. The name also bares a visual resemblance to the Roman numeral "XV" used in popular decorations for quinceañeras. In cis-gendered quinceañera celebrations, the importance of biological sex is often erased as bodies are assumed to conform to what are viewed as "normal" sexual characteristics.

The three primary performance pieces under discussion here are "Solia un hombre, ahora soy una quinceañera" and "Mis XXY años: Pino Suarez" in 2015 and "Habitar femenino" in 2013. Each of the presentations embodies Lía's desire to close physical and emotional gaps between people—gaps that are seen to bolster hatred, violence, and systemic oppression. Revisiting her goal of presenting "encuentros afectivos," Valerie Leibold distills the notion from a spatial perspective as she analyzes Lía's mermaid encounters, also presented in Mexico City:

> No se trata de un trabajo artístico que mantenga la separación entre el artista y el público, sino de una convivencia y una transformación colectiva descolonializadora basada en los afectos.

> (This is not an artistic work to maintain the separation between the artist and the public, but a coexistence and a collective decolonialized transformation based on affection.) (Leibold 150)

Lía's work, from this vantage point, is fundamentally about the reorientation of a public space that alienates bodies and minds to one that allows people to be vulnerable enough to connect with other human beings, in the hope that such contact can spur social transformation. Through her adoption of quinceañera practice, Lía artistically asserts that the quinceañera is a place of affect, of contact, of intimacy over alienation.

## QUINCEAÑERA REPRESENTATION SPACE

Quinceañeras are not simply reproductions of social norms or expectations of gender presentation; they also evince an internal system of representation. Lía's creative work recognizes and challenges the internal assumptions made by viewing audiences by reproducing familiar symbols on a body that defies the clear borders of binarized gender presentations. Through self-conscious representation Lía transforms her body as a site of contextual innovation into traditional practice. Stuart Hall describes representation as the process by which meaning is produced and exchanged between members of a culture through various forms of symbolic mediation such as language and through which meaning is socially constructed (1). Following the discursive or constructionist approach undertaken in this book, I understand meaning to be made differently in diverse quinceañera performances where vulnerable bodies matter. In this case the members are participants in a community of practice. The following three performance spaces constructed by a mujer trans add to the practice of quinceañeras as a shared micro-representative system among Latinas and Latin American communities. These performances claim territory within the cultural practice.

"SOLÍA SER UN HOMBRE, AHORA SOY UNA QUINCEAÑERA"

The first text is a 2015 mediated performance that I experienced through a quinceañera's recuerdo, her keepsake video. Recuerdo videos commonly capture the preparation process of the quinceañera on the day of her event, and older home videos and photographs are incorporated into the final cut to document the quince's coming of age, from birth to adolescence. Lía's keepsake video is meant to document her transition into womanhood, using personal photos, music, original voice-over scripts, and video clips of a version of her Mexican quinceañera produced on streets in Barcelona.[3]

"Solia" foregrounds Lía's self-production as a mujer trans through public quinceañera performance. The function of a keepsake video is to document a moment in personal history for the purpose of historical recognition. The video places people in space and time as they are in a moment of personal transformation. As such, it functions as a personal manifesto of gender transition, using the quinceañera as a metaphor of transformation and cultural integration. Lía's soundtrack is "Quinceañera" by Thalía, a classic choice for quinceañera celebrations that engineers an intertextual connection between teenage coming-of-age dramas and Lía's representational performance of transitional gender identification. The characteristic tune and the image of a plastic, pink and white quinceañera-girl cake topper are used to inform the viewer that this is a quinceañera performance space being documented, implicating connections to celebrations across the Western Hemisphere but also her own body of work. To understand Lía's transformation from her own perspective, one must first understand that her life, from her perspective, began with a lie. The video begins by introducing a baby, Gerardo García, being held in his mother's arms in a hospital just after his birth. The image is immediately called into question. The viewer is told that looks may be deceiving and is offered a corrective narrative to complicate the image of the baby boy. In front of a pale pink flower- and feather-accented background are Lía's words:

> Cuando el doctor me entregó en brazos
> de mi madre le dijo que yo
> "Era Niño"
> siempre supe que esto era una mentira

> (When the doctor put me in
> my mother's arms he told her that I
> "Was a Boy"
> I always knew that this was a lie)

Through this statement Lía takes control over her right to identify as a woman. In this simple statement she anticipates and reflects on the barrage of criticism she might expect as she moves through her adult life as a mujer trans who would be burdened with justifying her life that others would see as a lie. Rather, Lía uses the quinceañera keepsake video as a form of familial documentation to unapologetically rewrite her life story as a trans woman who owes no one any justification for her existence, only acknowledging the mistake of the doctor who delivered her. Her creation of the trans quinceañera keepsake video calls into question the way nominally natural females are born and identified as such but still must go through a socializing process to prove their social status, emphasizing the contrived nature of womanhood. Her video calls attention to the crack in the façade of idealized womanhood, but it is precisely in the crack that her own womanhood flourishes. Her assertion of the doctor's mistaken interpretation of her gender identity, which in fact he could not have known, paves the way for the quinceañera to make sense as a woman coming into herself, even if later in life than the traditional celebration.

As Lía's words scroll, the song "Quinceañera" plays over the visual narrative, creating a complex amalgam of auditory accompaniment to the visual but also two complementary narratives, a personal decision linked with a culturally recognized and socially realized event. She explains the ritual as a celebration of the transition from "niña a mujer" (girl to woman) at the same moment that Thalía sings, "No sé por que mi cuerpo cambia día con día" (I don't know why my body changes day to day). Lía uses the song to show the similarities in her development into womanhood and that of Latina teenagers, albeit with significant differences, especially that of self-defined femininity. Her transitioning body is the perfect representation of the social power of the quinceañera celebration as an adornment of the Mexican nation-state, yet it also erodes her social stability within the state. The quinceañera serves as a bridge between her body and the social body, facilitating transformation through spectacle. In a voiceover of images Lía says,

> Se presenta al cuerpo ante la sociedad . . .
> pero un cuerpo socialmente tiene que
> ser pretendido, llevado al espacio privado
> y listo para la reproducción
>
> (The body is presented to society . . .
> but socially the body has
> to be claimed, taken to the private space
> and ready for reproduction)

After these lines are delivered, the visual narrative trails off, and Lía's voice, deep and masculine, accompanies the black and white image on her Mexican military registration card that fills the screen. As she speaks, a new image is superimposed, not replacing, only obscuring the previous one. It is an image of Lía in a red quinceañera gown with black and white zebra-print accents. She is holding a matching *ramo*, bouquet of faux flowers. The music is now replaced by her voice, stating clearly and firmly,

> Soy Lía y solía ser un hombre.
> Ahora soy una quinceañera.
> Mi cuerpo es un ir y venir de historias.
> Tengo muchas voces dentro de la piel.
> Construyo una historia para respirar y sacar la voz.
> Hoy, mi cuerpo no solo es mío.
> Es una cuerpa colectiva
> de carne y metáfora.
> De sueños y confusiones
> Habitar un espacio que es lejano, que es muy lejano a mío.
> Pero que también es mío, y siempre lo será.
> Vengo de las profundidades
> Soy muy profunda.
> Pensaron que era débil, incómoda
> Pesada y traumada.
> Hoy soy solo los reflejos de esos ojos.
> El olor de esa piel
> La sonrisa que leo en esos labios
> Que siempre he querido besar
> Que siempre he querido tocar
>
> Mi transición es una fiesta.
> Bailo sobre mi propio género
> Construyo redes afectivas
> Yo soy afectiva.
>
> No más violencia del estado para nosotras
> Nos queremos vivas
> Ni una más
> Lo personal es político
>
> (I am Lía, and I used to be a man.
> Today I am a quinceañera.

My body is a pathway of stories.
Many voices emerge from my skin.
I build my story to breathe, and release my voice.
Today, my body is not only mine.
It's a shared body
Made of flesh and metaphor.
Of dreams and disarray
I inhabit a space that is distant, distant from me.
But it is also mine, and will always be.
I come from the depths
I am very deep
They thought I was weak, uncomfortable
Weighed down and traumatized.
I am now only a reflection from those eyes.
The scent of this skin
The smile that I read on those lips
That I've always wanted to kiss
That I've always wanted to touch

My transition is a celebration.
Dancing atop my own gender
Creating affective networks
I am affecting.[4]

No more state violence for us
We want to live
Not one more
The personal is political)

This narrative offers Lía's framework for understanding her affective performances, not just her quinceañera presentations but also those of La Novia and La Sirena. These performance ask audiences and onlookers (or reluctant audiences) who find themselves sharing public space with Lía's encuentros to consider the body as a space of occupation, a porous vessel for experiences and voice, not a conclusion but a beginning.

As Lía's voice reaches the lines "Vengo de las profundidades," the viewer transitions to watching her exit a large van with eight trans men serving as her chambelanes in a quinceañera encuentro in Barcelona. While I have been discussing quinceañeras in an inter-American circuit of knowledge, this performance becomes especially poignant as we see the tradition, which is not practiced in Spain, represented by a mujer trans from Mexico City whose work has been globalized through visits to the United States and western Europe but also through her active social media presence. In this performative moment when a conventional quinceañera would be displaying images with her biological family, Lía honors her trans family as integral to her open and honest transitional process. The group takes its place on a public street with crowds waiting. Lía walks into an open space in the crowd and is greeted with affection and smiling faces. Her body moves through the public street as a mujer trans, and the dress on her body making soft curves declares her feminine transition as she moves from one chambelan to the next, blowing out the candles they hold as any other quinceañera would. As she moves through her court, an unprecedented addition to the ritual occurs as each chambelan touches her arm. A new voice-over begins with Lía's personal transformation to feminine womanhood coupled with the reality that her transition during this ritual event must be accompanied by chemical intervention. Her own biological process is made visible rather than hidden by the flourishes of the quinceañera celebration. Instead of simply functioning to reveal her feminine secondary sexual characteristics, the development of breasts, the curve of hips, the softening of facial features, Lía narrates the functions and side effects of her supplemental hormone therapy, Oestraclin, an estradiol gel. She highlights the unwanted effects, "depresión, comezón, enojo, llanto" (depression, itching, anger, crying) as results that are exacerbated by what she refers to as "otros voces" (other voices). These other voices represent the critical voices of members of the wider queer community "que se abunden al su alrededor" (that abound all around you) and that she revoices as invasive and insulting questions that worsen the complex and emotionally exhausting physical process of gender transition.

The most disturbing question Lía narrates is a hypothetical question of her choice to begin supplemental hormone therapy: "Y que onda? Vas a hacer trabajo sexual, o que? A que vas a dedicar?" (What's up? Are you going to do sex work or what? What are you going to do with yourself?). The audible voice-over at this moment and during each of the aggressive revoiced questions is coupled with a very different visual reality. As each of these questions is read, including the one that flippantly references Lía's potential future as a sex worker, the viewer sees exactly what Lía will do with her life despite the voices. She is surrounded by smiling faces and applause, being whirled around and smiling as she spins a bright pink parasol to the beat of 1930s dance music. The structure of this keepsake video articulates the ambivalence of Lía's own daily experiences, inundated by external expectations of living as a mujer trans, coupled with the public life she is making for herself through affective encounters that bring people together to openly acknowledge the lived experience of a mujer trans. Through this public ritual, Lía lays claim to her identity as a mujer trans whose road to trans womanhood is similar to those of other young Latinas, in particular in their fundamentally contrived nature. Lía applies hormones that absorb through her skin, but this does not make her a mujer trans. She chooses to become a mujer trans at the hands and acknowledgement of her community, which she builds through her affective encounters. In this encounter, her body becomes a space of intimate transformation during the quinceañera process. Making her process of gender transition a public process, even if confined to audiences and community circles that are trans-accepting, is fundamentally dangerous but in her view absolutely necessary to reaching a place of self-acceptance.

In the final image the screen fades to black and Lía is surrounded by arms outstretched toward her. She is smiling, with her chin in the air and two wide-open arms, one clutching a parasol high in the air, the other extended to what looks like a wide embrace. Her final words advocate silencing the voices that would ask trans bodies to suffer at their own hands.

No más disforia de género
Mejor euforia de género
México, D.F.
2015

(No more gender dysphoria
Better, gender euphoria
Mexico City
2015)

### "MIS XXY AÑOS: PINO SUAREZ"

In the spring of 2015, Lía and a cohort of transgender Mexican men as her escorts staged an affective encounter that took the form of a quinceañera ritual in the Pino Suarez metro station in the heart of Mexico City. Her work, including her metadiscursive 2016 *encuentro* "Lía García: La experiencia del cuerpo transgénero como una pedagogía afectiva" (The transgender body experience as an affective pedagogy), situates her body as a contingent artifact telling a precarious story about personal and social trans-gression. This public encounter mobilizes metaphors of space to initiate a narrative of acceptance around transgender lives. I accessed the encounter through Lía's personal archive of video documentation of her performances. She does not perform alone, and she consistently documents her encounters by photography, video recording, or both. She edits and produces keepsake videos that she circulates for pedagogical purposes. Her work has been seen across Latin America and in Germany and Spain.

For this presentation, Lía secured city permits to occupy a space in the bustling metro station Pino Suarez in the Cuauhtémoc district. It is an important linking point to the center of the city and the transfer point for two of the busiest train lines, 1 and 2, which traverse the center of the city along east-west and north-south routes, respectively. The Pino Suarez sign that marks the space for commuters above ground documents the crossing of lines 1 and 2, resembling a transgender community flag with (colloquially masculine) blue and (feminine) pink stripes joined by a central white stripe. Many of Lía's personal Facebook photos include this image as a constant representation of the struggle toward transgender rights in Mexico. Lía, who is a self-described lover of metaphors, sees in this public space a chance to overlay trans activism and community zymology in the disinterested public space of the metro station, which normalizes aloof public engagement, the opposite of her affective encounters.

The intersection of the lines, by color and the indexical symbolism of contrived gendered symbology of babies and young children, makes an intertextual link between the performance and Lía's keepsake video depicting her own birth and misidentification as a baby boy. Reinforcing the contrived gendering process is what for women Judith Butler calls a semiotic "girling" process (232). Lía represents her own gendering process by arriving at the Pino Suarez station by metro in her journey on a constantly moving stream of unstable and overlapping gendered identifications, some claimed and others ascribed. The entourage of eight hombres trans as chambelanes and DJ Laura legally occupy a roughly twenty-by-twenty-foot area of the station during commuter traffic. Their presence, more than just bodies in immediate spaces, can be heard down tunnels as Tchaikovsky's "Sleeping Beauty Waltz" and "Como la flor" by Selena resound through the station far beyond the confines of the circle of onlookers cum guests who surround the event. The micro context of the event resonates deeply as people stop to gawk and observe, to take photos and dance with the quinceañera.

The performance takes control of the gendering process of Lía as an individual who uses it to assert her feminine identification as it calls attention to the fluid and socially contrived nature of gendered performance in general. The presentation, like any quinceañera, uses dance and dress to draw in gaze. Gaze is the precursor to desire, and as gaze deepens, so desire emerges. Lía uses the familiarity of the quinceañera ritual in Mexico as a way to draw the public into conversations about gender difference and human rights. Although her cause is urgent, her claims are never aggressive. Instead, she chooses tenderness as her methodology, attracting people with affection and touch.

At one point during the presentation, Lía makes her way around the gathered crowd with a tiara, the quinceañera's crown, in her hand. She walks around, reaching out to the gathered crowd, not saying a word, only extending her hand, touching cheeks and faces gently with the tiara in a offering of affection and blessing. DJ Laura narrates as Lía circulates:

> This is also an emotional and affective ritual
> A ritual of blessing
> An invitation to life,
> An invitation to love
> Everyone comes to this world with a strong energetic force
> So, sharing this energy and letting it flow is our happiness . . .
> It is our objective

This gesture closes the space between bodies. Lía hugs strangers, some of them hug back, others simply stay still, but no one pushes her away. It is as though she has entranced them, the quinceañera exposed in public; she enthralls the crowd and generates a liminal space of potential understanding made possible by Lía's disclosure of her transgender subjectivity. In this moment the celebration ceases to be simply about disclosure and becomes a recognition of celebration and appreciation. One of Lía's collaborators, Michel, intimates his view:

> For starters, I think celebrating with trans friends independent of thinking about gender, but thinking about trans diversity, I mean transgender, transsexual, cross-dresser, or whichever of these, is about building affective connections that we need because we are and we live in a society and we cannot live alone and far away from ourselves and our desires.

Affective encounters become ways of creating community through understanding and shared celebrations, even when celebration is a violation of social expectation. While trans youth have a rough road to walk, they are not without joy. Lía's work illustrates that creating a space for queer subjectivities to be included in a nationally recognized cultural tradition is one step closer to recognizing the shared humanity of the transgender community in Mexico and beyond. Likewise, the erasure of queer identification in US quinceañeras, even if peripherally accepted, demonstrates a vilification of this community among US Latinxs.

## "HABITAR FEMENINO"

This affective performance places Lía's trans quinceañera body at the World Trade Center Hotel in Mexico City on October 6, 2013, for the biannual quinceañera product exposition 15 Fest Expo. The hotel is in the Nápoles area on the large Avenida Insurgentes in the center of Mexico City and is positioned as one of the most prestigious multi-use buildings in the city's financial district. Much like expos across the United States, the goal of 15 Fest Expo is to bring together consumers with quinceañera-serving professionals to realize and materialize quinceañera celebrations in and around Mexico City. Lía said these events are for the wealthy, the upper classes of Mexico City, as evident by the "200 peso entrada," around US$10 entrance fee, a parallel fee one would find to enter *Quinceañeras Magazine* expos all over the United States. Unlike their US equivalents, these expos reach only a small proportion of Mexican teens and their families in the capital city. Most instead opt to shop for their quinceañera goods in area markets such as Mercado Lagunilla and Mercado Merced that offer lower-cost, lower-quality dresses and decorations, making the tradition accessible to less affluent citizens. Her initial desire was to participate in the quinceañera dress fashion show as a trans woman and host a booth in the expo to integrate her body into wider quinceañera culture in the city. She was not able to secure permissions to participate in the fashion show, and the cost to rent a booth as a vendor was prohibitive. So, Lía chose to perform just outside the expo event.

Dressed in a light-pink taffeta quinceañera gown with vintage styling and gold sequin applique, sky-blue opera gloves, and sparkling tiara, Lía spoke with girls and their mothers outside the expo doors. The dress, the centerpiece of her presentation, implied intimacy between teens, mothers, and Lía. It was one of a kind and handmade by a friend's aunt. It was loaned to her by that same friend, who had celebrated her own quince years before. Lía asked participants to answer brief questions about their quinceañera experiences, write down answers on small, blue slips of paper, and pin them on her dress. Some questions were "What does turning 15 mean to you?" and "What does having a quinceañera party mean to you?" The encounter combined sharing quinceañera experiences in a commercial zone while also asking individuals to risk their personal space by approaching her and touching her dress. She described the event as follows:

Un encuentro afectivo que explora la concepción de la feminidad que tienen actualmente las mujeres que serán ejecutantes del ritual de la quinceañera e invita a un intercambio con mi feminidad a través de un acto afectivo como metáfora de extensión del discurso y reconocimiento social entre mujeres que estamos en un estado de celebración por medio de este ritual, desde nuestras propias experiencias y afectos.

(An affective encounter that explores the current concept of femininity possessed by young women who are performing the ritual of the quinceañera, it invites an exchange with my femininity through an affective act as a metaphor that extends discourse and social recognition among women who are celebrating this ritual through our own experiences and feelings.)

Unlike her other performance texts, this encounter was not met by wholesale acceptance, but that was due more to the commercial nature of the event where she was staging her encounter than to her presence as a trans quinceañera celebrant in public. Before she could complete her educational encounter inside the expo, she and her cameraperson were asked to leave the hotel by local police. It was not until her voice was heard, after she arrived at the second level of the hotel, where the entrance to the expo was, that she encountered resistance to her expressing herself. Lía's voice is one of the few aspects of her manner that someone could regard as telling. She even claims that unless she opens her mouth, others are hard pressed to peg her as a mujer trans on a city street. While Lía desired to speak with whoever wanted her removed, simply to explain her motives and the pedagogical value, she was not allowed access or explanation.

Much like her previous encounters, her public presence was an overlay of quinceañera symbology in space, even as her version of the coming-of-age drama did not match the upper-class consumer event that was also sharing space with a pet expo and a baby expo. Her art went unappreciated when it might have dissuaded consumerism. But the encounter revealed how in Mexico, quinceañera practice, much like that in the United States, is a function of lifestyle clustering, where communities share class trappings and quinceañera practice in public when linked to consumption in a high-class and exclusive endeavor catering explicitly to a female audience. Lía commented on her own concepts of gendered public space as

un espacio poblado en su mayoría por mujeres, ya que las niñas
que asistían lo hacían en compañía de sus familias pero marcado
más [por] la presencia de sus madres y hermanas.

(a space mainly populated by women, as girls who were attending
were accompanied by their families but with the marked presence
of their mothers and sisters.)

These mothers, sisters, and daughters were marked as upscale consumers with
the resources and social status to pay US prices to simply browse the performative options. While Lía might be able to pass in this specialized environment as a quinceañera, she was not able to pass as upper class.

These three performances represent one node of a wider body of queer
revisionist discourse that challenges the primacy of heteronormative cultural
identification among US Latinx communities. *Quinceañera* is a stage production written in 1998 by Paul Bonin-Rodriguez and Alberto Araiza as an
interdisciplinary theatrical performance piece that narrates the experiences of
queer Latinx men in their thirties and forties "addressing the first 15 years of
the AIDS pandemic" (258). Joe Salvatore notes that the piece "borrows the
ritual that young Latinas undergo at 15 as a way to draw a parallel between
reaching adulthood and *surviving* adulthood, while also serving as a healing
ritual for all involved" (258).

Bonin-Rodriguez and Araiza mobilize bodily narratives of illness and loss
to set aside a space for audiences to participate in a process of shared cathar-
sis and the building of community around the ritual event as a collectivity.
The work uses the quinceañera celebration as a framework for understanding death and loss as a function of social and cultural marginality. It uses
the quinceañera to discuss the lives of gay men. It does not engage with the
tradition directly but instead borrows the cultural visibility and intelligibil-
ity of the quinceañera frame to speak of issues facing gay Chicano men. In
the play's final scene, titled "The Creed," Bonin-Rodriguez's, Araiza's, and
Danny Bolero Zaldivar's characters together chant affirmations for the future
as a light-timbre bell rings. One of the most powerful statements asserts the
need for critical vulnerability in Latinx communities: "I believe compassion
is revolution" (Bonin-Rodriguez and Araiza 298). The line forms an affective
link between this queer revisionist narrative, which is private and intellectual,
with Lía's public presentations.

In a tragic-comedic narrative, comedian and queer Chicana Monica Palacios pens a personal experience of her proto-queer self forced to participate in

a quinceañera celebration. Her work emphasizes the experience of the often overlooked reluctant quinceañera. Hers is an observable personal narrative of the celebration that deemphasizes her own role in the planning of the event and instead envisions her as a subject of cultural and familial expectations. She undergoes the coming-of-age process but not of her own accord. Some reluctant quinceañeras narrate the reasoning behind their distaste for the event as one of personality politics—they simply do not want to be in the spotlight. Others have deeper cause for resisting. Rather than simply shying away from the process of female formation, some young women find the performance of conspicuous heteronormativity to go against their own developing feelings about gender identification and sexual desire. The coming-of-age drama centralizes stereotypical hyperfemininity and female fecundity and idealizes heteronormative coupling. It materializes a kind of cultural betrayal in which queer identifications are rendered wrong even before they fully flourish in young lives. Such is one theme reinforced in "The Dress Was Way Too Itchy." In it, Palacios narrates her own experience as a reluctant participant in quinceañera traditions of her youth in San Jose.

For this community of participants, who look back at the quinceañera as a betrayal of their true selves stifled under layers of tulle and taffeta, pomp and propriety, honor and chastity, their forced participation is more than reluctant—it is a rejection of their true selves and a reification of the emotional baggage many will carry into adulthood. The reluctant quinceañera narrative transcends gendered identifications, as the celebration is steeped in ritualized heteronormativity for both female- and male-identifying participants. Yet the work of Bonin-Rodriguez and Arabize and Palacios remains private, closed to the public view, accessible to the English-language-literate and interested academics.

To those who can access them, queer quinceañera narratives reflect the very best of quinceañera traditions as they expose the worst about Latinx community prejudice and social inequity. The stories depict sincere affective bonds between individuals as kin, fictive and blood, as well as discrete narratives of space and enactment. They integrate personal space into extracultural space, temporarily overlapping the affective and the disinterested. The stories make people nervous and force some to feel and see in ways they did not previously. In many ways, these narratives challenge the secular version that would foreground corporatization and conspicuous consumption characteristic of twenty-first-century quinceañera culture. The tragic irony must be acknowledged that it is a body of queer narratives of those excluded and erased who offer the most beautiful and moving quinceañera performances. They reinscribe the value of family, culture, and belonging lost among generations that take their heteronormative privilege for granted.

## QUINCEAÑERA PERFORMATIVITY AND ENGAÑO

Lía's artistic use of the quinceañera tradition employs a frame for embodied social performance that marks personal transformation in culturally specific, public space and serves as representation of the work of gender identification that is dramatized through the quinceañera ritual performed by Latinx teenagers. As such, Lía's performances as well as those of quince girls call attention to the way quinceañera celebrations are "dramatic realizations" of Latina womanhood and to how contrived the notion of womanhood they represent at their material surfaces truly is (Goffman 30). Erving Goffman has noted that patterns of dramatic realization pervade everyday experiences. The quinceañera is not an everyday occurrence but does implicate daily life external to the ritual context. Goffman asserts, "The world, in truth, is a wedding" (36). The social performance of matrimony, much like the social performance of coming of age among Latina teens, is a performance of reality. The wedding is a contextually and temporally specific reality that exists in a constant state of formation and reformation. One cannot presume that the quinceañera ritual is systematically progressing in the sense of liberal identity politics. It is continuously changing in a web of influences and affirmation that is facilitated by extracultural influences that render the celebration a marker of more than ethnicity and race but one of socially visible class standing. I have been examining the materialization of the quinceañera ritual through a lens of economic and commercial influences, but the work of performance artists to recast the celebration sits between "dramatic self-expressions" of individual teens and families and the "commercially organized fantasies of the nation" (Goffman 31). These performances provide counternarratives to the conspicuous consumption and neoliberal identity politics that pervade the competitive quinceañera marketplace but do not affectively replace it.

What these performances reveal is the nature of quinceañera celebrations to conceal poverty as much as they reinforce economic certainty. They can be taken up as a materialization of performative cynicism, framed by Goffman as the disbelief in one's representational face (18). Although Goffman asserts that everyday performances of self reside on a continuum from "sincere" to "cynical," quinceañera artistry of teens and professional performers resides in a gray area between the sincere and cynical. In this theoretical context, a sincere performance is one that the actor accepts as true, that is, what might be called living in an authentic way. On the other hand, a cynical performance is a social performance an actor knows is untrue yet performs anyway based on desired social results in a given context. Quinceañera performance that is locally dramatic self-expression and patterned practice, a "commercially organized fantasy of the nation," is neither wholly sincere nor wholly cynical.

As a representation of Latinx communities, it embodies a social and cultural ambivalence realized in the daily lives of Latinx Americans who are marked by social scripts that programmatically deny Latinx citizens the ability to live unquestionably as unmarked middle-class Americans.

Class performance becomes one of the subsumed narratives revealed through the materialization of the quinceañera ritual. The concept of revelation becomes a key trope of the celebration—revealing age, revealing biological capacity, revealing affluence, and revealing networks of support are all parts of the social presentation. And yet, these revelations are received differently by myriad audiences. Representations of the ritual presentation allow rethinking of the reception of youth performance as a cynical performance of middle-class passing in which social perceptions of Latinx Americans render a disconnect between social performances of aspirational and realized class advancement read as vicious deceptions of class standing.

It was the only commentary email I received from the *New York Times* article that featured my interpretation of the quinceañera as a performance of class and economic aspiration in the United States. The gentleman, whom I will not name, was a Jewish doctor from Connecticut and very interested in asserting that while I had noted that Jewish families are often not critiqued for large-scale bat-mitzvahs as Latinx families are for quinceañera celebrations of similar scale, Jewish communities were more affluent than their Latinx counterparts. He suggested that my interpretation of spending as strategy was not justified by virtue of his generalized assumption that Latinx people are poor. I resisted the urge to respond to him with an equally dismissive turn, but I realized his patronizing tone that assumed I did not understand how statistics work made me recognize the widespread social resistance toward the idea of the existence of middle- and upper-class Latinos. It is not so much that these communities exist by virtue of access to education, technology, and overall household income, but that the social history of any ethnic community would render them open to critiques on how they choose to spend their hard-earned money that astounded me.

I realized from the commentary of this individual that it was not the spending that bothered him but rather spending by people he assumed did not truly have the money to spend. In his logic, the bat-mitzvahs of affluent Jewish families, presumably on the East Coast that he was familiar with, reinforced a family's class standing, while the "overpriced" events of Latino households only pretended to match their true economic resources, rendering the events false. His interpretation was veiled by pity, claiming it was a "shame" that families were "forced" to live outside of their income brackets. This discussion allows me to imagine where notions of engaño fit into economically oriented narratives of quinceañera performance. Such discussions are fundamentally tinged with the residual classist assumptions of racialized economics that would assume not only that brown (and black) communities are poor and unable to manage money but also that they have no money to manage. As such, any spending that is not externally deemed "necessary" is deserving of paternalistic critique. Such paternalism emanates from extracultural contexts that frame difference by way of ethnic and race identification as well as from intracultural contexts that would have highly educated Latinos criticize the economic choices of a undereducated underclass. As acts of perceived of social cynicism, of dishonest performance, quinceañeras occupy a rebellious spirit that exists at the periphery of presumed respectability. Much like the "crime of the confidence man," the true crime of the quinceañera is that it challenges the socially accepted "belief that middle-class manners and appearances can be sustained only by middle-class people" (Goffman 18).

Quinceañera presentations become visual markets of social passing where genuine middle-class identity is seen as elusive to average Latino Americans. Rather then dwell on negativity, I instead lean into the notion of passing as an effective social survival strategy and examine how queer performance artists work this notion of engaño into their creations that use the quinceañera ritual as a performance frame, offering audiences a different lens through which to reinterpret the coming-of-age drama.

# RIGHTS/RITES AND REPRESENTATION

Reading Latinx Social Performance

On June 12, 2018, Alexa Lopez danced her quinceañera waltz outside the federal immigration detention facility in Richmond, California, where her father, Raul Lopez, was being held. She proceeded through the crowd of demonstrators with her cousin, who carried a photo of her father. Mr. Lopez, who had been in detention for more than a year, has resided in the United States over three decades since arriving from Guatemala. Alexa used her Latina spectacle to raise awareness not only of her father's case but the cruelty of separating families at the border and beyond. In the process, she illustrated the potentiality to effect social change in the United States through Latina spectacle ("Teen Holds Quinceañera").

In her public address during the 2017 Human Rights Campaign gala in Los Angeles, the Latina actor America Ferrera made the powerfully simple statement "Representation is how most of us learn what is possible" (qtd. in Moreno). She was speaking of the predicament of media and how the film and television industry still lacked sufficient representation of people of color, among other minority groups. Her words, which circulated through the HuffPost Latino Voices thread online, resonate, as my work in these chapters has, to illuminate in more ways than one, how the quinceañera tradition serves as a vehicle of representation for US Latinxs. The quinceañera serves the community and disrupts a social trajectory of compulsory heteronormativity through an aesthetic of aggressive visuality. The result of this functional repurposing is an investment in social documentation—to document oneself and craft one's own narrative in the public sphere. As such, the myriad representations of quinceañera practice, those labeled defiant, outlandish, indulgent, and even garish, fundamentally change the socioracial landscape into which subsequent representations enter. The performance of quinceañeras changes the social scripts of Latinx social performance, offering a space steeped in the possible rather than the permissible. Representation in the form of self-documentation founded in the present lays the groundwork for a persistent social narrative; these representations influence over time and thus help foment a sense of collective remembering in the form of Latinx commemoration.

Beyond gender presentation, quinceañera practice is also about coming out Latinx. This public declaration of Latinx identity reflects an interpretation of cultural citizenship that is documented in and facilitated through the quinceañera spectacle. The spectacle exposes contemporary issues of gendered, raced, classed, and localized experiences of cultural citizenship that are amplified by an aggressive visual style. The style is a response to poverty-stereotyping in a USAmerican social imaginary. Rather than simply being about aspirational wealth, the style is also a marker of being neither financially needy nor socially at risk. Rather than being firm declarations of wealth, quinceañeras instead disrupt victimizing social scripts that are embedded in popular representations of Latinx communities. Such public performances of unexpected affluence offer visual counternarratives that challenge the authority of social elites who would presume to know how Latinx communities live and should live. The material representations of these moments of strategic visuality serve as self-guided documentations of lived experiences of Latina youth and their families. The notion of self-documentation, as a basic yet powerful understanding of the collective motivations of communities of practices—to be acknowledged, recognized, even if not completely understood, and remembered—resides at the heart of contemporary folklore studies and as a central point of relevance to communities of color whose lives are continuously rendered "outsider" within mainstream notions of accepted normativity. The concept and language of documentation hits immigrant communities particularly poignantly, as the possession or absence or merely the presumption of documentation has the legal capacity to break up families and render whole communities of individuals as presumed criminals. In the United States to be "documented" means more than a legalistic claim to civil and human rights. It represents a distinct fissure between communities determined to be socially worthy and those marked as disposable.

While I am not a scholar of immigration, I do see clear connections between how individuals establish belonging to place and people, especially as they move between spaces and statuses making and defending meanings as they traverse social, cultural, and political environments. The term "documentation" becomes increasingly relevant, as it has a salient tie to the popular discourse surrounding Latinx communities across the United States at this very moment. The power of *papeles*, papers, has saturated Latino pop culture and humor as a coping mechanism for the lived reality of surviving legal placelessness. In the juridical sense, the most common context under which the term appears in popular media and new discourses references legal authorization to be within the national boundaries of the United States—be that through work or travel visas, deferred action, or US birth certificates. The discourses are much like those around trans-identifying communities, whose experiences and struggles for recognition first ask those who are not transgender to mark themselves as "cis" rather than reinforce their unmarked social privilege. The term "documented" is often taken for granted, as many Americans would sooner define themselves as "normal Americans" than as "documented Americans."

At this historical moment Latinx voters are said to be shifting the tide in presidential elections in swing states. The 2016 presidential election season, which started much earlier than anyone wanted, was built upon cruel and insidious public discourse that began with candidate Donald J. Trump flippantly calling "Mexicans," specifically characterizing undocumented migrants who fuel US service industries and agricultural economy, rapists and murderers. Many of us thought, "Certainly, this is both the beginning and the end of Donald Trump's outrageous presidential ambition?" And yet, here I sit taking in the day's worth of horrific news stories, fearing that the antigay, antiwomen, antipoor, and most definitely anti-Latinx campaign being waged by what is the new party of Trump has ignited a burning ember in the racist hearts of a huge number of USAmericans fearful of the apparent and inescapable loss of white cultural supremacy in the United States in the twenty-first century.

The anger of white nationalists can only be matched by their fear—a fear that the neoliberal identity politics that once supported their rise to power has since been utilized by unspecified *others* whose racial profiles are incompatible with the tenets of innovative entrepreneurial acumen, savvy marketing, and a fierce competitive ethos. The only difference is that after generations being told everything they could not and should not do, a new generation of Latina and Latino cultural producers and consumers who will not be defined by solely racial and ethnic categories has emerged, and they are using their culture knowledge as resources for social success. It is the work of anthropological folklorists to examine the manifestations of their cultural knowledge, of folklore, as resistive social strategies of adaptation and ultimately survival that constitutes everyday life.

Folklore does work in the world. The field in which I was trained, American folklore, struggles with the transnationality and diversity of the Americas/Américas and as such fails to make strong connections between patterns of practice as fundamentally rooted in intersectional social experiences, particularly with regard to communities of color. The *work* of folklore in communities of color functions far beyond social entertainments to represent the spectrum of embodied experiences, from the precarious to the triumphant, of individuals and groups in public and private life. Such experiences cannot and should not be excised from their historical contexts rooted in oppressive coloniality. Coloniality, alongside legacy social hierarchies that institutionalize structures of symbolic and material violence against minoritized populations, continue to function under rebranded terms as classism, racism, ableism, queerphobia, regionalism, and misogyny. The cultural work being done by folk practice in such a social environment is observed to function as cultural gatekeeping, either drawing in or keeping out audiences, creating divisions between authentic and inauthentic "others." Folklore itself is a product and process of documentation mobilized in the service of nondominant communities. In US Latinx cultural contexts, it further serves as in-group representative practice that asserts a need for a documented self in the neoliberal western marketplace. Latinx folklore is situated in both material and digital space where the act of self-branding coupled with conspicuous visibility of racial signifiers mark social privilege.

This niche marketplace, before "Hispanic" and now "Latinx," has been used to characterize and constitute communities. But it has been constructed through the use of stereotypes that attempt to compose community by "the construction of a Hispanic market based on the notion of Hispanics as a nation with a nation" (Dávila, *Latinos, Inc.* 88). Such a construction is invested in a fantasy of pan-Latinx solidarity that overlooks deeply entrenched racial hierarchies that divide communities by colorism, racism, classism, and regionalism. The nation within a nation is a fantasy, but like the quinceañera it is a coming-of-age fantasy that facilitates a discourse by communities of consumption that binds Latinx social actors together across diasporic ethnonational affiliations through shared practice.

In the era of Trump, the politics of representation of nonwhite Americans and of women has normalized the objectification and dehumanization of people of color across levels of economics, race, religion, gender, sexuality, and region. At this moment in US history, naming and claiming the ways communities and individuals choose to make themselves visible/invisible as publics provide insight into the ways individual cultural practices become collective strategies of social survival. Here, "survival" is defined as the ability to stave off social erasure in a society that, through the democratic process, collectively determines whose lives matter most. Cultural practices that emphasize and publicize a nonwhite narrative of "Americanity" (Quijano and Wallerstein 549) are both resistive and dangerous, as they reveal processes that aid in the timely emergence of new economic and political publics. Aníbal Quijano and Immanuel Wallerstein note that in the formal postcolonial period in the Americas, such publics develop coping strategies through the introduction of claims to ethnic categories made material through self-defined cultural forms. Ethnicity was not self-sustaining and required "conscious and systemic racism" to endure (551). US Latinx communities are diverse yet grounded in a few shared factors that normalize their collective discrimination in the United States: personal experiences of migration, the attributions of migratory legacies, and systemic marginalization due to such experiences and attributions. Collective experiences allow Latinx folklore scholars to examine folkloric practices as representations of situated knowledges that link self-described Latinx cultural forms with legacies of hemispheric coloniality of power.

In *Quinceañera Style* I have examined the representational impact of quinceañera events and cultural knowledge formation in an inter-American context. Quinceañera celebrations take place across the Americas, and anecdotal origins are located in pre-Columbian Central America. Given Alexandra Stern's assertion of an inter-American circuit of knowledge that moves with historical patterns of migrations across the hemispheric Americas, it is difficult if not inaccurate to attempt to categorize quinceañera practices as simply "American," read as US or Anglo-American, or even "transnational," as that term holds a distinct meaning linked to crossing national boundaries still delineated by political geographies. Rather, the quinceañera in this body of representational contexts operates beyond a singular sense of nationality, instead being situated in between them. Quinceañera practice, particularly representations of the tradition, resides amid a flow of global circuits of cultural production and consumption, most intensely through the Americas first, through economic migration, and second, virtual connectedness of advanced digital visual technologies. The industrial manufacturing of dresses in China adds another node in the global circuit of quinceañera culture. The assertion of an inter-American quinceañera represents an undefined relation between America and América that is always in a state of flux while also precipitating a conversation that is not limited by place, city, territory, reservation, or nation (Raussert 4). Yet one must also recognize how the idea of "America" and the agency and diversity it indexes on a global stage have impacted the production of the contemporary quinceañera event.

Inter-American quinceañeras utilize the currency of the term "American" where the term "functions as a discourse of neoliberalism making possible struggles for rights through consumerist practices and imaginaries that [comes] to be used both inside and out[side] the territorial boundaries of the United States" (Grewal 2). Such a framework allows one to situate the tradition in space yet out of place, where placelessness need not be tragic or faulty. Instead this situated interstitial identity serves as an acknowledgement of continuing streams of ideological and social mobility where cultural productions take on entangled forms and meanings that cannot be located neatly within constructed physical boundaries. While previous scholarship on the topic of quinceañeras has investigated the tradition where performance context overlaps with the bounded territoriality of cities, regions, and entire countries, my intention has been to focus on the material aspects of the ritual in ephemeral spaces of production. The quinceañera event then becomes a place where patterned iterations laminate in one temporary space to facilitate a form of community-inspired albeit temporary place making.

## STRUCTURES OF SEEING IN THE AMERICAN QUINCE

Within the quinceañera event, the quinceañera girl is in a position of constant oscillation between her USAmerican roots and her inter-American lifestyle. She wears her ambiguous associations on her body and generates a space in which spectators who consume her image as quinceañera are ushered into that postnational position that enlists the power of a self-conscious image of Latinx in a USAmerican context. Structures of seeing may be defined as the social and cultural constraints that affect visual perception of images and identities. Borrowed from discourses of film theory, structures of feeling are often coded in terms of gendered perceptions that allow certain subjects (usually men) to arrange images on the screen that become intelligible to a particular audience. They are the subtle and often hegemonic ways the spectator is corralled into a particular culturally and socially defined gaze (Doane 75-76). This formation for the orchestration of seeing negates the role of individuals in a community to be agents in the construction of their own visual narratives. Participation in the quinceañera event, even by proxy, is rooted in beholding the quinceañera girl in her lavish adornments, as it is through the beholding—the attracted gaze—individuals are able to "escape their flawed lives" through beauty (Shukla 30). In its current iterations the quinceañera dress in and out of its ritual contexts materializes a counteraesthetic. This counternarrative through contextualized dress, as adornment on raced and classed bodies, is a way of controlling gaze, demanding to be seen, but understanding reception will range from enamored romanticism to revulsion. Self-portraiture is a representative composition, both material and digital, that serves as a conspicuous platform for embodiment and presencing in American society that cannot simply be reduced to acts of economic expenditure.

Focusing on representation over ritual and returning to Jennifer González's concept of autotopography—the narrating of identity through the surrounding material display—it can be seen that quinceañeras do work in communities that transcend ethnoracial identity confirmation and the oversimplified standardization of feminine gendered behavior. Through the customization of space, quince girls are rearticulating a context of reception that foregrounds style as a mechanism for navigating society, an approach characterized as strategy over tactic. Certeau notes in *The Practice of Everyday Life* that "strategies" are the purview of the powerful, social institutions, and governments, where as "tactics" are the work of everyday people, where one may read "everyday" as weak or socially subordinated. Deconstructing Certeau in "The Practice of Everyday (Media) Life: From Mass Consumption to Mass Cultural Production?" the new media scholar Lev Manovich asserts that "tactics are the ways in which individuals negotiate strategies that were set for them" (322). While I initially wanted to categorize the work of quinceañeras to reform their contexts of reception as "movidas," Spanish for the social tactics they use to evade systems of power to meet their own ends, I came to realize how this in many ways is a form of rhetorical violence, as it presumes the flouting of rules instead of the creation of new contexts with new rules for reception.

The rhetorical positioning of "movidas" indexes a community origin; it obscures the ways people are working and succeeding to reframe themselves at the center of their social environments. Rather than being adept at the margins, communities are envisioning a new center. One can see the process of neocapitalist logics running though contemporary quinceañeras, where tactics are being commoditized and sold back to communities as strategies. Manovich goes on to assert that in this process "what was ephemeral, transient, unmappable, and invisible became permanent, mappable, and viewable" (324). This holds true for the quinceañera as a practice of representation that was once cloistered behind ethnoracial walls and has been rendered readable as a process of assembling material commodities, the process of which is laid bare to the community, creating a deregulated cultural context for the event's production and changing the rules of community engagement and ritual functionality. Rather than "tactics," I would return to the term "amasamiento" from Gloria Anzaldúa's work:

> *Soy un amasamiento*, I am an act of kneading, of uniting, and joining that not only has produced both a creature of darkness and a

creature of light, but also a creature that questions the definitions
of light and dark and gives them new meanings. (103)

This interstitial positioning posited by Anzaldúa, the space of ambivalent
in-betweens, is also a space of creativity and interrogation. The process of
amasamiento is implicitly taken up by quinceañera girls as they look to find
solid ground for their own cultural instabilities.

Drawing on rhetorics of tradition becomes tricky, as many participants
are the first in their families to have had a quinceañera for generations. Cultural practices become part of a sociocultural documentation process in
which form, context, and content become metadiscursive representations of
community—regardless of the accepted function of the practice. The goal
is therefore to make visible not static identities but the creative processes
by which quinceañeras move beyond characterizations dominated by heteropatriarchal and conservative Catholicism to imagine them as secular strategies of selfhood, visibilizing processes of self-determination that push back
against the problematic hypervisibility that haunts US Latino communities
daily—in particular the specter of illegality. In the case of American quinceañera practice, such strategies or amasamientos recast shallowly interpreted
moments of indifferent pageantry into forms of multidimensional artifice,
defiant visibility, and embodied commemoration while drawing on an inter-
American circuit of knowledge.

## RECLAIMING THE SPECTACLE WITH STYLE

In a society ruled by the profitability of spectacle that draws in a consumptive
gaze as in the contemporary Americas, image management is paramount. In
a social world that is driven by the exchange in visual currency, control over
one's brand profile allows for finding creative autonomy but also the capacity
to influence one's audience and control one's performance context. This is
accomplished through the modulation of quinceañera style.

I have presented style as a cultural resource and a social strategy instrumentalized by quinceañera girls as a set of "signifying practices," a coded set
of communications in which meaning is group-specific. For Dick Hebdige
in his 1979 work *Subculture: The Meaning of Style*, style is an ever-changing
composition of self-indexing intersectionality. For Hebdige this manifested
in the clothing, dance, music, makeup, and drug use of British punks. Even
though quinceañera style does not maintain a concrete everyday presence
in the lives of young participants, it functions as an intense, compressed
moment of performative risk; the celebration opens up a short period of

the expressions of style and exerts a lingering influence that continues but in indirect ways. Here, it is not enough to understand who is an intended interlocutor to such embodied communication but also who sits outside of comprehension. In the case of US quinceañeras, I assert that quinceañera girls forging identities are not using style to set themselves against a cultural mainstream but are positioning themselves against antiquated interpretations of their previous selves—in a way embodying a kind of futurity as they frame their events' positionality potential rather than re-creations of the past to literally and ideologically refashion traditional practice and the contexts of that practice's reception as ritual event that are themselves double coded as models of and for reality. Style cannot be interpreted outside of neoliberal capitalism or indeed, a framework of racialized economics. Here again, the chuntara quinceañera serves as a fascinating example of these dynamics at play. Her social position, wandering the mall seemingly unaffected, embodies the kind of social posturing of an unmarked citizen—one who is serving only herself. In a social performative context that could render her out of place in style and form, she designs her own sense of place in public space. She comes to embody a sense of longing and belonging.

## SELF-DOCUMENTATION AND AN AESTHETIC OF DESIRE

"Self-documenting" is both a verb and a noun. It represents a process through which people are actively building a public image of themselves that they share with the wider world. In modern society they would have many options. But it is also an ongoing process of revisions, especially as the objects of documentation, the documentation itself circulates through venues open to audience critique. In a neoliberal social context, this process is part of a self-marketing paradigm in which individuals are eager to gain group approval, even if the group is a small, discerning, niche audience of a like-minded minority. The primary goal of self-documentation is to be seen. Although being seen does not always require a public audience, it could mean being acknowledged by one's family as a core sentiment in quinceañera practice. It is also not an naturalized process but being seen as a temporary, curated ideal self, a self that is variable and variegated.

I claim that self-documentation is therefore a process by which individuals make themselves present, visible, and culturally accountable on their own terms. It is a form documenting personal experiences from the margins of social life by virtue of categories of race, ethnicity, class, region, and gender and sexuality politics. As a method it is a process that prioritizes telling one's own story and in the process asserting the value of such a story and the individual behind it. Self-documentation is practically fluid but in the twenty-first century has an amplified technological component as youth communities parlay digital connectedness into social art meant to draw in public gaze to their lives. Patterns of self-documentation potentially reinforce social norms or by their visibilized presence disrupt social expectations based on myriad social factors including but not limited to age, race, class, and gender.

Staging a Latinx quinceañeras is a way to assert citizenship through performance. The social experience that is reified through style is then preserved through memory as well as material remembrances. Memory objects serve to index family histories traced back through photographic narratives that can be passed on from one generation to the next. But more immediately, the young women amass quinceañera images as part of a profile of a curated public self. The quinceañera draws together much more than material accessories or coordinated if over-the-top fashion choices. At the core of contemporary events, those of young Latinas in the twenty-first century exhibit a truly transgressive styling guided by an aesthetic of desire.

Digital quinceañera narratives enter the mass circulation of social media to connect communities of practice through a process of comparative remembering. In the video "Women Try [on] Their Old Quinceañera Dresses," hosted by the popular Latinx media outlet Pero Like, millennial Latinas use their quinceañera dresses as vehicles of remembering their teenage years. The participants respond by trying on their dresses while also sharing the memories fostered through their mock fashion show. While the tone of the video is playful, what happens is that it utilizes desire in two significant ways. First, Pero Like's media influencers utilize the quinceañera practice as a way to draw in Latinx audiences to attract traffic to their sites, brokering in likes and shares within the visual economy of online social media. The video was so popular it was followed by two more quinceañera-themed videos, "Latinas Try $50 Quince Dresses from Amazon" and "Latinas Try on Quinceañera Dresses for the First Time." Both follow-up videos soon garnered more than 1.5 million views. Second, the desire that is leveraged by drawing in those who recognize the tradition also facilitate an esoteric space for the sharing of memories among Latinx women. The comment thread burst with comments that shared a collective message that quinceañeras are not simply practices of celebration but a cultural motif that brings about ambivalent discussions of financial literacy and economic capacities of families.

Women share their own quinceañera counternarratives, those that specifically reveal their own families' inability to host events for them and how they processed those decisions. Similarly, comments take on a more assertive tone when women note their own choices to not ask for the celebration and their own admission of self-abnegation, a sign of maturity and responsibility to their families. The quinceañera is thus used as a means to foment desire and as a cultural site of negating that same desire.

Style is a form of self-documentary practice. Using the vantage point of traditional practice, namely the quinceañera coming-of-age celebration contextualized in US Latinx communities, allows the consideration of how young women are using cultural practice as a mode of self-documentation in an era when they simultaneously experience invisibilization and hypervisibilization as a product of structural violence and intracultural body policing. Style is then an intentional, agentive strategy for social presencing and survival. It serves as a method for engineering stateless personhood, humanity at the borders of the body when connected to dress. Quinceañera style works as a form of self-documentation that commemorates ethnoracial histories and experiences while facilitating the visibility of emergent publics whose common ground is neither ethnically or racially predetermined but must be read intersectionally. In this context of creative self-fashioning, belonging is predicated on reading citizenship from the vantage point of consumer agency and the public claiming of "America" as home.

In quinceañera performance contexts, I have examined the use of dress in rituals as a process of self-documentation and as an approach to Latinx cultural studies and folklore studies that I have termed "critical Latinx folkloristics." This framework for the study of USAmerican folklore that prioritizes racialized perspectives aims to collaborate with communities with the understanding that creative cultural practices are part of how communities intellectualize their own identities and representations in public and private spaces. This approach prioritizes the idea that people actively create meaning through practice rather than allowing practices to passively hold meaning. The job of academics working among such communities is to acknowledge community authority by recognizing practices of survival and resistance through creativity as self-documentation.

The system of dress and adornment, namely professionally designed hair and makeup services, are part of a signifying system that amplifies the quinceañeras' social presence and opens up quinceañera discourse to extracultural audiences through appearances in unexpected places. The term "unexpected" used in this context assumes social erasure and really a lack of confidence in the capability of certain raced, classed, and gendered communities. Among Latinx youth, the elaborate self-adornment in cultural practice becomes an exercise in conspicuous citizenship and allows girls to take their social capital from the salon to the statehouse. Makeup and hairstyle art forms part of quinceañera portraiture that follows young women into other stages of quinceañera performance where the heteronormative aesthetic of desire draws in gaze from general, unconnected audiences who see in the presence of elaborately adorned young women an enticing spectacle. The desire that captivates onlookers at the state capitol in Texas or those who "like" and "love" images of quinceañera girls at the capitol grounds in Des Moines can also be harnessed in other ways, such as the 2017 quinceañera protests at the Texas capitol to oppose SB4, a state Senate bill to prohibit sanctuary-city declarations in Texas.[1] These embodied strategies that draw in gaze need not simply objectify young women but can subvert normative assumptions of belonging, particularly in social and historical narratives of statehood and national citizenship.

Lía Garcia's practice of encuentros afectivos also illustrates the way desire is mobilized through quinceañeras' capacity to bring people together and manifest community in the process. This manifests desire to share space with a quinceañera celebrant, as the star of a specifically legible social moment draws people into celebrations even when uninvited. Public celebrations customary in working-class neighborhoods in Mexico City have a more elite analogue in young people entering more exclusive parties as uninvited party crashers. These spatial dynamics further render the quinceañera girl an object of desire as the central focus of each individual element in the event, from custom lighting to unique cake flavors that elevate the spatial social experience by reinforcing the elite identity of everyone invited and present. Lía mobilizes this sirenlike desire that surrounds the quinceañera girl, indexed by her elaborate ritual dress to draw varied publics into a small, temporary community in the bustling Mexico City metro station. Her work uses the quinceañera aura that is socialized into Mexican peoples through the ambient sociohistoric story of quinceañeras that is present from one generation to the next and that continues to be supported in the miles of quinceañera industries teeming from shop stalls and vitrines across the city. This aura transforms into desire, as metro travelers close the physical gap between themselves and Lía's performance mediated by her trans body but utilized with the primary tools of her artwork, tenderness and affection.

Lía again subverts the typical interpretations of desire that are politically mapped onto the body of trans women across the Americas by engaging with the sensual and not the sexual. Lía's performances are affective and draw on the kind of affection between people who care for one another as chosen family. Although people are drawn to her public performances, her work removes the stigma of sexual desire from her trans body and instead places her out in public, literally potentially laying her life on the line to call attention to the capacity for a desire without sexual exploitation. Her work portrays how the manifestation of a quinceañera can change the relations between bodies in space, even if only temporarily making friends from strangers.

Lía's work draws on the implicit tension in quinceañera celebrations, that of a wish to render young women sensual but forbidding them to be sexual. In many ways, this tension is at the heart of the quinceañera dress selection process. The dress is the primary signifier of femininity in the celebration, but it is also linked to social values of families and class performativity. In the case of Jazmin and her mother, the dress was one part of a larger process-ing of bringing beauty into their celebration, where beauty was defined by particular western values while modified by sociocultural interpretations of morality. Color codes that are overlaid with the spectrum of propriety, both implicit and explicit, become negotiating points in the customization of the larger event as it relates back to the socializing of the young Latina body. There is fine line between a generically beautiful gown and a seductive one. Seduction is the first step in fulfilling sexual desire, and although stories of first sexual experience can also be coupled with quinceañera stories, these are often stories shared in embarrassment or shame. Upon looking at the dress as a form of self-documentation, one can see it as a tool for social advancement and goals that exceed fulfilling a sexualized desire. The acquisition narrative of the dress tell a deeper story of personal and familial aspiration that begins with a establishing memories of youth that will serve as building blocks for a socially mobile future. Moreover, memories, like their material reminders, become high-value commodities in the cultural economy and preserve the reliquary of social media. Families come to understand this as antithetical to notions of coupling or even marriage, claiming that their daughters may never fulfill those social contracts and may choose different lives for them-selves. The selection of dress, the finding of oneself on material and digital racks, promotes a sense of self that is autonomous and provocative, calling attention to the power of cultural wealth when wielded beyond the bound-aries of traditionally accepted cultural logics. From this assessment, one may find that girls learn that they must desire themselves if they are to find social success in the wider world and that quinceañera practice is one venue to cul-tivate this sense of self-love.

These examples are meant to illustrate the revision process that quincea-ñera practice is undergoing, bolstered by an expansion of performative con-texts that widen the impact of this tradition that generates hope. The quincea-ñera thus becomes a metonym for the larger coming-out process of Latinx communities around the United States that cannot and should not be ideo-logically separated from US mainstream culture or material and nostalgic transnational links. As these images manifest and are circulated through communities in a variety of media, they move from performance to representation and as such, enter a cycle of influence as subsequent generations of quinceañera celebrants seek out inspiration in wider sociocultural experiences.

## LATINX FEMINIST PRAXIS AND THE DEREGULATION OF FEMININITY

Sartorial choices and an increasing demand for bodily autonomy are fundamentally dangerous, given the cultural context of gendered normativity in Latino communities, where a woman's value continues to center on heteronormative pairing and having children. In the context of domestic priorities, women are prized as disciplined and self-sacrificing—embodying the archetype of *la mujer abnegada,* the abnegated woman. This is an idealized woman who gives of herself to others, emotionally, physically, and intellectually, and asks for nothing in return. She wants nothing and as such dies a martyr. And by living out her suffering, she passes the scaffolding of internalized pain along in a cycle of abuse to the next generation. Desire is a distraction from her responsibilities as a mother, a wife, a daughter, and a sister. Her life only has shades of meanings that are offered by others. She lives a relational life, not a life of relationships. Quinceañera style has developed to push back on this idea of idealized self-negation—the quinceañera girl as an American consumer and as a product of American consumerism wants publicly and unashamedly. The practice of the tradition at this moment in time reframes traditional practice to open up a context to display desire. This is a sign of change, a material and ideological rebellion against what bell hooks calls "traditional notions of gender and desire" (*Feminism Is for Everybody* 93).

The quince girl wants attention, draws in gaze, desires to be seen, and desires to define herself, inspire social change, and intensely control a feminine rhetoric she is free to discard the next day. This is the legacy of Chicana and Latina feminist theorists working tirelessly for civil rights. But the quinceañera girl remains an ambivalent messenger, as beauty and teenage narcissism were not supposed to be the poster child of Latinx feminisms in action. The embrace of an aesthetic of desire—wearing what one wants proudly, demanding the right to make demands of the world—is a revolution for every woman who suffers in silence at the hands and fists of a dominating partner, every queer woman who was forced into feminine performance against her will, every young girl who has been socialized to believe "Calladita te ves mas bonita" (You're prettier when you're quiet), every woman who has internalized a rhetoric that motherhood defines a woman's worth in the world. An aesthetic of desire disrupts cultural logics of the past and reframes embodied technologies—the use of gaze, of sexualization, of the hypervisible—in order to reframe young Latinas as the authors of and agents in their own stories, their own spectacles, and their own futures.

This is an understanding that the material manifestations of the quinceañera celebration code meaning beyond an adherence to or disavowal of traditional cultural forms but instead serve as a kind of visual code switch. The quinceañera as a communicative register and a consumer practice becomes a form of modeling of desire fundamentally linked to class performance. What is desired in particular is what young women, Latina women, have been socialized to expect or not expect from themselves as social actors in US Latinx cultural contexts. Consumption becomes an index of desire. More than marking desire, the events become the legible manifestations of the fulfillment of desire—a rightful sense of personal indulgence. The events' legibility stems from their traditional context and the ritual scaffolding understood to be at the core of the events' constructions, namely religiosity, community service, and female modesty in holistic form, where the template of quinceañera events as celebrations of young womanhood continues to document a positionality of young womanhood from the perspective of a newer, culturally hybridized American Latina.

Rather than only considering the quinceañera or genre of folkloric practice, the idea of "self-documentation" serves as an umbrella term from which to examine multiple genres of personal and public performances that span genre, language, community affiliation, and style in the service of documenting personal practices of identification, in this case focusing on Latinx communities in the United States. Rather than a categorical arrangement, the frame of self-documentation is a tool through which to analyze and link material and ephemeral cultural forms and their communities of practice. Such a frame specifically focuses on the present rather than examining detailed relations to past forms; it is not in the service of authentication. Instead, it attempts to bridge creative folkloric formations to larger structures of power.

Class is a social performance. And much like folklore, class is dependent on its racialized context of reception. I have examined the quinceañera from a variety of entry points that link back to modes of consumer practice in different contexts. The work of this event extends beyond the marking of time in a lifespan of a girl turned young woman, but through its analysis it reveals hidden fissures between the construction of self and the interpretation and reception of that self in the public sphere including spaces of digital remediation. For US Latinx communities, class is a transient resource that is dipped into and instrumentalized. It is a product of practice and not statistics and is potentially fleeting but nonetheless real. Quinceañera style materializes class performance for Latinx communities who make economic choices based on a sense of social investments in children as fundamentally connected to the socioeconomic system of the United States. Rather than rhetorics of being "middle class," again one sees a recategorization based on community perspective—spending leading the push toward marketing luxury goods and services thus creating the category of upscale Latinos. This market circulating in the public sphere bolsters an image of upwardly mobile Latinx communities. Such a practice bypasses the legacy of racialized wealth gaps that would limit the economic strength of nonwhite, particularly black Americans. Even more significant is that the performance of class mobility implicitly confronts the moralization of poverty in which it is the right of the rich to dictate how those with less cash use their own economic leverage. This is most egregiously manifest in coethnic contexts where middle-class legacy immigrants critique the lifestyles and expenditures of newer, often undocumented migrants.

While fissures between intracultural classed experiences grow, a divide that also falls along racial lines frames those who are deemed to be pathologically poor as irrational economic actors, thus explaining away their inability to achieve the American dream by instead investing in heritage practices. Through the quinceañera Latinas annex the territory of their own bodies to materialize a middle-class fantasy, even for just one day indulging in Oluo's Boston cream pie. The examination of the power of representation within and around quinceañera practice illustrates how class experiences are not about financial ledgers (although they help) but about perspectives, both historical and contemporary, of the capacities of US Latinx communities to be "American" when neoliberal economic ideologies dictate that being American is spending like an American. Class identification therefore is not approached like an achieved plateau but a fluid and fluctuating social performance that may be enacted at different points in one's life; it can be chosen or even denied. Class identification becomes dependent on an accumulation of social performances, not on one singular fact. The quinceañera represents one such possible performance accessible to US Latinx communities. Those who would and do criticize the rationality or value of spending on coming-of-age celebrations over establishing a college fund or a first-car fund are questioning the consumer sovereignty of individuals but more so fomenting ideologies that mark staunch divisions between generations of US Latinxs. If Americans are defined by an ethos of spending, to chastise and marginalize those who do choose to invest in their daughters and sons is to want to limit their capacity to spend and curtail their opportunities to achieve full social citizenship.

LATINX COMMEMORATION INSTRUMENTALIZING MEMORY
UNDER CULTURAL AUSTERITY

With visibility come vulnerability and change (Rice-González 158). Coming out Latina is a dangerous proposition in the United States today. Embracing the spectacle and attracting gaze in ways that risk criticism imply an unearned freedom. Acceptable Latinxs are admirable and working class, having pulled themselves up from their bootstraps. They are grateful for minimal rights and social obscurity. Socially mobile Latinxs destabilize the status quo. They disrupt the social logics of white privilege and are therefore dangerous. Public representations of quinceañeras work to counter a mainstream media stereotype that "reaffirms whiteness as dominant in understandings of American citizenship" (Lieu 128), carving out fragile ideological and cultural spaces between nations. The character of consumer citizenship, where consumption practice is at the heart of deterritorialized social experiences, is one of constantly vacillating between feelings of longing and belonging bridged by practice. But where are these experiences, these representations emerging from?

Quinceañeras as consumer practices like other traditions are the product of cultural memory, both real and imagined. My research does not prove a link between quinceañera practice and pre-Columbian ritual. I believe that communities who mobilize that narrative believe those connections sincerely and derive value from those historical links. As I study Latinx folklore using a lens that foregrounds the realities and perceptions of inter-American migration, memory becomes a powerful tool through which to understand the functionality of practice and the tie between communities. Latinx Americans, who represent a variety of raced and classed diasporas, share an imaginary of a time before colonial rule. This imaginary is a cultural resource of survival that sustains people in the worst, most oppressive moments. As peoples of diaspora, there is also a distinct disconnect from histories and gap in knowledge and understandings. These are black holes, cold obscurities that are by-products of the first colonial encounter. Latinx cultural practices therefore serve a deeper meaning, something beyond their material worth or their presentist cause, that of unification of communities of practice via commemoration. Latinx commemoration is a function of cultural practices that serve as affective and political forms of collective remembering for the purpose of resisting narratives of social marginalization and erasure that would ignore past trauma and extinguish the possibility of an autonomous Latinx future. Commemorative practices help stave off the fear of symbolic annihilation through the legibility of deeply or newly embedded cultural traditions that cannot be geared toward preserving a romantic past but must also be a renewed investment in inter-American circuits of knowledge and people. We cannot mourn the passing of the familiar but instead embrace the emergent value of amasamiento—that which is constantly changing, that which unsettles us, that which challenges us to rethink who tradition serves and whose traditions lay the groundwork for our own and how we can disrupt structures of power simply by choosing to remember together.

PREFACE

1. In this work I examine ideas of belonging that are difficult to contain in traditional vocabularies of nationhood. I use the term "USAmerican" to refer to mainstream, white, cis-male-dominant culture in the United States.

INTRODUCTION

1. When I began my research in 2008, the company and the magazine had the name "Quinceañeras," plural. Since 2011 the name has become singular on the magazine covers. It is used interchangeably on the company websites, and I will use it as it initially appeared in my research, a plural.

2. "Interrogative gaze" refers to hostile public reception of bodies deemed to have questionable social value. I use it as a way to think about being seen that is hostile because viewers are incredulous at the value of the social phenomenon they are witnessing despite its material reality. I find this particularly valuable when discussing racialized encounters of quinceañeras in public, not specifically Latinx cultural spaces.

3. Here I refer to the process of subjectification proposed by Rabinow and Rose. Srinivasan notes that the process of self-governance as one of subjectification may or may not lead to positive results for the individual, and in fact the results may even be harmful. "Subjectification essentially refers to the process by which individual entities self-govern, i.e., work upon themselves, in accordance to various truth discourses about individual and collective wellbeing" (Srinivasan 2014, 11).

4. Under the current administration, quinceañera travel is still possible and likely is thriving, especially as families seek to affirm their ethnonational Latinx identities, which are actively disparaged in current political rhetoric about the national economy and immigration. Although under President Trump travel to Cuba has been limited, more specifically travel that supports the patronage of military-run businesses, travel for visiting as well as cultural events is still permissible. Most commonly, the purpose of "support of the Cuban people" is a rationale that one can apply to travel legally to the island, and it specifically requires travelers to discuss society with the local people, engage in cultural activities such as museum visits and musical performances, learn about independently owned local industries such as tobacco, and support local nonmilitary-owned businesses. A quinceañera trip would facilitate both of those factors quite easily.

CHAPTER 1

1. Rogelio Díaz-Guerrero discusses the theoretical concept of national personality types, presenting a paradigm for the characterization and study of the Mexican personality. I use it to extrapolate personality typing that specifically comes to affect patterns of Mexican parenting that then travel with families as they relocate to the United States.

2. Founded in 1996 as the Association of Hispanic Advertising Agencies, the Culture Marketing Council: The Voice of Hispanic Marketing is a national trade organization of marketing, commu-

nications, and media firms with trusted Hispanic expertise. In 2018 the association was renamed the Culture Marketing Council as it expands beyond Hispanic American markets ("AHAA Rebrands Itself").

3. The data appear to have been collated and published on September 16, 2013, to coincide with National Hispanic Heritage Month, September 15–October 15. The data release could be interpreted as ideally timed to rank and promote Hispanic-affinity group activities on Facebook.

## CHAPTER 2

1. Formerly narrated as being "queen for a day" (Ortiz), the quinceañera is advertised in contemporary planning magazines as a princess moment. The change shows a functional shift in the implied purpose of the event, from initiating a child into adulthood to acknowledging an intermediary state of young adulthood.

2. The terms "quince años" (fifteen years) and "fiesta de quince años" (fifteenth-year party) are more commonly used in Mexico to refer to the event, and the celebrant alone is termed the "quinceañera." In the United States, likely through the mixing of languages and the dominance of English among Latinx youth communities, the term "quinceañera" has been used as shorthand for both the event and the person being celebrated. The sociolinguistic investigation of this transformation could be its own project. The term can be masculinized, as it is used to apply to the growing number of parties for young male celebrants known as "quinceañeros."

3. In "Performing Nation Diva Style in Lila Downs and Astrid Hadad's La Tequilera," Angelique Dwyer observes that "Greater Mexico," a term coined by Américo Paredes in his 1958 study *With His Pistol in His Hand*, was initially used to describe the American Southwest or the US-Mexico border, an area that Gloria Anzaldúa later named "the borderlands." The concept of Greater Mexico is further explored by José Limón in *American Encounters*; he explains that the term refers "to all Mexicans, beyond Laredo and from either side, with all their commonalities and differences" (3). Héctor Calderón calls it "América Mexicana" in his book *Narratives of Greater Mexico*, in which he studies the work of Chicano writers and their incorporation of the borderlands in their work as a location, subject, or framework. In "Expanding Borderlands," Lynn Stephen suggests that due to current scholarship the term "Greater Mexico" may be used broadly to incorporate other US cities that have large populations of Spanish speakers of Mexican heritage, like Chicago, New York, and Philadelphia.

4. Beginning in 2018, Mary's has rebranded its quinceañera lines into Mary's Quinceañera Dresses, Mary's Ball Gowns, and Alta Couture. The new ball gown lines only come in shades of champagne, ivory, and off white and are cross-listed in the bridal section. Mary's Quinceañera Dresses blend the styles and color palettes of the former Beloving and Princess lines, which can be found under their original names at other retailers.

5. As these retail sites are constantly changing, I use the Internet Archive Wayback Machine to maintain access to the version of digital content that I consulted. Doing so gives me a representational archive of trends in economic, stylistic, and technical developments. As fashion and thematic trends change on the ground, so does their marketing by retailers. The Vizcaya narrative of January 2019 expresses content in a similarly joyful tone as in 2016, although a close reading might reveal more interesting rhetorical shifts that have yet to be assessed. It says, "Turning fifteen is a big deal. We know. Your Quinceañera dress should be a beautiful reflection of the woman you're becoming, and a symbol of your style and taste. Our Vizcaya Collection is a stunning array of bold colors, large flowing princess ball gown skirts, and all the sparkle you've been dreaming of. . . . Morilee's Vizcaya Collection is second to none when it comes to our gorgeous beaded embellishments on flowing organza, or cascading tulle adorned with delicate jeweled beading. Can you really go wrong? Your

Quinceañera is your day to steal the show. So reach big for the stars and make sure you find your extra twinkle" ("Turning Fifteen").

## CHAPTER 3

1. This phenomenon has been popular in Japan since the 1990s and has been the subject of pop news stories on the Latinternet (Martinez). Stories on it also appear in the media streams of the Latinx pop culture site Remezcla, such as Andrea Gompf's "Check Out These Japanese Cholos. Jolos, If You Will." The website Mitú has posted the short documentary *Chicano* by the filmmakers Louis Ellison and Jacob Hodgkinson on the topic of a Japanese community especially interested in Chicanos from Los Angeles (Villegas).

2. Variations of the handkerchief-hemline style skirt have been popular in quinceañera dress industries in the United States since at least 2011, when I began seeing these pañuelo skirts advertised by *Quinceañeras Magazine* Bay Area edition. They were made popular in the United States by the brand Bella Será.

3. This subject's full name was published two weeks later by BuzzFeed in a parallel story about the same exhibition (Cadena). Remezcla and BuzzFeed's Pero Like serve the same online communities and piggyback on one another's trending content. The recirculation of the same story demonstrates this point while also reproducing a similarly themed line of commentary with critiques of spending practices of the poor and self-righteous assertions of inexpensive alternatives to celebrating a quinceañera to socially and culturally come of age.

4. In 2019 these videos had been moved to a different playlist, "For All Your Quince Needs!" as Giselle shifts her channel's themes toward offering more generalized beauty and fashion tips.

5. Giselle's newest link is to her own online store, Risueña, where she designs and models merchandise. It is an independent online boutique powered by Shopenvy, which offers the infrastructure to host online retail spaces. Giselle is working toward designing and marketing her own indie brand.

## CHAPTER 4

1. In the summer of 2016 I passed just such a scene on TX-16 headed south into Bandera, Texas, on my way to a powwow event.

2. This term of reference fits under a rubric of queer Latinx in the hemispheric context of migration. Luis uses his home state of Guanajuato as a key identity marker in his Facebook profile, which helps inform his community and business connections in the greater Kansas City, Missouri, area.

3. I visited Jonathan in his salon in San Antonio in the summer of 2017 to discuss his work. I made an appointment for a cut and color, and he ended up bleaching and dyeing my roots electric blue. He was generous and sincere, and I am indebted to him for his patience.

4. I met with Luis at different times over the 2011–2016 quinceañera seasons at expos hosted by *Quinceañeras Magazine* in the Midwest. In July 2017 I interviewed Luis and his sister directly about their quinceañera business venture in their home in Kansas City.

## CHAPTER 5

1. The epigraph is from Lía as she reflects on her process of staging her quinceañera performance as a form of activism at La Plaza de Solidaridad in Mexico City on March 31, 2014 (in Quintana Guerrero and Conn).

2. Lía actively identifies as a "mujer trans," a trans woman, and I have chosen to keep the Spanish term, as her identity and experiences come with very specific regional cultural politics.

3. Quince años celebrations are not a tradition in Spain. Lía's invitation to perform there as a trans activist represents an interesting reversal of colonial culture flow, from Latin America to Europe, Mexico to Spain. Lía's work in the quinceañera tradition was globalized expressly as a performance of trans activism, not as a product of the folklore-popular cultural borderlands.

4. Lía and I discussed this translation, particularly the word "affectiva," which is central to her creative pedagogy. Sorting out feeling, affect, emotion, and love are at the center of her work. She was eager that I translate my interpretation of the term because she felt that the definition can be fluid and really depends on how it is being received by the audience. While she felt that "Yo soy afectiva" could have been translated "I am emotional," I thought the use of "I am affecting" spoke more to how she intellectualizes her focus in her work. I decided to go with the latter, as it reflects how I was affected by her performance.

CONCLUSION

1. On July 19, 2017, the multi-issue, Latinx-focused organization Jolt Texas hosted a quinceañera-themed demonstration in Austin to protest SB4. Jolt promoted the event on its website, stating, "Join us on Wednesday, July 19, at the South Steps of the Texas Capitol for Quinceañera at the Capitol. Come and rally around 15 young women who will share the 15 reasons that they're resisting SB4. We're going to combat hate and racism by celebrating Latino culture" ("Quinceañera at the Capitol").

Aageson, Thomas. "Cultural Entrepreneurs: Producing Cultural Value Ad Wealth." *The Cultural Economy*, edited by Helmut K. Anheier and Yudhishthir Raj Isar, vol. 1, Sage, 2008, pp. 92–107.

"About Us." *Quinceañeras Magazine*, www.quinceanerasmagazine.com/about-us. Accessed January 17, 2019.

Abundmer, Inc. Dresses. *Ambifi: Business Directory You Can Trust*, abundmer-inc.houston. tx.amfibi.directory/us/c/2959453-abundmer-inc. Accessed June 3, 2017.

Agius Vallejo, Jody. *Barrios to Burbs: The Making of the Mexican American Middle Class*. Stanford University Press, 2012.

"AHAA Rebrands Itself as Culture Marketing Council: The Voice of Hispanic Marketing." Association of Hispanic Advertising Agencies, January 31, 2018, www.prnewswire.com/news-releases/ahaa-rebrands-itself-as-culture-marketing-council-the-voice-of-hispanic-marketing-300591294.html. Accessed January 12, 2019.

Alvarez, Julia. *Once upon a Quinceañera: Coming of Age in the USA*. Viking, 2007.

Anzaldúa, Gloria E. *Borderlands/ La Frontera*. Aunt Lute, 1999.

"Are You a Vendor?" *Quinceañeras Magazine*, quinceanerasmagazine.com/are-you-a-vendor. Accessed January 19, 2019.

Asante, Molefi K. *It's Bigger than Hip-Hop: The Rise of the Post-Hip-Hop Generation*. St. Martin's Press, 2008.

Banet-Weiser, Sarah. *Authentic™: The Politics of Ambivalence in a Brand Culture*. NYU Press, 2012.

Baudrillard, Jean. *Simulations*. Semiotexte, 1983.

Bhabha, Homi K. *The Location of Culture*. Routledge, 2004.

Blank, Trevor J., editor. *Folklore and the Internet: Vernacular Expression in a Digital World*. Utah State University Press, 2009.

Bonin-Rodriguez, Paul, and Alberto Araiza. "Quinceañera." *The Color of Theater: Race, Culture, and Contemporary Performance*, edited by Roberta Uno and Lucy Mae San Pablo, Bloomsbury, 2002, pp. 261–302.

Butler, Judith. *Gender Trouble: Feminism and the Subversion of Identity*. Taylor and Francis, 2006.

Cadena, Daniela. "This Photographer Shows the Sacrifices Families Make for a Quinceañera." BuzzFeed, August 25, 2016, www.buzzfeed.com/danielacadena/this-photographer-shows-the-sacrifices-families-make-for-a q?utm_term=.wwAkXMO96#.qfbKmDjWX. Accessed January 19, 2019.

Calderón, Héctor. *Narratives of Greater Mexico: Essays on Chicano Literary History, Genre, and Borders*. University of Texas Press, 2004.

Cantú, Norma E. *Canícula: Snapshots of a Girlhood en la Frontera*. University of New Mexico Press, 2015.

———. "Chicana Life-Cycle Rituals." *Chicana Traditions: Continuity and Change*, edited by Norma E. Cantú and Olga Nájera-Ramírez, University of Illinois Press, 2002.

———. "La Quinceañera: Towards an Ethnographic Analysis of a Life-Cycle Ritual." *Southern Folklore*, vol. 56, no. 1, 1999, pp. 73–101.

Carrasco, Mario. "The Persistence of Hispanic Culture in the Digital Age." *Media Post*, September

1, 2016, www.mediapost.com/publications/article/283902/the-persistence-of-hispanic-culture-in-the-digital.html. Accessed December 30, 2018.

Cereijido, Antonia. "You Are Cordially Invited to Hailey's Quinceañera." *Latino USA*, #1638, September 16, 2016, latinousa.org/episode/cordially-invited-haileys-quinceanera. Accessed September 20, 2016.

Certeau, Michel de. *The Writing of History.* Columbia University Press, 1988.

Colloff, Pamela. "Sweet 15: The Rise of the All-Out, Over-the-Top, Bank-Breaking Quinceañera." *Texas Monthly*, March 2009, pp. 140–208.

"Company Overview." Televisa, www.televisair.com/en/company-overview/at-a-glance. Accessed January 29, 2019.

Danielson, Marivel T. *Homecoming Queers: Desire and Difference in Chicana Latina Cultural Production.* Rutgers University Press, 2009.

Dávalos, Karen Mary. "La Quinceañera: Making Gender and Ethnic Identities." *Frontiers: A Journal of Women's Studies*, vol. 16, no. 2–3, 1996, pp. 101–127.

Dávila, Arlene M. *Culture Works: Space, Value, and Mobility across the Neoliberal Americas.* NYU Press, 2012.

———. *Latinos, Inc.: The Marketing and Making of a People.* University of California Press, 2001.

Dayton-Johnson, Jeff. "What's Different about Cultural Products? An Economic Framework." Department of Canadian Heritage, November 23, 2000, www.researchgate.net/publication/228551988_What's_Different_about_Cultural_Products_An_Economic_Framework. Accessed January 17, 2019.

Debord, Guy. *Society of the Spectacle.* Rebel, 1967.

Deiter, Kristen. "From Church Blessing to Quinceañera Barbie: American as 'Spiritual Benefactor' in la Quinceañera." *Quinceañera*, edited by Ilan Stavans, Greenwood, 2010, pp. 47–63.

Díaz-Guerrero, Rogelio. "La psicología de los mexicanos. Un paradigma." *Revista Mexicana de Psicología*, vol. 1, no. 2, 1984, pp. 95–104.

Doane, Mary Ann. "Film and the Masquerade: Theorizing the Female Spectator." *Screen*, vol. 23, 1982, pp. 74–87.

Durán, Javier. "Border Voices: Life Writings and Self-Representation in the U.S.-Mexico Frontera." *Border Transits: Literature and Culture across the Line*, edited by Ana Maria Manzanas, Rodopi, 2007, pp. 61–78.

Dwyer, K. Angelique. "Performing Nation Diva Style in Lila Downs and Hadad's La Tequilera." *Race and Cultural Practice in Popular Culture*, edited by Domino Renee Perez and Rachel Valentina González, Rutgers University Press, 2019, pp. 132–151.

Erevia, Angela M.C.D.R. *Quince Años: Celebrating a Tradition; A Handbook for Parish Teams.* Missionary Catechists of Divine Providence, 1996.

Estill, Adriana. "From Big Screens to *Pasarelas*: Studying Beauty in Latin America." *Latin American Research Review*, vol. 52, no. 1, 2017, pp. 173–182, doi.org/10.25222/larr.95.

Ewen, Stuart. *All Consuming Images: The Politics of Style in Contemporary Culture.* Basic Books, 1988.

———. "Marketing Dreams: The Political Elements of Style." *Consumption, Identity, and Style: Marketing, Meanings, and the Packaging of Pleasure*, edited by Alan Tomlinson, Routledge, 1990, pp. 41–56.

Falicov, Celia J. "The Cultural Meanings of Money: The Case of Latinos and Anglo-Americans." *American Behavioral Scientist*, vol. 45, 2001, pp. 313–328.

Flores-Gonzalez, Nilda. *Citizens but Not Americans: Race and Belonging among Latino Millennials.* NYU Press, 2017.

Foster, Hal. *Vision and Visuality*. Bay, 1999.

Franco, Jean. *Plotting Women: Gender and Representation in Mexico*. Columbia University Press, 1988.

Fraser, Nancy. "Rethinking the Public Sphere: A Contribution to the Critique of Actually Existing Democracy." *Social Text*, no. 25/26, 1990, pp. 56–80.

Frazer, James George. *The Golden Bough: A Study in Magic and Religion*. 1922, www.bartleby.com/196/index.html#chap3. Accessed January 17, 2019.

Fregoso, Rosa Linda. "Re-imagining Chicana Urban Identities in the Public Sphere, Cool Chuca Style." *Between Women and Nation: Nationalism, Transnational Feminism, and the State*, edited by Caren Kaplan, Norma Alarcón, and Minoo Moallem, Duke University Press, 1999, pp. 72–91.

Gerth, Karl. *Consumer Nationalism*. Sage, 2012.

Goffman, Erving. *The Presentation of Self in Everyday Life*. Doubleday, 1990.

Gompf, Andrea. "Check Out These Japanese Cholos. Jolos, If You Will." *Remezcla*, September 13, 2012, remezcla.com/culture/check-out-these-japanese-cholos-jolos-if-you-will. Accessed January 15, 2019.

Gonzalez, Carolina Dalia. "This Quinceañera Photo Series Highlights the Sacrifices Parents Make for This Rite of Passage." *Remezcla*, August 12, 2016, remezcla.com/lists/culture/photos-quinces-in-colombia-delphine-blast/. Accessed January 19, 2019.

González, Jennifer A. "Autotopographies." *Prosthetic Territories: Politics and Hypertechnologies*, edited by Gabriel Brahm and Mark Driscoll, Westview, 1995, pp. 133–150.

González-Martín, Rachel V. "Digitizing Cultural Economies: 'Personalization' and U.S. Quinceañera Practice Online." *Cultural Analysis*, vol. 15, no. 1, 2016, pp. 57–77.

Gottschild, Brenda Dixon. *Digging the Africanist Presence in American Performance: Dance and Other Contexts*. Praeger, 1998.

Grewal, Inderpal. *Transnational America: Feminisms, Diasporas, Neoliberalisms*. Duke University Press, 2005.

Grimes, Ronald. *Deeply into the Bone: Reinventing Rites of Passage*. University of California Press, 2002.

Hall, Stuart. *Representation: Cultural Representations and Signifying Practices*. Sage, 1997.

Halter, Marilyn. *Shopping for Identity: The Marketing of Ethnicity*. Schocken, 2002.

Hansen, Karen Tranberg. "The World in Dress: Anthropological Perspectives on Clothing, Fashion, and Culture." *Annual Review of Anthropology*, vol. 33, 2004, pp. 369–92.

Härkönen, H. "Becoming a Woman: Quince as a Moment of Female Sexuality." *Kinship, Love, and Life Cycle in Contemporary Cuba*, 2016, pp. 89–105.

Hebdige, Dick. *Subculture: The Meaning of Style*. Taylor and Francis, 2013.

Hernández, Hilda Gabriela. "Rose Quartz and Serenity Are the New Colors of 2016!" *Quinceanera.com*, www.quinceanera.com/decorations-themes/rose-quartz-serenity-are-the-new-colors-of-2016. Accessed January 20, 2019.

Hernandez, Jillian. "Miss, You Look Like a Bratz Doll: On Chonga Girls and Sexual Aesthetic Excess." *NWSA Journal*, vol. 21, no. 3, Fall 2009, pp. 63–90.

Hernández i Martí, Gil-Manuel. "The Deterritorialization of Cultural Heritage in a Globalized Modernity." *Transfer: Journal of Contemporary Culture*, vol. 1, 2006, pp. 91–106, www.llull.cat/rec_transfer/webt1/transfer01.pdf#page=93Accessed. Accessed May 10, 2016.

Herrera, Andrew. "Our Story." Remezcla, 2016, remezcla.com/about-us. Accessed October 2, 2017.

Hinojosa, Sara V., and Dolores Inés Casillas. "'Don't Be Self-Conchas': Listening to Mexican Styled Phonetics in Popular Culture." *Sounding Out*, May 5, 2017, soundstudiesblog.

com/2017/05/05/dont-be-self-conchas-listening-to-mexican-styled-phonetics-in-popular-culture. Accessed March 11, 2018.

*Hispanic Marketers' Guide to Cable: Hispanic Cable Facts and Cultural Cues.* Diversity Marketing Center, Cable Advertising Bureau, 2008.

hooks, bell. *Feminism Is for Everybody: Passionate Politics.* Routledge, 2015.

———. "The Oppositional Gaze: Black Female Spectators." *Movies and Mass Culture,* edited by John Belton, Rutgers University Press, 1996, pp. 247–264.

Horowitz, Ruth. "The Power of Ritual in a Chicano Community: A Young Woman's Status and Expanding Family Ties." *Marriage and Family Review,* vol. 19, no. 3–4, 1993, pp. 257–280.

Hoyt-Goldsmith, Diane. *Celebrating a Quinceañera: A Latina's 15th Birthday Celebration.* Holiday House, 2002.

Huggins, Harry. "Chicago's Dress Shop Economy." *Medill Reports Chicago,* March 16, 2016, news.medill.northwestern.edu/chicago/chicagos-dress-shop-economy.

King, Elizabeth. *Quinceañera: Celebrating Fifteen.* Dutton Juvenile, 1998.

Kudialis, Chris. "Quinceañera Tradition Has Grown into Booming Industry in Las Vegas." *Las Vegas Sun,* August 21, 2016, lasvegassun.com/news/2016/aug/21/quinceaera-tradition-booming-industry-las-vegas/.

"*Las 20 mejores telenovelas: Quinceañera.*" *People en Español,* March 31, 2010, peopleenespanol.com/gallery/las-20-mejores-telenovelas. Accessed April 28, 2013.

Leibold, Valerie E. "La sirena decolonial: Lia la Novia y sus interrupciones afectivas." *Extravío,* vol. 8, 2015, pp. 148–164.

Lieu, Nhi T. "Remembering 'The Nation' through Pageantry: Femininity and the Politics of Vietnamese Womanhood in the Hoa Hau Ao Dai Contest." *Frontiers: A Journal of Women's Studies,* vol. 21, no. 1/2, 2000, pp. 127–151.

Limón, José E. *American Encounters: Greater Mexico, the United States, and the Erotics of Culture.* Boston: Beacon, 1999.

———. "Transnational Triangulation: Mexico, the United States, and the Emergence of a Mexican American Middle Class." *Mexico and Mexicans in the Making of the United States,* edited by John Tutino, University of Texas Press, 2012, pp. 236–256.

Llopis, Glenn. "Facebook to Help Brands Convert 55 Million U.S. Hispanics." *Forbes,* January 6, 2014, www.forbes.com/sites/glennllopis/2014/01/06/facebook-to-help-brands-convert-55-million-u-s-hispanics/#124b685438cf. Accessed January 13, 2019.

Lorde, Audre. "The Master's Tools Will Never Dismantle the Master's House." *Sister Outsider: Essays and Speeches,* Crossing Press, 1984, pp. 110–113.

"Made in China?" *The Economist,* March 12, 2015, www.economist.com/news/leaders/21646204-asias-dominance-manufacturing-will-endure-will-make-development-harder-others-made.

"Madeline Gardner (Mori Lee): Biography." *Brides Do Good,* www.bridesdogood.com/designers/madeline-gardner-mori-lee. Accessed April 15, 2016.

Maines, Don. "Father-Daughter Duo Share a Dance in Coca Cola Commercial." *Houston Chronicle,* June 29, 2016, www.chron.com/neighborhood/bellaire/news/article/Father-daughter-duo-share-a-dance-in-Coca-Cola-8331494.php.

Manovich, Lev. "The Practice of Everyday (Media) Life: From Mass Consumption to Mass Cultural Production?" *Critical Inquiry,* vol. 35, no. 2, Winter 2009, pp. 319–331.

Marling, Karal Ann. "Quinceañera Debutante: Rites and Regalia of American Debdom." *Quinceañera,* edited by Ilan Stavans, Greenwood, 2010, pp. 3–6.

Martinez, Fidel. "Japanese Cholos: From East L.A. to East Asia." *Splinter,* April 23, 2014, splinternews.com/japanese-cholos-from-east-l-a-to-east-asia-1793841387. Accessed January 15, 2019.

"Mary's Bridal/P.C. Mary's Inc." Dallas Market Center, dallasmarketcenter.com/exhibitors/detail. aspx?exhibitor=2546. Accessed January 13, 2019.

"Mary's Quinceañera." Mary's Bridal, www.marysbridal.com/quinceanera-dresses. Accessed December 31, 2018.

McCracken, Angela B. *The Beauty Trade: Youth, Gender, and Fashion Globalization*. Oxford University Press, 2014.

McCracken, Grant David. *Culture and Consumption II: Markets, Meaning, and Brand Management*. Indiana University Press, 2005.

———. "Living in the Material World: Marketing and Meaning." *Market Leader*, Quarter 3, 2012, www.warc.com/content/paywall/article/mkt/living_in_the_material_world_marketing_and _meaning/97108.

Moreno, Carolina. "America Ferrera: Representation 'Is How Most of Us Learn What Is Possible.'" *Huffington Post*, March 21, 2017. www.huffingtonpost.com/entry/america-ferrera-represen- tation-is-how-most-of-us-learn-what-is-possible_us_58d162dae4b0ec9d29dfd410.

Morse, Parker. "Six Facts about the Hispanic Market That May Surprise You." *Forbes*, January 9, 2018, www.forbes.com/sites/forbesagencycouncil/2018/01/09/ six-facts-about-the-hispanic-market-that-may-surprise-you.

Nájera-Ramírez, Olga. "Of Fieldwork, Folklore, and Festival: Personal Encounters." *Journal of American Folklore*, vol. 112, no. 44, 1999, pp. 183–199.

Napolitano, Valentina. "Becoming a Mujercita: Rituals, Fiestas, and Religious Discourses." *Across the Boundaries of Belief: Contemporary Issues in the Anthropology of Religion*, edited by Morton Klass and Maxine Weisgrau, Westview, 1999, pp. 64–82.

Noriega, Chon A. "Fashion Crimes." *Aztlán: A Journal of Chicano Studies*, vol. 41, no. 2, Fall 2016, pp. 195–205.

Oakes, Tim, and Louisa Schein. Preface. *Translocal China: Linkages, Identities, and the Reimagining of Space*, edited by Oakes and Schein, Routledge, 2006, pp. xii–xiii.

Ochoa, Marcia. *Queen For a Day: Transformistas, Beauty Queens, and the Performance of Femininity in Venezuela*. Duke University Press, 2014.

Oluo, Ijeoma. "Poor People Deserve to Taste Something Other than Shame." *Medium*, May 12, 2016, medium.com/the-establishment/poor-people-deserve-to-taste-something-other -than-shame-90eb3aceabf9.

Ortiz, Almudena. "Fiesta de Quinceañera: Queen for a Day." Master's thesis, University of California, 1993.

Ortiz Cofer, Judith. "Silent Dancing." In *Short Fiction by Hispanic Writers of the United States*, Arte Público, 175–184.

Ortner, Sherry B. *New Jersey Dreaming: Capital, Culture, and the Class of '58*. Duke University Press, 2003.

Paredes, Américo. *With His Pistol in His Hand: A Border Ballad and Its Hero*. University of Texas Press, 1958.

Paulsen, Krista. "Ethnography of the Ephemeral: Studying Temporary Scenes through Individual and Collective Approaches." *Social Identities*, vol. 15, no. 4, 2009, pp. 509–524.

"People Try Salvadoran Food for the First Time." Pero Like, March 5, 2016, www.youtube.com/ watch?v=tidV2tYAnVY. Accessed October 2, 2017.

Perez, Domino Renee, and Rachel Valentina González. "Re-imagining Critical Approaches to Folklore and Popular Culture." *Race and Cultural Practice in Popular Culture*, edited by Domino Renee Perez and Rachel Valentina González, Rutgers University Press, 2019.

Pérez, Emma. *The Decolonial Imaginary: Writing Chicanas into History*. Indiana University Press, 1999.

Pertierra, Anna Cristina. "Quinceañera: Coming of Age through Digital Photography in Cuba." *Consumer Culture in Latin America*, edited by John Sinclair and Anna Cristina Pertierra, Palgrave Macmillan, 2012.

Petrelli, Daniela, et al. "AutoTopography: What Can Physical Mementos Tell Us about Digital Memories?" *Proceedings of the SIGCHI Conference on Human Factors in Computing Systems*, Association for Computing Machinery, 2008, pp. 53–62, ACM Digital Library, doi:10.1145/1357054.1357065.

Pina, Pedro. "Between Scylla and Charybdis: The Balance between Copyright, Digital Rights Management, and Freedom of Expression." *Digital Rights Management: Concepts, Methodologies, Tools and Applications*, vol. 1, GI Global, 2012, pp. 1355–1367.

Pine, B. Joseph, and James H. Gilmore. "Welcome to the Experience Economy." *Harvard Business Review*, July-August 1998.

Potowski, Kimberly, and Lillian Gorman. "Hybridized Tradition, Language Use, and Identity in the U.S. Latina Quinceañera Ritual." *Bilingual Youth: Spanish in English-Speaking Societies*, edited by Kimberly Potowski and J. Rothman, John Benjamins, 2011, pp. 57–87.

Puar, Jasbir. "A Transnational Feminist Critique of Queer Tourism." *Antipode*, vol. 34, 2002, pp. 935–946.

"QuickFacts: Houston City, Texas." US Census Bureau, www.census.gov/quickfacts/houstoncity-texas. Accessed January 19, 2019.

Quijano, Aníbal, and Immanuel Wallerstein. "Americanity as a Concept, or the American in the Modern World-System." *International Social Science Journal*, vol. 44, no. 4, 1992, pp. 549–557.

"Quinceañera at the Capitol." Jolt, July 17, 2017, jolttx.org/event/quinceanera-at-the-capitol-2. Accessed November 10, 2017.

Quintana Guerrero, Jaime, and Clayton Conn. *Trans-gresión para desafiar los prejuicios de género*. March 25, 2015, feministas.lamula.pe/2015/03/25/trans-gresion-para-desafiar-los-prejuicios-de-genero/feministas.

Rabinow, Paul, and Nikolas Rose. "Biopower Today." *BioSocieties*, vol. 1, no. 2, June 2006, pp. 195–217.

Ramírez, Catherine Sue. *The Woman in the Zoot Suit: Gender, Nationalism, and the Cultural Politics of Memory*. Duke University Press, 2009.

Raussert, Wilfried. Introduction. *The Routledge Companion to Inter-American Studies*, Routledge, 2017, pp. 4–5.

Restuccia, Danielle. "Upscale Latinos Drive the U.S. Market." *La Opinión*, April 30, 2014, laopinion.com/2014/04/30/upscale-latinos-drive-the-u-s-market.

Rice-González, Charles. "Latino/a Visibility and a Legacy of Power and Love." *QED: A Journal of GLBTQ World Making*, vol. 3, no. 3, Fall 2016, pp. 157–159.

Rodriguez, Gregory. "The Emerging Latino Middle Class." Pepperdine University, Institute for Public Policy, 1996.

Rodriguez, Richard T. "X Marks the Spot." *Cultural Dynamics*, vol. 29, no. 3, 2017, pp. 202–213.

Romo, Laura F., and Rebeca Mireles-Rios. "Latina Mothers' and Daughters' Expectations for Autonomy at Age 15 (La Quinceañera)." *Journal of Adolescent Research*, vol. 20, no. 5, 2013, p. 24.

Ruiz, Vicki L. *From out of the Shadows: Mexican Women in Twentieth-Century America*. Oxford University Press, 2008.

———. "Star Struck: Acculturation, Adolescence, and the Mexican American Woman." *Building with Our Hands: New Directions in Chicana Studies*, University of California Press, 1993, pp. 109–129.

Russell, Douglas A. *Costume History and Style*. Prentice-Hall, 1983.

Salcedo, Michele. *Quinceañera: The Essential Guide to Planning the Perfect Sweet Fifteen*. Henry Holt, 1997.

Saldívar-Hull, Sonia, ed. *Feminism on the Border: Chicana Gender Politics and Literature*. University of California Press, 2000.

Salvatore, Joe. "Collaboration/Celebration: Introduction to Quinceañera." *The Color of Theater: Race, Culture, and Contemporary Performance*, edited by Roberta Uno and Lucy Mae San Pablo, Bloomsbury, 2002, pp. 257–260.

Sandoval, Chela, and Guisela Latorre. "Chicana/o Artivism: Judy Baca's Digital Work with Youth of Color." *Learning Race and Ethnicity: Youth and Digital Media*, edited by Anna Everett, MIT Press, 2008, pp. 81–108.

Scharmer, Claus Otto. "Presencing: A Social Technology of Freedom." *Trigon Themen*, vol. 2, 2002, pp. 1–4.

Schor, Juliet. *The Overspent American: Why We Want What We Don't Need*. Harper Collins, 1999.

"The Shifting Religious Identity of Latinos in the United States." Pew Research Center, May 7, 2014, www.pewforum.org/2014/05/07/the-shifting-religious-identity-of-latinos-in-the-united-states.

Shultz, Stacy E. "Latina Identity: Reconciling Ritual, Culture, and Belonging." *Woman's Art Journal*, vol. 29, no. 1, Spring-Summer 2008, pp. 13–20.

Shukla, Pravina. *The Grace of Four Moons: Dress, Adornment, and the Art of the Body in Modern India*. Indiana University Press, 2008.

"Social Media Fact Sheet." Internet and Technology, Pew Research Center, February 5, 2018, www.pewinternet.org/fact-sheet/social-media. Accessed December 31, 2018.

Solís-Cámara, Pedro, et al. "Parenting in Mexico: Relationships Based on Love and Obedience" *Parenting across Cultures: Childrearing, Motherhood, and Fatherhood in Non-Western Cultures*, edited by Helaine Selin, Springer Science and Business Media, 2013, pp. 349–366.

Stephen, Lynn. "Expanding the Borderlands: Recent Studies on the U.S.-Mexico Border." *Latin American Research Review*, vol. 44, no. 1, 2009, pp. 266–277.

Stern, Alexandra. "An Empire of Tests: Psychometrics and the Paradoxes of Nationalism in the Americas." *Haunted by Empire: Geographies of Intimacy in North American History*, edited by Ann Laura Stoler, Duke University Press, 325–343.

"Teen Holds Quinceañera outside Richmond Detention Facility while Father Remains Detained." NBC Bay Area, June 10, 2018, www.nbcbayarea.com/news/local/Teen-Holds-Quinceanera-Outside-Detention-Facility-Housing-Her-Father-485075671.html. Accessed January 20, 2019.

*"Thalia recibe premio tvnovelas por actriz revelacion en quinceañera." YouTube*, February 13, 2010, www.youtube.com/watch?v=uWQELqT9kGo. Accessed August 5, 2014.

Tomlinson, John. *Globalization and Culture*. University of Chicago Press, 1999.

Turner, Terence B. "The Social Skin." *Reading the Social Body*, edited by Catherine B. Burroughs and Jeffrey Ehrenreich, University of Iowa Press, 1993, pp. 15–39.

"Turning Fifteen Is a Big Deal." Vizcaya Quinceañera Dresses, Morilee, www.morilee.com/browse/quinceanera-dresses/vizcaya. Accessed August 1, 2016.

"Understanding Diversity among Hispanic Women Entrepreneurs." National Women's Business Council, September 15, 2017, www.nwbc.gov/2017/09/15/hispanic-women-entrepreneurship-understanding-diversity-among-hispanic-women-entrepreneurs. Accessed January 13, 2019.

"US Hispanic Affinity on Facebook." Facebook Business, www.facebook.com/business/a/us-hispanic-affinity-audience. Accessed January 15, 2019.

Valdivia, Angharad N. *Latina/os and the Media*. Polity, 2010.

Villegas, Omar. "Watch a Mini-Doc about Japan's 'Chicanos.'" *Mitú*, February 6, 2017, wearemitu.com/newsfeed/watch-a-mini-doc-about-japans-chicanos. Accessed January 15, 2019.

Wang, Shan. "BuzzFeed Launches Pero Like, a Distributed Project for the 'English-Speaking Latinx' Community." *NiemanLab*, February 12, 2016, www.niemanlab.org/2016/02/buzzfeed-launches-pero-like-a-distributed-project-for-the-english-speaking-latinx-community. Accessed July 4, 2018.

Watters, Bert. "Quinceañera: The Mexican-American Initiation Ritual of Young Women." *The American Ritual Tapestry*, edited by Mary Jo Deegan, Greenwood, 1998, pp. 145–158.

"What Does Conflei Mean?" Pero Like, February 23, 2016, www.youtube.com/watch?v=nYuAQ8mBREU. Accessed October 2, 2017.

Williams, Raymond. *Marxism and Literature*. Oxford University Press, 1977.

Wollen, Peter. *Addressing the Century: 100 Years of Art and Fashion*. London, Hayward Gallery, 1998.

Ybarra-Frausto, Tomás. "The Chicano Movement/The Movement of Chicano Art." *Exhibiting Cultures: The Poetics and Politics of Museum Display*, edited by Ivan Karp and Steven Lavine, Smithsonian Institution Press, 1991, pp. 128–150.